Indian Economy and Entrepreneurship Prophecies Amidst Pandemic

"Atmanirbhar Bharat: From the Perspective of Young Entrepreneurial Skills and its Financial Implications"

भारतीय अर्थव्यवस्था तथा महामारी के मध्य उद्यमी पूर्वानुमान

''आत्मनिर्भर भारत : युवा उद्यमशीलता एवम् कौशल और उसके वित्तीय निहितार्थ के दृष्टिकोण से''

Indian Economy and Entrepreneurship Prophecies Amidst Pandemic

भारतीय अर्थव्यवस्था तथा महामारी के मध्य उद्यमी पूर्वानुमान

Edited by

DR. KAVITA YADAV

Department of Commerce - SBSEC

Shaheed Bhagat Singh Evening College

University of Delhi

RESEARCH INDIA PRESS

New Delhi (INDIA)

Indian Economy and Entrepreneurship Prophecies Amidst Pandemic

ISBN : 978-93-5171-076-9

Price : 1100/-

First Edition: 2021

Published by :
RESEARCH INDIA PRESS
E-6/34, Sangam Vihar
New Delhi-110062
Phone: 011-26047013, (M) 9818085794
E-mail: researchindiapress@gmail.com

Type Setting & Design by
G. R. Sharma

Disclaimer

Every care has been taken to verify the authenticity of the contents of this complementary endeavor of Department of Commerce- SBSEC, an edited book. The study intends to participate in the academic discourse sans any other expressed or implied intention. The contents, opinions, write-ups, findings and recommendations expressed in the book are that of the author(s) and do not reflect the opinions of the Distinguished Editorial board, College Principal, any of the editor, publisher and/or any member of the College Fraternity related with this work. However, the information, presentations, and articles contained in the chapters are believed to be reliable and free from plagiarism, the college and the member of the Editorial board, publisher or printing press shall not be held responsible for any errors in accuracy, misrepresentation and/ or omissions in the contents or any consequences of using such information now or later in future. The onus shall completely lie on to the writers and author(s) in any/every such case.

Principal's Address

Prof. S. K. Sinha
Principal

It is a matter of great pleasure for me to write a special note for this book brought about by efforts of the Department of Commerce, Shaheed Bhagat Singh Evening College. The topic of this book is of contemporary relevance and I congratulate the Department of commerce for taking this initiative. Since first five-year plan, there have been three main objectives of Indian planning: Growth with Modernisation, Self-Reliance and Social Justice. However, the meaning of 'Self-reliance' has been changing in different five-year plans, depending on the needs of the country and in the varying global, economic and political context. 'Atmanirbharta' has assumed a greater significance in this pandemic as the world economic system is in deep stress. India needs to prepare itself for the present crisis as well as for the crisis that may take place in the future. The government policy of 'Atmanirbhar Bharat' would lead to utilisation of local resources - both physical and human, which have been lying unutilized. This will have huge impact on Indian economy as this will result into higher economic growth, balanced regional development specially development of backward areas and distributive justice. In totality it will help in building robust economy, hitting at the roots of poverty and inequality. In this book we will get to learn from the view points of the learned authors and I hope we will be able to understand what 'Atmanirbharta' means in today's context and what should be the roadmap to achieve it in present scenario. I once again congratulate Department of Commerce for their efforts to compile this book on such a relevant topic. Dr Kavita Yadav deserves a special mention for her untiring efforts. I am confident that readers would be greatly benefited by this book.

Prof. S.K. Sinha
Principal

On Invitation

An Act of Beneficence

Message

Prof. R. K. Singh
Head & Dean
DSE, DU

The fertile academic mind of the Department of Commerce, Shaheed Bhagat Singh Evening College, University of Delhi, deserves compliments for bringing an edited academic piece of work on a contextual and contemporary issue, 'Indian Economy and Entrepreneurial Prophjecies amidst Pandemic.' This culmination of efforts has been able to explore some of the interesting issues about Atmanirbhar Bharat, e-learning, digitization, AI, ML, automation, etcetera. I am sure these themes would not only add value to readers in bringing critical perspective instead help look at a grand narrative in pandemic times. These efforts pave the way for academics, society, and policymakers to bring the economy on the path of recovery.

College Fraternity and Principal deserve notable accolades for bringing this informative and educative book. I am sure this fervor and flavor of college would remain intact to reach college to newer heights.

I wish college a great success

Prof. R. K. Singh
Head & Dean
DSE, DU

Message

Prof. A. Kundu
Eminent Economist
JNU

Indian economy being increasingly exposed to global forces, the possibility of its being seriously impacted by new waves of the present Pandemic or some other virues cannot be ruled out, In such eventualities, there is a need to ensure that the foundation of the economy that provide sustenance to large segments of the population, particularly the poor and vulnerable, is not jeopardized. Pandemic demands a new socio-economic order and has, indeed, forced the planners and policy makers to consider reorganising the production base to create stable employment, even during the periods of economic crisis and restrictions on mobility.

Given this macro context, it is important to bring down excessive dependence of the national production system on the global market so that the uncertainties and recession of the post industrial societies are not automatically imported into our domestic economy. More importantly, the production environment must promote growth of small and medium scale industries, utilising local resources and generating employment on a sustainable basis. There is also need for revising the urban development strategy in compliance with SDG Goal 11 for developing small and medium-sized towns and balanced spatial development, to facilitate the aspiring youth to seek, find or create employment. Promotion of small and middle scale industries can contribute in the achievment of this goal and, at the same time, strenghthen the resolve of making India self-reliant.

I am very happy that the Department of Commerce, Shaheed Bhagat Singh Evening College, University of Delhi has brought out this volume, analysing the prospects and possibilities of promoting growth of small and medium scale industries through engagement of young entrepreneurial talents. I congratulate the college management for this impotant initiative with special mention of the efforts of Dr Kavita Yadav.

Amitabh Kundu
Senior Fellow, World Resources Institute
The 3rd July 2021

Message

The book "Indian Economy and Enterpreneurial Prophecies Amidst Pandemic" is a great effort by the team in trying circumstances. The topic is important in view of the turbulence in the economy and associated institutions. Its a perfect example of collaborative research involving academics from different areas. I believe it will add value to the experiences and knowledge of those working in the field. Heartiest congratulations to the team.

Prof. Jaideep Sharma
Eminent Academician
IGNOU

Prof Jaideep Sharma
IGNOU

Message

Prof. Naseeb Ahmad
Eminent Academician
JMI Delhi

I am pleased to know that Department of Commerce, Shaheed Bhagat Singh Evening College, University of Delhi is making a significant academic contribution through this edited book on a very significant contemporary theme, "Indian Economy and Entrepreneurial Prophecies Amidst Pandemic" which is focussed on the spirit of "Atmanirbhar Bharat: From the Perspective of Young Entrepreneurial Skills and its Financial Implications.

As the covid – 19 pandemic has adversely affected the global economy and brought the ill effects of globalisation especially for the developing economies which are heavily dependent on foreign trade, it has forced the policy makers across the globe to explore various measures to minimise the impact of the pandemic on economy. The pandemic and subsequent Chinese intrusion and hostilities has made us realise our dependency on china for various products like pharmaceutical Ingredients, chemicals, electrical, electronics & IT hardware etc. The present circumstances has proven to be a blessing in disguise for the Indian manufacturers especially the Micro, Small and Medium Enterprises (MSME) sector and the Prime Minister has announced a Rs. 20 lakh crore economic package under the 'AatmaNirbhar Bharat Abhiyaan', for making the economy self-reliant and give boost to the home grown industries.

In the present pandemic time battling all odds; conceiving and bringing about an edited book on this emerging issue is indeed an entrepreneurial endeavour. I would like to thank and congratulate the whole team of Shaheed Bhagat Singh Evening College and other contributories for this academic adventure.

Dr. Naseeb Ahmad
Professor, Department of Commerce and Business Studies
Jamia Millia Islamia (Central University), New Delhi

Word of Wisdom

Advisory Editorial Board

Message

Dr. S. K. Grover

It gives me immense pleasure that Department of Commerce, Shaheed Bhagat Singh Evening College has brought out opportunities for the students, academic fraternity, and practitioners, through its formal Commerce Association-VARICO.

The department has called for interdisciplinary research papers on ATMANIRBHAR BHARAT: From the Perspective of Young Entrepreneurial Skills and Its Financial Implications from academics and practitioners alike.

The Concept Note vividly raised the ground situational reference to global crisis caused by the COVID-19 pandemic. It set the tone for transforming the crisis into an opportunity.

India has charted its own unique trajectory showing remarkable resilience through the most stringent lockdown at the onset of the Pandemic and then continually calibrated its response while gradually unlocking and easing economic activity. Thus, the call for papers was on lines of role and contribution of global economies in self-reliant India.

The papers, from academicians and practitioners, were provided with specific but varied themes to revolve around. The indicative themes cover areas on humanitarian, health-care Initiatives, women, youth and minority inclusivity, sustainable economic developments, political fallouts, IT, digitalisation & communication, HR, transportation, finance, international dimensions, entrepreneurship, education tourism, etc.

The response has been tremendous and encouraging, particularly when our efforts are at its infancy stage of evolution. We hope the papers published will contribute to the existing knowledge base and expand horizons of practicality. The papers have unveiled latent/ impending talent amongst stakeholders that provide new shape and direction to the existing thinking and action. Hope this attempt sets new rules for higher standards of accomplished institutional efforts.

Dr. S. K. Grover

Message

Dr. H Kumar

The present book entitled, 'Indian Economy and Entrepreneurial Prophecies Amidst Pandemic ' is making an attempt to foresee the future of Indian Economic System when there'll be tremendous use of Online Technology. This is an open secret that all of us are getting globalized. Even backward communities are making progress in searching new opportunities for earning livelihood. Modern education and information system have spread in the whole world like anything through active media and open cultural value system. Gone are the days when people had blind faith in Superstitions and Dharamgurus. Today almost every indian thinks on the lines of modernization in every sphere of life be it business, politics, health and so on. In the race of economic development all of us are trying to move ahead in absolute as well as relative terms. An era of perfect information and perfect competition has got prevalent in the whole marketing system. A direct link between producers and consumers has been established significantly. Traditional intermediaries like wholesalers, distributors, Aarhtis, brokers etc. are getting eliminated who used to exploit producers as well as consumers particularly in markets of agriculture products. Now professional agencies like Amazon, Paytm etc. are cropping up which facilitate promotion of Trade and Commerce. Fortunately our Government has been supporting the modernization move consistently. In brief I would like to say that the entire social system of earning livelihood is getting revitalized and consequently all of us are constrained to mould ourselves accordingly. With these words I wish a bright future for the upcoming book.

Thanks.

Dr H Kumar

Teacher-in-Charge

Department of Commerce

2020 - 2021

संदेश

Dr. Poonam Chaudhary

वैश्विक महामारी कोविड-19 ने विश्व को हर तरह से प्रभावित किया है सबसे ज्यादा दुष्प्रभाव आर्थिक जगत पर हुआ। प्रस्तुत संकलन में महामारी की विभीषिका से आगे निकलकर भविष्य के उत्पादन, उपभोग और विनिर्माण के नवीनतम आयामों पर विद्वतजनों के अमूल्य विचार संग्रहीत किए गए हैं। मानवीय चेतना शाश्वत उत्थानमयी है और भौतिक जगत में ह्रास एवं विकास की लुकाछिपी का खेल सतत चलता ही रहता है। आशा बदलवती होती है। वह चिता की चिंगारियों में भी चारु चित्रावलियों के रचनात्मक चमत्कार की अपेक्षा के लिए कटिबद्ध है। वर्तमान युग सूचना क्रांति का है कम्प्यूटर का है नवीनतम और उत्कृष्टतम अन्वेषण करने वाली अप्रतिम प्रतिभाओं का है। एक वर्ष से अधिक समय बीत गया विश्व महामारी की भीषण विभीषिका के चुंगल से पूरी तरह अब भी छूट नहीं सका है परन्तु आनलाइन की आभारी (वर्चुअल) पद्धति ने अपने पंख पसार कर जहां बंद बाजारों के गेट सीधे उपभोक्ता के दरवाजे पर खोल दिए। वही विद्यालयी पठन-पाठन से लेकर ऑफिस वर्क तक सब कुछ बड़ी सहजता और सरलता से आनलाइन चलने लगा। इन सभी पहलुओं पर इस पुस्तक में एक विस्तृत विवेचन, कदम यही होता है कि परिस्थितियों को जब अपने अनुकूल बदलना असंभव लगे तो अपने को परिस्थितियों के अनुकूल ढालना चाहिए। यह हमारे आर्थिक, बौद्धिक, वैज्ञानिक और भौतिक विकास का परिणाम है कि विश्व को पूरी तरह तहस-नहस करने की क्षमता वाले कोरोना काल में भी बड़ी द्रुतगति से हमने स्वयं को संभाला और कई को पूरी तरह आत्मसात कर चुका है इंटरनेट के जादुई चमत्कार ने मानवीय पहुंच को असीमित विस्तार दे के अनगिनत व्यापारिक प्रतिष्ठानों का अजस्र स्रोत बना दिया है यही कारण है कि युवाओं के सामने स्टार्टअप के रूप में एक ऐसा ''रनवे'' उपस्थिति है जहां से वे मनोवांछित उड़ान भर सकते हैं। कृषि, रक्षा, फर्मास्युटिकल, आटोमोबाइल, इलेक्ट्रॉनिक, हास्पिटैलिटी जैसे क्षेत्रों में अपार संभावनाओं के नवद्वार नव उद्यमियों के स्वागत के लिए आतुर है।

इस सम्पूर्ण पुस्तक का उद्देश्य यह है कि नवयुवकों को जो नवीनतम अवसर मिल रहे हैं उसका मानव कल्याण और अपनी उन्नति के लिए अवश्य अपनाएं अंत में ''सुमन'' की पंक्तियों के साथ हम अपनी बात को विराम देते हैं–

इसलिए समय के सैलाबों को मत रोको
खुशहाल हवाओं में न खिड़कियां बंद करो,
हर किरन ज़िंदगी के आंगन तक आने दो
नवनिर्माणों की लपटों को मत मंद करो।।

डॉ. पूनम चौधरी
पुस्तकालय अध्यक्ष

Introduction

Prof. O. S. Deol

Since the outbreak of deadly conoravirus early in 2020, nation-wide lockdown was preferably imposed by the Government of India as to save its people from this unknown or medically little known (as global studies and research are still being carried out to verify claims about the origin and impact of the virus on human life). Gradually, lockdown had been lifted in phased manner, primarily with the concern to boost Indian Economy and save the livelihoods alongwith lives of its citizens by the authorities. In May 2020, to accomplish this objective, the Government of India prompted rupees twenty Lakh Crore package in order to make country self-reliant, i.e. Atmanirbhar Bharat, whereby in this parcel, academicians and researchers found themselves engaged in crystallization for young entrepreneurs.

The current book is the brainchild of the Department of Commerce, in the times of national crisis – an attempt to appraise the efforts of an audacity of Indian authorities in harmony with the goals of young aspirants. India is now successfully placed itself in the league of young nation as it's around 62% population consists of young population. In the growth trajectory of Indian Economy in this decade, this is the prime time and manoeuvre to essentially be steep in participation of the youngsters in democratic process of employment and entrepreneurship.

Amidst world wide pandemic, battered Indian Economy is leaving no stone unturned to bounce back, whereby the contribution of the youngsters in this mission is inevitable. It may be assessed through two parametres - one, in Modern India, also Digital India, has been shifted on e-mode during pandemic, and stay at home work-culture came into existence during this time, here, technology played vital role. ICT (information, Technology and Communication) came into rescue to keep the economy functional as all its functions now been carried out from WFH (Work From Home), & WFA (Work From Anywhere), flexibi-hours and staying safely with family in respective house came as a relief. Secondly, youngsters' flamboyance filled the economy with a hope that with their skills and innovation they may pioneer themselves in modern technology driven India.

It is learnt that Pandemic and subsequent lockdown could not diminish the spirit of Youngsters. Several reports shows that how wisely they utilised their time to learn and polish their digital, technological and similar skills alongwith pursuing their creative- interest and hobbies kept them occupied in this time of home bound. Gone are the days when, in order to create the lavish empires, youngsters depend on their inherited money, muscle or any kind of influence. Sunderesan, a 32 year old billionaire went on to become the role-model of young aspirants, who emerged as a successful entrepreneur in this gloomy times, patronizing his entrepreneurial set up based on digital innovation.

Colossal opportunities in industrial growth and worldly interrelations can be utilised now by an entrepreneur with the help of technology, while seating in front of his device. A huge democratisation of wealth is enabling youngsters who do not own any inherited tangible properties or networks to beat inheritance by creating, buying and selling new ideas and concepts in Atmanirbhar Bharat.

Professor O S Deol
Editor-in-Chief

Preface

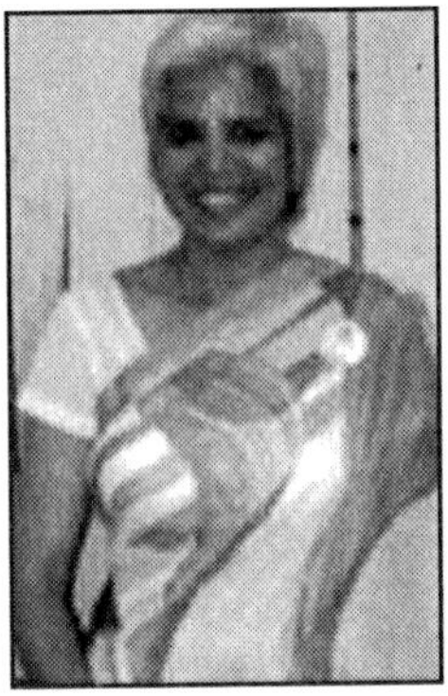

Dr. Kavita Yadav

The upcoming literary work of Department of Commerce on 'Indian Economy and Entrepreneurial Prophecies Amidst Pandemic' is comprehended prolific care towards the youngsters entrepreneurship possibilities amidst severe wave of corona, lockdown and despair Indian Economy in Pandemic. In the middle of Pandemic, on one hand anxiety, depression and uncertainty looms the academic future of youth. Contrary to it, technological transformation is a sigh of relief for not only students, but academicians, researchers, industrialists and political leaders equivalently. Unlike the business environment of the nation in pre-pandemic years, an entire remodelling in the economic operations have come into foray, which propel us to the basis of our current academic work.

Digital transition of Indian Economy during Pandemic furnishes new opportunities to young entrepreneurs amid imposition of challenges. Indian Economy is operationalised through online mode with foods & FMCG, pharmacies, groceries and information & entertainment are few sectors witnessed incessant shift on to e-business, Big-Basket, Reliance Fresh, Grofers, PharmEasy etc are name a few. Major advertisements and marketing dominate steeply on social media regarding products, services or any information during the nationwide lockdown.

In schools, colleges and universities teaching and learning went on to online mode, embraced by the stakeholders including teachers, students and parents albeit reservations. This online shift, blended L&D - Learning & Development opens numerous avenues for the post-pandemic phase too. Cyboard - the Online School claims to revolutionise the Indian Schooling by offering a boundaryless fun-learning academic environment for kids is considered the elementary step in this direction.

Tech-skills are quintessential for Fourth Industrial Revolution when automation is being adopted by more and more industries in the time to come, like Python, Block-chain, Artificial Intelligence & Machine Learning, Cyber Security, Cloud Computing have come up with the optimism among youngsters, They are being guided to take up any of these courses to strengthen their skills and organisational abilities during the Pandemic for staying relevant.

Medical Practitioners and ICMR Authorised Medical Bodies astonished the third wave of deadly coronavirus on young children, timely medical preparation to safeguard the health is another objective with inoculation before the formal governing bodies, Medical, paramedical, psychologists role is a calibrated move in the economy in this time. Online, Tele-consultancy, video calls, e-medical facilities are apparently booming in the Corona crisis for patients who require severe medical assistance.

The bruised Indian Economy with economic slowdown, inflation and unemployment as a resultant of announcement of lockdown, devastating effect of corona wave on loss of lives and livelihoods, fiscal deficit and negative GDP are challenges before the Government of India to be resolved by creating employment and entrepreneurial opportunities early in the time to come.

Digital India has thrived to catapult innovative amendments in work-culture and behaviour of people with them to stay safe and healthy at home through WFH and online purchasing. It opens the door for the youngsters to employ digitally with modernised, ease of doing sustainable online business & marketing practices through calibrated, collaborative & competitive approach in Atma Nirbhar Bharat, towards making India a self-reliant nation sans (de)globalised tacties, whereby world premium bodies like WHO, World Bank, Stock Market etc are committed to extend the requisite funds, vaccination and technological aid in order to empower youngsters to bounce back early in next national financial year.

Dr Kavita Yadav
Senior-Editor

Acknowledgement

The e-book is aimed to bring all the thinkers, academicians, research- scholars and executives under one roof to initiate and participate in deliberations around the Indian Economy, entrepreneurship in Atmanirbhar Bharat and emerging prospects for youth during Pandemic. I have triumphed over the dissemination of this literary work albeit it got delayed due to the unprecedented COVID crisis in the nation, and subsequent lockdown since it's resurgence of second wave.

The e-edited book is an effort of the Department of Commerce-SBSEC, I take this opportunity to express my sincere gratitude to all the members involved in this venture in various capacities.

At the onset, I express my thankfulness to our Respected Principal Prof S K Sinha for his constant support and guidance.

On behalf of the Department of Commerce - SBSEC, I extend sincere Gratitude and warm wishes to Prof R K Singh, Head & Dean, DSE, DU; Prof Amitabh Kundu, JNU; Prof Jaideep Sharma, IGNOU; and Prof Naseeb Ahmad, JMI, our Distinguished Editorial Board for their act of beneficence. It is our absolute honor to collaborate with these stalwarts in this academic affair of our department.

I consider it a privilege to work closely with Dr S K Grover, Dr H Kumar - Teacher-In-Charge (2020-2021) and Dr Poonam Chaudhary, our advisory Editorial Board members, I am grateful to them for collaborating so well in this multidisciplinary academic affair. Dr O S Deol, Editor-In- Chief, remains a source of inspiration and extends his full support, guidance and encouragement to make this work a reality.

With immense satisfaction, I take the opportunity to appreciate the hard work put in by Dr Aditi Goel, Dr Amrita Kaur, Dr Anshu Jain-Editors, and tech-savvy members, in bringing this venture, in its current shape, into the public domain. This endeavour would not have been easy, had it not been for Ms Shilpy Malhotra's time and effort to prepare strategy to propagate on social media.

I owe profound credit to Dr Shalu Suri and Dr Suman Swami in this incredible journey of making e-book for their instant availability to us.

With colossal pleasure, I would like to put emphasis on the contribution of the respected members of our Department of Commerce - SBSEC in completing the task organically with ease. In order to acknowledge their contribution, I would like to mention their names - Mr M C Sharma (Teacher-in-Charge, session 2021-2022), Mr Dinesh Kumar, Mr Vinod J Kaul, Mr Sunil Kumar, Mr Sunder Singh, Ms Viney Narang, Ms Khushboo Gupta, Ms Geeta Devi, Ms Versha Dhusia, Dr Triveni, Dr Ritika Chaudhary, Mr Rajan, Mr Shakti Singh, Mr Manish Kumar, Mr Tauseef Alam, Mr Ghanshyam Yadav, Ms Shivalik Veen, Ms Aruna Singh, Ms Tuba Shamim, Ms Pranita Srivastava, Mr Rupesh Sharma, Mr Suzanne Malhotra, Dr Sandeep Singh, Ms Manika Gupta, Dr Sonam, Ms Trishala Chauhan, Ms Seema Chaudhary, Mr Abhimanyu Bhardwaj, Dr Nand Lal, Mr Mohd Ehtesham, Mr Varinder Kumar, Mr Raj kumar Akela, Mr Vikram.

This academic affair would not have been possible without the support & involvement of the college fraternity, Office & Administrative personnel. Mr Dinesh Dhawan, Administrative Officer, deserves a special mention here. My gratitude to Mr J C Joshi, Mr Dharmender, Mr Chirag Malik for providing immediate official support, as & when required during the process of making this undertaking.

I appreciate the academic contribution from the authors (list enclosed), whom we are associated with from various colleges, universities and industrial/corporate sectors for their valuable submissions and imposing trust in us.

I am thankful to Research India Publication, its proprietor Mr Pathak Jee and Mr. G. R. Sharma for their active role in composing this manuscript in order and looking after the publication work with great enthusiasm.

Dr Kavita Yadav
Senior Editor

Contents

List of Contributors

1. **Abhishek Sharma,** Research scholar, Lovely Professional University, Jalandhar, Punjab, India.
E-mail: abhisheksharma36934@gmail.com
2. **Ankitha Lohia,** Research scholar, Lovely Professional University, Jalandhar, Punjab, India.
E-mail: ankithalohia07@gmail.com
3. **Ms Anju,** Commerce Dept, Delhi University, Miranda House College, New Delhi, India.
E-mail: anjuvekny895@gmail.com
4. **Ms Shweta,** Commerce Dept, Delhi University, Deen Dayal Upadhyaya College, New Delhi, India.
E-mail: shwetasah4@gmail.com
5. **Dr. Brijesh Kumar,** Department of Tourism Management, Govt. College, Sector – 9, Gurugram, Haryana, India.
E-mail: brijeshkumar8787@gmail.com
6. चन्दन कुमार, शोधार्थी (विधि) शारदा विश्वविद्यालय ग्रेटर नोएडा
E-mail: chandankumar621988@gmail.com
7. **Prof. Smt. I. K. Mathad,** B. V. V. Sangha's, Basaveshwar Commerce College, Bagalkot-587101
E-mail: surekha849@gmail.com
College Mail Id: bvvscommerce@gmail.com
8. **Dr. Indu Singh,** ARSD College, Department of Commerce, University of Delhi
E-mail: indu141182@gmail.com
9. **Mr. Krishan Dahiya,** Former Associate Professor, Government Colleges in Haryana.

10. **Ms. Khushbu Dahiya,** Former Assistant Professor, Dr. B. R Ambedkar National Law University, Sonipat.
E-mail: dahiya.khushbu02@gmail.com

11. **Ms. Namita,** Research Scholar, HNB Garhwal University, Srinagar, Uttarakhand
E-mail: namitakaushik35@gmail.com

12. **Nikita Chhatriya,** Shri Guru Gobind Singh College of Commerce, Teaching Center.
E-mail- chhatriyanikita2000@gmail.com

13. **Dr. Niraj Kumar Singh,** Head and Assistant Professor, Department of Geography, S.M.S.G. College Sherghati, Gaya, Magadh University, Bodh-Gaya, Bihar.
E-mail: nirajcsrd@gmail.com

14. **Ms. Poonam,** Department of Political Science, Assistant Professor, Mata Sundri College.
E-mail: poonam20051972@gmail.com

15. **Prof. Smt. S. S. Charantimath,** Asst. Professor, PG Department of Commerce, Basaveshwar Commerce College, Bagalkot.
E-mail: charantimathshilpa@gmail.com

16. **Prof. S. M. Khot,** Asst. Professor, Department of Commerce, Basaveshwar Commerce College, Bagalkot.
E-mail: shreekhot33@gmail.com

17. **Ms. Stuti Ghosh,** Assistant Professor (Visiting Faculty), Accounting and Finance at Banasthali Vidyapith, Rajasthan.
E-mail: stutighosh2018@gmail.com

18. **Sheetal V Barshi,** BBA, Basaveshwat Commerce College, Rani Channama, Belagavi.
E-mail: sheetalbarshi3@gmail.com

19. **Dr. Shephali Mathur,** Assistant Professor, School of Management, BBD University, Lucknow.
E-mail: shephalimathurscm@gmail.com

20. **Dr Prashant Kumar,** Assistant Professor, Department of Business Administration, Feroze Gandhi Institute of Professional Studies, Raebareli.
E-mail: prashant_kumar015@yahoo.com

21. **Smt. Y. H. Bilagi,** B.V.V. Sangha's, Basaveshwar commerce college, Bagalkot-587101
E-mail: yasmeenbilagi@gmail.com
College Mail id: bvvscommerce@gmail.com

22. **Ritu Raj Sinha,** Teacher
E-mail: sinharituraj77@gmail.com & rituraj011777@gmail.com

23. **Dr. Harikishni,** Assistant Professor, Bharti College, Delhi University, Delhi.
E-mail harikishni@gmail.com

24. **Sandeep Kumar Pandey,** Department of Commerce, Pondicherry university, Pondicherry.
E-mail: sandeeppandeycommerce@gmail.com

25. **Archana Kumari,** Faculty of Commerce, Banaras Hindu University, Varanasi
E-mail: archanak846@gmail.com

Chapter - 1

Aatmanirbhar Bharat – A Mission to Make India Self-reliant

Abhishek Sharma and Ankitha Lohia

Abstract: Atmanirbhar Bharat is the concept to make India self-reliant with entirely focus on local producers and service providers. This will boost the economy, improve living standards and most of all improve the nation's trade imbalance and net surplus. The purpose of this paper is to recognize the Atmanirbhar Bharat Abhiyaan vision of modern India proposed by the Honourable Prime Minister Shri Narendra Modiji. The main focus of this paper is on the five pillars of self-reliant India. This paper also discusses the contribution made by the government of India under this scheme so far to make India self- reliant. This paper also suggests the major changes that government of India can implement to achieve the mission of Atmanirbhar Bharat. This is a review-based paper that has used existing literatures and other secondary sources to study the major step taken by Indian government for Atmanirbhar Bharat.

Keywords*:* Atmanirbhar Bharat, Economy, Infrastructure, Technology driven system, Vibrant demography, Demand

Introduction

In the middle of the coronavirus pandemic (COVID-19) lockdown, the Indian prime minister Sri Narendra Modiji used a term Atamnirbhar Bharat in regards to economic growth in the nation which refers as self-reliant India or self-sufficient India.

On May 12, 2020 Prime minister Narender modi explained that self-reliant India depends mainly on five pillars of aatmanirbhar bharat. Giving the address to the country, PM Modiji stated the five pillars are namely economy, infrastructure, technology driven system, vibrant demography and demand. Defining each pillars, PM explained that the economy need not have to change incrementally but should preferably have a quantum jump. The infrastructure sector is eminently responsible for boosting India's overall advancement and enjoys strong attention from government for establishing policies that would assure time-bound construction of first-class infrastructure in the nation. The infrastructure ought to be world-class and it must describe India. The third pillar i.e. system of India must not be regarding last century instead should be technologically driven. He also said that about the demography of India which is largest and has vibrant demography. Lastly the demand and supply chain of the country needed to be utilized to its fullest level to make India self-reliant. (*India's Self-Reliance Stands on 5 Pillars of Economy, Infrastructure, Technology-Driven System, Vibrant Demography and Demand: PM Narendra Modi | India News | Zee News*, n.d.).

In the time of pandemic, three Atamnirbhar Bharat package worth Rs. 29.87 lakh crore were provided by the government. On 12 may 2020, Indian government introduced an economic package worth Rs. 20 lakh crore, on 12 october 2020, the government introduced an economic financial aid worth Rs. 73000 crore, which was defined as Atmanirbhar Bharat Abhiyan 2.0. And then on 12 November 2020, the Indian government introduced an economic financial package worth Rs. 2.65 lakh crore, which was defined as Atmanirbhar Bharat Abhiyan 3.0 (Sodhi *et al.*, 2020). Various government initiatives have been taken in the context of the Atmanirbhar Bharat, including an amendment in the definition of MSMEs, increasing the limits for private involvement in various sectors and rising FDI in the defence industry. In July 2020 Reliance Jio chairman Mukesh Ambani confirmed that Jio has developed a full 5G solution from scratch, which will be 'Made in India' 5G network. Slogan introduced under Atmanirbhar Bharat are 'vocal for local', 'local for global' and 'make for world' (Sethi *et al.*, 2020).

Discussion

Five pillars of Atamnirbhar Bharat

1. Economy
2. Infrastructure
3. System
4. Vibrant demography
5. Demand

Economy

The Indian economy is defined as a middle-class income emerging market economy. In nominal GDP India is fifth largest economy in the world and it is third largest country by purchasing power parity. The fastest growing sectors in Indian economy are agriculture sector, industry sector, services sector, manufacturing sector and food processing (Mi *et al.*, 2020). Recently there has been a lot of development in these sectors under AatmaNirbhar *Bharat scheme. To meet crop loan requirement of* Rural Cooperative Banks and Regional Rural Banks (RRBs), *NABRAD* (National Bank for Agriculture and Rural Development) is providing finance support of Rs. 120000 crores, this will assist 3 crore farmers (Lee *et al.*, 2020). To strengthen agriculture infrastructure government has decided to spend Rs. 100000 crores, this will enable quick and efficient harvesting, storing, processing, packaging, and selling. In order to maintain credit flow to animal husbandry, diary and fisheries sectors, the government will invest Rs. 16.5 lakh crore. If we talk about industry sector, government has made a big change in the industry sector by changing the definition of Micro,small and medium enterprise (MSME) (K. T. Çalıyurt, 2020). Previously manufacturing and service enterprise were taken in different categories but now government has made amendments in MSMED Act, 2006 by keeping manufacturing and service enterprise in one category. Government has increased investment and turnover limit for micro, small and medium enterprises, by this many companies will come under MSME category and they can get cheaper loans and tax rebates (Asher & Novosad, 2020). In recent union budget 2021, government has announced Rs. 1.97 lakh crores Production Linked Incentive Schemes, this will assist India to become global leader in manufacturing. In service sector, the government has decided to spend Rs. 64,180 crores on a centrally supported scheme 'AtmaNirbhar Swastha Bharat Yojana' in the next six years. To give post metric scholarship to 4 lakh schedule cast students, government is spending Rs. 35,219 crore for six years. In order to reach good health and quality of life, government is spending Rs. ₹ 2.87 lakh crores to provide universal water supply to 4378 urban bodies (Sarkodie & Strezov, 2019).

Infrastructure

More crucial and troublesome work in the development procedure of the nation is to supply the essential infrastructure facilities (*Infrastructure Development in India*, n.d.). Union budget 2021 has given most important and necessary consideration to infrastructure development which would decrease transaction cost and exchange cost and enhance factor productive capacity (*Infrastructure Development in India: Market Size, Investments, Govt*

Initiatives | IBEF, n.d.). Additionally, the concentration on railways and roads will establish a consolidated market in India for consistent transit of human resources and goods and services. The Indian government planned to make high investment in infrastructure sector, more predominantly, urban transport, highways and renewable energy (*Union Budget 2021: Infrastructure Clearly the Focus Area in the Budget - The Financial Express*, n.d.)

Infrastructure financing - Development Financial Institution (DFI): A effectively administered Development Financial Institutions is essential to act as a supplier, catalyst and facilitator for infrastructure financing. The aspiration of the government to have a key portfolio of minimum Rs 5 crore for DFI in the span of 3 years and also to capitalize DFI the government has granted amount of Rs. 20,000 crore.

Roads and Highways Infrastructure: Finance minister declared the length of roads exceeding 13000km, at value of 3.3 lakh crore, has so far been granted by the 5.35 lakh crore bharatmala pariyojana project.

Railway Infrastructure: Indian railway have planned a National Railway Plan for India 2020. The aim of the plan is to build a 'future ready' railway framework by 2030. Reducing the logistic costs of our industry is the foundation stone of our plan to empower 'Make in India'.

Urban Infrastructure: The government will progress ahead to increase the portion of the public transport in urban region by developing the metro rail system and enlargement of city transport facilities, and for this a new scheme of Rs 18,000 crore will be incorporated.

Power Infrastructure: Finance minister planned to initiate improve reform-based result connected to power allocation sector with cost of Rs 3, 05,984 crore over a period of 5 years. **Ports, Shipping and Waterways:** Budgets intends to give more than Rs. 20,000 crore by crucial ports and Public Private Partnership mode in financial year 2021-2022 (*Union Budget 2021: Infrastructure Clearly the Focus Area in the Budget - The Financial Express*, n.d.)

System

Under AatmaNirbhar Bharat system means a framework that does not follow the proceeding century norms. It should be capable of fulfilling our modern era vision and be technology oriented. To provide students the fundamental understanding of space technology and to raise their interest in new areas of space activities, the Indian Space Research Organisation (ISRO) has initiated a particularly unique program for school children named the "Young Scientist Program" (Yuvika) (Chaurasia, 2019). To make India a strong player in space technology, ISRO made history by launching Cartosat-3 which is earth observation satellite. It is able to take closest photos of any object from space. ISRO successfully launched "Emisat' which is electronic intelligence satellite. Emisat is created for Defense Research Development Organisation (DRDO) (Aggarwal *et al.*, 2020). It is also very useful to keep a close eye on border movements. Its primary goal is to track electronic or any type of human action on the Pakistani border. ISRO has built India's first human space flight centre in Bangalore. This will launch the first human space mission by the end of 2022. ISRO is also planning to build India's own space station by 2030 after Gaganyaan mission (Fairweather & Sutton, 2020). To make India strong in defense sector the next important organisation which is being contributing a lot is Defence Research & Development Organisation (DRDO). Its most important contribution is Integrated Guided Missile Development Programme (IGMDP), which was led by Dr. APJ Abdul Kalam. It was aimed to achieve self sufficiency in the area of missile technology. Under IGMDP India developed missiles like Short-range surface-to-surface ballistic missile – Prithvi, Intermediate-range surface-to-surface ballistic missile – Agni, Short-range low-level surface-to-air missile – Trishul, Medium-range surface-to-air missile – Akash, Third generation anti-tank missile – Nag Recently DRDO listed 108 system and subsystem for industry to build, create and produce to achieve "Atmanirbhar Bharat". DRDO recently launched 5 young science laboratories, the implementation of these laboratories builds the groundwork for high tech technology research and innovation (Redmond & Nasir, 2020). It recently launched Air Defence Fire Control Radar (ADFCR) 'Atulya',the primary goal of which is efficient level defence against all short and very short air attacks at day and night in all climatic conditions. It has launched many other defense system equipment system like Software Defined Radio-Airborne for secure communication, Advanced Light Weight Torpedo (ALWT) for detection of enemy target through sonar onboard ship or aircraft, 3rd Generation Helicopter Launch Anti-Tank Guided Missile (Dhruvastra) this is one of the world's most powerful anti-tank weapon systems, Anti Drone System which use a laser-based Directed Energy Machine gun to damage drones. These are some the big steps taken by DRDO to achieve aim of making India Atmanirbhar in modern world defense technology system (Singhal *et al.*, 2020)

Vibrant Demography

Government of India require the economy of India to be a vast contributor to worldwide development. Moreover a vibrant and powerful India can lead to stabilisation of nation's economic order. In the Virtual Global Investor Roundtable 2020, PM discussed about the four D's- diversity, democracy, demand and demography. This is why India is said to be diversified as it has numerous markets inside one market (*India to Play the Role of Global Growth Engine, Says PM Narendra Modi | Business Standard News*, n.d.). The population of India is youngest among the entire world. More than 65% of India population is below 35 years of age, i.e youth population, so there is a need to tap the potential of the youth population for economic growth of India (*Demographics of India - Wikipedia*, n.d.) In the coming year by 2022, the average age of the Indian population will be 28 years, which makes India's working age of the population a long step ahead of non- working age population. Tackling the demographic gain rely on the employability of the youth population, their wellbeing, professional training and skills, good governance and education. India can get the advantage of the demographic opportunity only if the programmes and the policies are associated to the shift in the demography. UNICEF 2019 stated that minimum 47% youth of India is not in the path to have the education and skills which are essential for employment in 2030. As the result of hich there is requirement of effective workforce that is properly educated and efficiently skilled (*Youth Can Be a Clear Advantage for India - The Hindu*, n.d.).

Demand

The COVID-19 outbreak is a 'extreme demand shock' for the economy of India and would result in moderation in the country's GDP growth as the COVID-19 pandemic caused lockdown which affected crucial disruption over different sectors (*COVID-19 Pandemic "severe Demand Shock" for Indian Economy: D&B - The Economic Times*, n.d.). The new package of atmanirbhar bharat focuses on demand instead of huge cash transfers. The development centres are making an environment which facilitates domestic demand, encourages companies to create jobs and increase production. The economy of India is moving into a year of instability. As the result of which it is crucial for supply chain managers to realise the challenges in front of them and be prepared to overcome the below challenges- Inventory and assets should be utilised fully, supply chain networks need to be converted to assist the growth of e-commerce, supply chain leaders should find approaches to leverage suitable transport policy changes, balance investment in labour and technology (*The Key Theme of Atmanirbhar Packages: Spur Demand Rather than Cash in Hand | Explained News,The Indian Express*, n.d.)

Conclusion

Government's recent new reforms, like the enabling of private enterprises in the strategic sectors, farm reforms, labour reforms and the commercial mineral extraction of coal, among many others, have served as central pillar of Indian economic development. India has a big pool of highly educated and enthusiastic youth, India has the benifit in the growing number of start ups and independent businesses supporting indegenous talent. With a population of 130 billion people, India has a large customer segment. In addition,increasing use of the internet and changing customer lifestyles have offered the local market a boost, encouraging new entrepreneurs and start ups. India has so many possibilities and resources in abundance. Including the greater level of skillset, this is one of the different factors that has made the nation the world's IT hub. India has good technical and engineering abilities, supported by world's best educational institutions working to educate India's youth. The government has introduced a new education policy, in order to meet the changing criteria of good quality education, innovation and research which will further work to make India a hub of knowledge. The 'Make in India' initiative is playing a major role in strengthening the

Indian manufacturing industry and decreasing dependence on imports. A move to self reliant ability in sector such as artificial intelligence,machine learning, fuel cell automobiles, bettery storage and components etc. can contribute more to make India Aatmanirbharat.

Reference

Aggarwal, S. C., Das, D. K., & Banga, R. (Eds.). (2020). *Accelerators of India's Growth—Industry, Trade and Employment.* Springer Singapore. https://doi.org/10.1007/978-981-32-9397-7

Asher, S., & Novosad, P. (2020). Rural roads and local economic development†. *American Economic Review, 110*(3), 797–823. https://doi.org/10.1257/aer.20180268

Çalıyurt, K. T. (2020). *New Approaches to CSR, Sustainability and Accountability, Volume I* (Kıymet Tunca Çalıyurt (Ed.)). Springer Singapore. https://doi.org/10.1007/978-981-32-9588-9

Chaurasia, A. R. (2019). Population and sustainable development in India. In *Population and Sustainable Development in India.* Springer Singapore. https://doi.org/10.1007/978-981-32-9212-3

COVID-19 pandemic "severe demand shock" for Indian economy: D&B - The Economic Times. (n.d.). Retrieved February 25, 2021, from https://economictimes.indiatimes.com/news/economy/finance/covid-19-pandemic-severe-demand-shock-for-indian-economy-db/articleshow/75081249.cms

Demographics of India - Wikipedia. (n.d.). Retrieved February 24, 2021, from https://en.wikipedia.org/wiki/Demographics_of_India

India's self-reliance stands on 5 pillars of economy, infrastructure, technology-driven system, vibrant demography and demand: PM Narendra Modi | India News | Zee News. (n.d.). Retrieved February 25, 2021, from https://zeenews.india.com/india/indias-self-reliance-stands-on-5-pillars-of-economy-infrastructure-technology-driven-system-vibrant-demography-and-demand-pm-narendra-modi-2283062.html

India to play the role of global growth engine, says PM Narendra Modi | Business Standard News. (n.d.). Retrieved February 23, 2021, from https://www.business-standard.com/article/economy-policy/

india-to-play-the-role-of-global-growth-engine-says-pm-narendra-modi-120110501857_1.html

Infrastructure Development in India: Market Size, Investments, Govt Initiatives | IBEF. (n.d.). Retrieved February 16, 2021, from https://www.ibef.org/industry/infrastructure-sector-india.aspx

Infrastructure Development in India. (n.d.). Retrieved February 16, 2021, from https://www.economicsdiscussion.net/india/infrastructure-development-in-india/20948

Lee, K., Miguel, E., & Wolfram, C. (2020). Does household electrification supercharge economic development? In *Journal of Economic Perspectives* (Vol. 34, Issue 1, pp. 122–144). American Economic Association. https://doi.org/10.1257/JEP.34.1.122

Mi, Z., Zheng, J., Meng, J., Ou, J., Hubacek, K., Liu, Z., Coffman, D., Stern, N., Liang, S., & Wei, Y.-M. (2020). Economic development and converging household carbon footprints in China. *Nature Sustainability, 3*(7), 529–537. https://doi.org/10.1038/s41893-020-0504-y

Redmond, T., & Nasir, M. A. (2020). Role of natural resource abundance, international trade and financial development in the economic development of selected countries. *Resources Policy, 66*, 101591. https://doi.org/10.1016/j.resourpol.2020.101591

Sarkodie, S. A., & Strezov, V. (2019). Effect of foreign direct investments, economic development and energy consumption on greenhouse gas emissions in developing countries. *Science of the Total Environment, 646*, 862–871. https://doi.org/10.1016/j.scitotenv.2018.07.365

Sethi, P., Chakrabarti, D., & Bhattacharjee, S. (2020). Globalization, financial development and economic growth: Perils on the environmental sustainability of an emerging economy. *Journal of Policy Modeling, 42*(3), 520–535. https://doi.org/10.1016/j.jpolmod.2020.01.007

Singhal, A., Sahu, S., Chattopadhyay, S., Mukherjee, A., & Bhanja, S. N. (2020). Using night time lights to find regional inequality in India and its relationship with economic development. *PLOS ONE, 15*(11), e0241907. https://doi.org/10.1371/journal.pone.0241907

Sodhi, -Garima, Singh, R., & Siddiqui, F. (2020). *THE ECONOMIC IMPACT OF OPEN SOURCE SOFTWARE ON COMPETITION, INNOVATION AND DEVELOPMENT IN INDIA.* https://economictimes.indiatimes.com/news/economy/policy/we-are-not-done-with-stimulus-nirmala-

The key theme of Atmanirbhar packages: spur demand rather than cash in hand | Explained News, The Indian Express. (n.d.). Retrieved February 25, 2021, from https://indianexpress.com/article/explained/atmanirbhar-bharat-fiscal-stimulus-sitharaman-budget-7049911/

Union Budget 2021: Infrastructure clearly the focus area in the Budget - The Financial Express. (n.d.). Retrieved February 19, 2021, from https://www.financialexpress.com/opinion/union-budget-2021-infrastructure-clearly-the-focus-area-in-the-budget/2190720/

Youth can be a clear advantage for India - The Hindu. (n.d.). Retrieved February 23, 2021, from https://www.thehindu.com/opinion/lead/youth-can-be-a-clear-advantage-for-india/article30897179.ece

Chapter - 2

Atmanirbhar Bharat from the Perspective of Young Entrepreneurial Skills And Its Financial Implications

ANJU AND SHWETA

Abstract: Atmanirbhar Bharat is the Vision of Prime Minister of India to make India self-reliant Nation however Self reliance does not mean isolating away from the world or closed economy but making National objectives a priority and translating India into bigger and more important part of the global economy.

"BUILD LOCAL TO GO GLOBAL" is the motto.

An Opportunities lie for young entrepreneurs in the packages announced by government for revival of the economy. Young entrepreneurs can invest and avail subsidies for themselves and helping economy to reach higher.

Introduction

The entrepreneurship is very a old concept according to which any one who runs business is called an entrepreneur. The more precise meaning of entrepreneur is; one who perceives a need and then brings together manpower, material and capital required to meet that need.

Entrepreneur is one who understands the market dynamics and searches for change respond to it and exploit it as an opportunity.

If we talk about the history of entrepreneurship in India then The history of entrepreneurship is important worldwide, even in India. In the pre colonial times the Indian trade and business was at its peak. Indians were experts in smelting of metals such as brass and tin. Kanishka Empire in the 1st century started nurturing Indian entrepreneurs and traders. Following that period, in around 1600 A.D., India established its trade relationship with Roman Empire. Gold was pouring from all sides. Then came the Portuguese and the English. They captured the Indian sea waters and slowly entered the Indian business. They forced the entrepreneurs to become traders and they themselves took the role of entrepreneurs. This was the main reason for the downfall of Indian business in the colonial times which had its impact in the post-colonial times too.Gradually we annexed by the British East India Company from the early eighteenth century and colonized by the United Kingdom from the mid-nineteenth century, India became an independent nation in 1947 after a struggle for independence that was marked by widespread nonviolent resistance. It has the world's twelfth largest economy at market exchange rates and the fourth largest in purchasing power. Economic reforms since 1991 have transformed it into one of the fastest growing economies however, and it still suffers from high levels of poverty, illiteracy, and malnutrition. Now The outbreak of COVID-19 has presented fresh challenges for the Indian economy.

The pandemic has devastating millions of people at risk of falling into extreme poverty and the possibility of increasing the number of undernourished people in the Economy. The damages caused by the deadly Coronavirus has taken everyone's life for a toss and has affected several businesses beyond repair. While the intensity of the impact differs from sectors to sectors. There are few sectors that have been hit the most and might continue to suffer until life turn back to normal.

Still India is facing the COVID-19 situation in fortitude and in a spirit of self reliance, that is evident in the fact that from zero production of personal protection Equipment before march 2020, India has created a capacity of producing PPE kits in lakhs and growing steadily. Additionally, India has demonstrated how it rises upto challenges and uncover opportunities therein By launching the Atmanirbhar Bharat, the vision of the Prime Minister Narendra modi ji of making India self –reliant Nation. First mention of this came in the form of Atmanirbhar Bharat Abhiyan or self reliant India mission during the announcement of the covid-19 pandemic related economic package on 12th May 2020,Announced package of 20 Lakh Crores about 10% of GDP of 2019

Meaning: Atmanirbhar Bharat means to Promote and give preference to Indigenous products and ensuring that these products match their imported counterparts in cost and quality by focusing on land, labour, liquidity and laws.

Objective

Strengthen local markets, production and supply chain: -Covid-19 has hit the local markets, their production and supply chain Atmanirbhar Bharat Abhiyan is a key to strengthen them.

Provide relief to various sectors including cottage industry, MSMEs, middle class and industries among others:-Various sectors are in distress, packages are announced to give some relief to these sectors

Empowering the poor, labourers, migrants both from organized and unorganized sector:- Poor and labourers got worst hit by pandemic the main objective of Atmanirbhar Bharat Abhiyan is to provide them relief

Complement Make in India initiative which intends to encourage manufacturing in India:- By producing in India at best quality complementing the make in India initiative launched in 2014

Building nation to compete at global level without adjusting counterparts, cost and quality of products:- Producing products in India should not adjust products counterparts and quality as of imported products and should be available as same price as those products in India so the manufacturers and consumers both will get same benefits.

Methodology

Here we have collected the secondary data through various magazines, newspaper and government websites for this study to make sure the results presented are Robust. This study focuses on descriptive research design.

Pillars of Self Reliant India

Bold reforms across sectors will drive the country's push towards self reliance.

To spur the growth and to build a self- reliant India, Atmanirbhar Bharat Abhiyan rests on 5 important pillars.

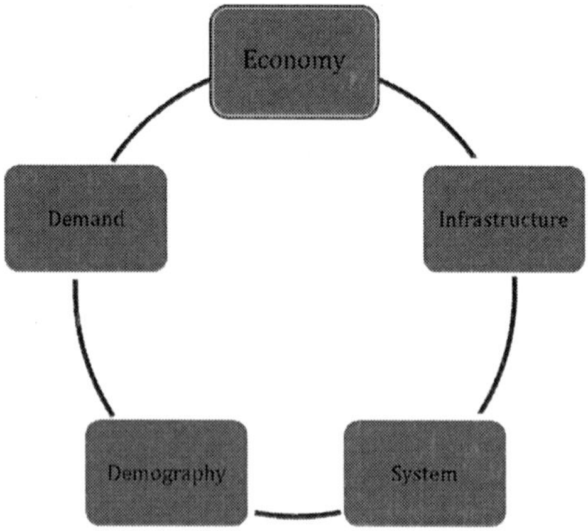

Economy: quantum jumps, not incremental changes so that India can covert the current adversity into an advantage

Infrastructure: that can be an image of modern India or it can be the identity of India

Systems: driven by 21st century technology and that is not based an old rule.

Democracy: A vibrant democracy that is the source of energy to make in India self reliant.

Demand: Where the strength of our demand and supply chain is utilized intelligently.

The five phases of Atmanirbhar Bharat focus on

Stimulus packages

Opportunities lie for young entrepreneurs in the packages announced by government for revival of the economy. Young entrepreneurs can invest and avail subsidies for themselves and helping economy to reach higher.

For MSMEs

The collateral free loans of worth Rs 3 lakh crore will be available for MSMEs it will help them crank up their operation.

The government has done well in extending a sovereign credit guarantee for the complete amount as bank may otherwise have been reluctant to support troubled borrowers.

The government could have specified the interest cap on these loans without leaving it to individual lenders as each of them has its own rate structure.

The Rs 20000 crore partially guaranteed subordinated debt programme and the 50000 crore fund of fund scheme will help boost the equity portion on MSMEs finances but again, the finer details need to be clear

Further, relaxing the definition of MSMEs addresses the perverse incentives of wanting to remain small.

This will incentivize MSMEs to scale up as and when the economy picks up, without worrying about not being able to take advantage of existing incentives
Classifications for MSME:

MSME Reforms

- New criteria for classification of MSMEs based on Investment and Annual turnover vis-a-vis criteria of investment:

Classification	Micro	Small	Medium
Manufacturing *(Existing)*	Investment<Rs. 25 lac	Investment<Rs. 5 cr	Investment <Rs. 10 cr.
Services Enterprise *(Existing)*	Investment<Rs. 10 lac	Investment< Rs. 2 cr	Investment<Rs. 5 cr.
Manufacturing &Services *(Revised)*	Investment < ₹ 1 crore & Turnover < ₹ 5 crore	Investment < ₹ 10 crore & Turnover < ₹ 50 crore	Investment < ₹ 20 crore & Turnover < ₹ 100 crore

For Finance intermediaries

NBFCs housing finances firms and micro finances entities get a much required liquidity boost in the form of a Rs 30000 crore scheme wherein their debt paper will be fully guaranteed by the government.

With this, and the partial credit guaranteed scheme of Rs 45000 crore, the government has broken the logjam wherein banks were unwilling to extend credit despite RBI's strong push.

This should largely attenuate the liquidity crisis in the non-banking space for now.

For DISCOMs

The government has also addressed the liquidity issues of power distribution companies through a Rs 90000 crore infusion to help them pay their dues till 31.03.2021 that will be securitized on their receivables and backed by a state government guarantee.

Discoms have been facing demand slumps due to the lockdown to contain covid-19

Current status: 68,000 crore has been sanctioned and around 25,000 crore is disbursed to discoms

Some of the discoms were not eligible for getting loans under package because they were not meeting working capital limit norms under Ujwal DISCOM Assurance Yojana (UDAY)

Earlier in August 2020, the Union Cabinet relaxed the working capital limit norms for discoms

The restriction was part of UDAY, banks and financial institutions are restricted to lend working capital up to 25% of discom's revenue in the previous year.

For Agriculture

Agriculture and allied sectors including dairy, animal husbandry and fisheries (1.5 lakh crore)

Rs. 1 lakh crore agriculture infrastructure fund for farm-gate infrastructure including using it for setting up cold-chain and post harvest management infrastructure.

20,000 crore to be provided to fishermen through Pradhan mantra Matsya Sampada Yojana and Rs 10,000 crore to formalize micro food enterprise.

Migrants and Street Vendors

Free food- grain supply to all migrants for the next 2 months, non- cardholder migrants, shall be given 5kg rice/wheat & 1 kg chana per family for 2 months

One nation card in three months- national portability of ration card with one nation one ration card will be implemented by august this year 67 crore beneficiaries will gain in 23 states, using this ration card in any corner of the nation in the next three months.

Affordable rental housing for urban poor- affordable rental accommodation for migrants labour and urban poor. A rental housing scheme will be incentivized to build affordable housing and converting government housing into rental housing under PM AWAS YOJNA

Rs 5000 crore special credit facility for street vendor which will be benefit 50 lakh street vendors. They will receive an initial working capital up to 10,000 within a month.

For Coal, minerals, defence production, civil aviation sector, space sector and atomic energy

Defence: FDI in defence manufacturing to be hiked to 74% from 49% under automatic route list of weapons and platforms are banned by government of India such items can only be produced from India

Young entrepreneurs can focus in this sector because it has a lot of potential to grow and achieving high.

Civil Aviation: restriction on utilization of the Indian air space to be erased for increasing of passenger aircraft to cut fuel usage and time to rake in 1000 crore per year benefit for the aviation sector 6 more airports to be privatized, India to become global hub for Aircraft Maintenance, Repair and Overhaul, tax rates rationalized

Here young entrepreneur can use their creativity and capitalize on opportunity created by government Coal and mineral: to introduce commercial mining in coal sector, entry norms to be liberalized, nearly 50 blocks to be offered immediately, coal gasification/liquefaction to be incentivized through rebate in revenue share Rs. 50,000 crore earmarked for infrastructure development in coal sector, coal bed machines extraction rights to be auctioned from coal India's mines to introduce seamless composite exploration Cumming-cum-production

Regime in minerals sector, 500 mining blocks to be auctioned, introduce joint auction of bauxite and coal mineral blocks, to rationalize stamp duty payable at the time of award of mining leases

Space: to allow private sector companies in satellites, launches and space-based services. Private sector will be allowed to use ISRO facilities and other relevant assets to improve their capacities

Atomic Energy : To set up research reactor in PPP(public-private partnership) mode for the production of medicals isotopes to help make available affordable treatment for cancer and other diseases, establish facilities in PPP mode to use irradiation technology for food preservation to complement agricultural reforms and assist farmers

Schemes

A few schemes have been discussed which we think giving best opportunities for new entrepreneurs

Production linked incentive (PLI) scheme

The production incentive scheme (PLI) is a central government scheme that was notified in April 2020 for large scale electronics manufacturing to provide financial incentives for domestic manufacturing of goods and also to attract large investment

The scheme was initially launched for domestic manufacturing mobile phones and specified electronic components and was later rolled out for pharmaceutical ingredients and medical devices. The PLI schemes resonates with the ambitious Atma Nirbhar Bharat campaign and make in INDIA initiative to make India a self reliant nation

Incentive Offered

This scheme is provides 4% to 6%incentive on incremental sales (over base year 2019-20) to eligible companies for manufacturing goods for 5 years period.

Eligibility: Companies that are registered in INDIA and are involved in the manufacturing of goods covered under the target segment of the scheme can apply under the scheme. The applicant can also operate existing and new manufacturing unit at one or more locations in the country.

List of sectors that are currently included under the scheme:

Sector	*Target Segments*
Mobile Phones Manufacturing	Mobile Phones Specified Electronic Components: SMT components, transistors, diodes, thyristors, resistors, capacitors, Printed Circuit Boards (PCB), PCB laminates, prepregs, photopolymer films, PCB printing inks, Sensors, transducers, actuators, crystals, System in Package (SIP), Micro / Nano-electronic components, Assembly, Testing, Marking and Packaging (ATMP) units
Manufacturing of Bulk Drugs	Pharmaceutical Ingredients (Drugs) Fermentation based KSMs/Drug Intermediates Fermentation based niche KSMs / Drug Intermediates / APIs Key Chemical Synthesis based KSMs/Drug Intermediates Other Chemical Synthesis based KSMs/Drug Intermediates/APIs

The Emergency Credit line Guarantee Scheme (ECLG)

Provides 100% Guarantee coverage to Banks and NBFCs to provide emergency credit facilities worth Rs. 3 lakh crore to MSMEs with outstanding credit of up to 50 crore as at February 20,2020 and Rs. 250 crore annual turnover in financial year 2019-20 to meet their working capital requirements ,without any requirement of providing additional collateral

Objective: To deal with issues of liquidity crisis, high default risks, supply shocks, shortage of labour and non-payments of dues caused by Covid-19 pandemic

Tenor – 4 years from the date of disbursement including a moratorium period of one year

Extended until March 31, 2021 and included 26 stressed (aviation, power, construction, roads and real estates, as identified by the KV Kamath Committee)and healthcare sectors as beneficiaries

In addition of MSMEs, individuals such as doctors, chartered accountants, lawyers, among others are also eligible to loan for professional purposes

Companies with outstanding dues of Rs. 50-200 crore as at February 29, 2020 are eligible to apply

Tenor- 5 years + one year moratorium

Current status: as of November 12, 2020, Rs 2.05 lakh crore of loans was sanctioned to 61 lakh borrowers

Operation Greens (Top to Total)

Ministry of food processing industries (MoFPI) has extended scheme from tomato, onion and potato(TOP) to all fruits and vegetables(TOTAL) for a period of six months on pilot basis as part of Atmanirbhar Bharat Abhiyan

Objective: protect the growers of fruits and vegetables from making distress sale due to lockdown and reduce the post harvest losses

Duration: extended till 31.03.2021

Eligible Crops: fruits -Mango, banana, guava, kiwi, lichi, papaya, citrus, pineapple, pomegranate, jackfruit Vegetables-French beans, bitter gourd, brinjal, capsicum, carrot, cauliflower, green chilies, okra, onion, potato and tomato

Any other fruit/vegetables can be added on the basis of recommendation by Ministry of agriculture or state government

Eligible Entities: food processors, FPO/FPC, co-operative societies, individual farmers, licensed commission

Agent, Exporters, state marketing/Co-operative federation, retailers engaged in processing and marketing of fruits and vegetables.

Subsidy: ministry will provide subsidy at 50% of the cost of the following two components

Air Transportation of eligible crops from surplus production cluster to consumption to Himalayan and North-Eastern States.

Hiring of appropriate storage facilities for eligible crops (for maximum period of 3 months) Subject to maximum Rs. 50 crore per project C) 70% for FPOs maximum Rs. 50 crore per project

Submission of claims: Eligible entities, who comply with the aforesaid essential criteria may undertake the transportation and/or storage of notified crops from notified surplus production cluster , without any prior approval from MoFPI and thereafter submit their claim on online portal

Mudra Yojana

Emphasis: On Women, backward classes, minorities, dalits and tribals who have been usually not provided the adequate opportunity of getting finances for their businesses

Objectives: For lying down policy guidelines for financing small/micro enterprises

Getting all the microfinance institutions and related entities registered and then regulating the same

Helping small businesses develop and grow further

Assisting lower income groups in building and expanding their business

For regulating all microfinance institutions that are dealing with trading, manufacturing and services

Limits: Shishu: up to Rs. 50,000 with interest being 12% annum, repayment time period is up to 5 years

Kishore: Loan from Rs. 50,000 up to Rs. 5,00,000 . The interest rate and loan repayment depends on guidelines of the schemes and bank keeping in view the applicant's credit

Tarun: Loan from Rs. 5,00,000 up to Rs. 10,00,000 The interest rate and loan repayment depends on guidelines of the schemes and bank keeping in view the applicant's credit

Loan is available: For car, commercial vehicle, Two wheeler, working capital, plant and machinery, revamping the business space

Eligibility: All non-farm income generating income businesses in trading, manufacturing and services whose credit requirements are lesser than Rs. 10 lakhs basically all individuals who want to avail loans below Rs 10 lakhs for micro units are qualified for such loan 60% the loans under the schemes to be offered via Shishu option and remaining 40% would be via Kishore and Tarun schemes

Pradhan Mantri Matsya Sampada Yojana (PMMSY)

Objectives: To boost production and exports in the fisheries sector

Allocation: Rs. 20,050 crore

Highest ever in Fisheries sector

Distribution: Out of 20,050 crore, Rs 12,340 is allocated for beneficiary oriented activities in Marine, Inland fisheries and aquaculture and about Rs 7,710 crore investment for fisheries infrastructure.

This scheme will not only benefit the fishermen, entrepreneurs, and cooperatives but by the multiplier and accelerator effects, many millions of families will earn decent income so this best opportunity option for young entrepreneur.

Findings and Discussions

Overall we have optimistic view that Atmanirbhar Bharat packages are never seen opportunities for existing and new young entrepreneurs Young entrepreneurs can seize the opportunities being available in form of packages to grow as an entrepreneur and help in boosting economy growth.

Schemes seem to give a strong supply side push by boosting the availability of capital on easy terms where the entrepreneur can capitalize these opportunities.

If implemented effectively, it can help in achieving the dreams of India being economically stable, technologically superior as young entrepreneurs would be able to help in achieving self-reliant needs.

Bibliography

1. Ray, R. (1992). *Entrepreneurship and industry in India, 1800-1947.* Delhi: Oxford University Press.
2. What is 'Atmanirbhar Bharat Abhiyan' announced by PM Modi. (2021). Retrieved 18 June 2021, from *https://indianexpress.com/article/india/atmanirbhar-bharat-abhiyan-pm-modi-economic-package-6406850/*
3. (2021). Retrieved 18 June 2021, from *https://www.jagranjosh.com/general-knowledge/atmanirbhar-bharat-30-1605177762-1 https://www.insightsonindia.com/2020/05/16/atmanirbhaabhiyan/*
4. New education policy key to making of 'Aatmanirbhar Bharat', says PM. (2021). Retrieved 18 June 2021, from *https://www.thehindu.com/news/national/other-states/new-education-policy-key-to-making-of-aatmanirbhar-bharat-says-pm/article33881844.ece*
5. discoms liquidity package: Latest News & Videos, Photos about discoms liquidity package | The Economic Times - Page 1. (2021). Retrieved 18 June 2021, from *https://economictimes.indiatimes.com/topic/discoms-liquidity-package*
6. vikaspedia Domains. (2021). Retrieved 18 June 2021, from *https://www.vikaspedia.in/news/atmanirbhar-bharat*
7. (2021). Retrieved 18 June 2021, from *https://economictimes.indiatimes.com/news/economy/finance/atmanirbhar-bharat-provides-vision-of-indias-plans-to-become-usd-5-trillion-economy-mea-official/articleshow/79342425.cm*
8. (2021). Retrieved 18 June 2021, from *https://bharatyojanas.com/atmanirbhar-bharat-scheme/*

Chapter - 3

Revival of Handicraft Sector in Tourism in India through Atmanirbhar Bharat Abhiyan

DR. BRIJESH KUMAR

Abstract: India has great tourism potentials for its unique diversification of cultural and natural attractions, which contribute the resources for this industry. Shopping being a basic component of tourism and India has always been famous throughout the world for its Handicrafts. Its rich heritage has played an important role in the economy of the country. The handicraft industries are commonly located in rural areas and the products are made for markets with personal touch. Whenever the visitors see that particular article which he has purchased gets happiness and reminds him of the days of visit. The attractive crafts have caught the imagination of the people abroad and earned rich dividends. Be it a metal craft, ivory carving, woodwork, jewellery, textile printing or leather embroidery. Indian craftsmanship adorns it with exquisite workmanship and superb artistry. These handicrafts are not only valuable earners of foreign exchange but also the interpreters of our country's art and culture to the people of other land.

India's tourism sector's total contribution to employment was 42 million jobs or 8.1% of the total employment and in the year 2018 contributed 9.3 % to India's GDP. This estimate shall increase considerably if the positive influence of tourism on the supporting industries is also considered.

But the current COVID-19 pandemic has added an unprecedented dimension of road blocks. It is likely to take at least a couple of years for the tourism industry and handicraft world to recover from this rude shock. Production for business came to a complete standstill. Many of the art lovers and stores have not only pulled back due to financial uncertainty but also galleries have shut doors and events such as crafts fairs have been cancelled. If there is no support and revival package from the government there could be job cuts in the textile sector, which has been severely hit by the on-going pandemic.

This new challenge can be tackled with the willing cooperation of the government by the introduction of "Atmanirbhar Bharat Abhiyan". The aim of this Abhiyan is to make country independent by empowering the poor, labourers, migrants working in handicraft sector and to make India a global hub for tourism and to strengthen our domestic tourism, Prime Minister of India urging each citizen to visit 15 tourist destination in India by 2022, so that both handicraft and tourism industry can be put back to the business.

Key Words: Atmanirbhar, Handicrafts, Tourism, Industry, Shopping

Introduction

Tourism is a basic and most desirable human activity deserving the praise and encouragement of all peoples and all government. It is an industry concerned with attracting people to a destination, transporting them there, housing, feeding, entertaining and shopping them upon arrival and returning them to their homes. Few decades ago travel was the privilege of a few rich people. Today, with the rise in the standard of living people in several developed and developing nations along with fast technological revolution in transport industry, overseas holidays are within the reach of middle and working class. Travel today, is sold like any normal consumer products through retail outlets, wholesalers and even departmental stores of many countries.

Tourism is not only an economic activity of importance to national development, but also an important medium of cultural changes among countries of the world. A lot of emphasis has been laid on the economic role of tourism, its contribution to the foreign exchange earnings of the nation and its potential for greater employment.

The full impact of tourism on the national economy is not just through expenditure on the front line tourist trade. It embraces all those industries, which have been called upon at various stages of the process to supply goods or services. The output produced by the industries which are outside the direct tourism sector are in very real sense due to the needs of the tourists who spends the money in the first place and sets the whole things going. According to the Richard an economist, there are two sets of links between tourist spending and the economy. First, the broad consumption items which have a direct affect. These relates to the actual expenditure involved on tourism e.g. transport, accommodation, food and drinks, shopping services etc. Secondly, the links between the traders directly involved in tourism and those traders and industries, which supply the tourism, trade with goods and services. (Negi, 1996).

Multiplier Effects

According to economists, tourism industry compared to other industry has much larger multiplier effect. In simple words, the money spent by the tourist circulates through the economy, as it changes hands and is spent and represent a number of times or every unit of Tourism Expenditure goes through several round of income creation and expenditure before its effect is exhausted.

The constant turnover of tourist expenditure is known as multiplier effect. Money spent by a tourist on hotel, accommodation, food, beverages, shopping, entertainment and transportation does not finish or ends but provides an income to hotel staff, taxi owners, shopkeepers and suppliers of goods and services. They, in turn, spend part of this income on their requirements of goods and services. The second round of recipients once again spends it to meet their needs. Thus, tourist money flows through numerous segments of the economy. It is just not a few hoteliers and travel agents who benefit from the tourism sector. Thus there is a chain reaction of spending money in Tourism Industry.

Growth of International Tourism

International tourism has grown steadily since 1950, as also tourism expenditure. Revenue from tourism means a lot to the host country, as foreign visitors in foreign exchange, which the host country can use for its economic development, contribute it. An idea of the growth of tourism and tourism expenditure can be had from the following table (Seth, 2003)

Table - I
World Tourism Growth 1996 – 2019

	International Tourist	*International Tourist*
Year	*Arrivals (million)*	*Receipts (US$ billion)*
1996	569.2	438.7
2000	682.0	478.0
2005	802.0	679.0
2010	940.0	919.0
2015	1195.0	1217.0
2016	1241.0	1246.0
2017	1333.0	1347.0
2018	1409.0	1457.0
2019	1460.0	1478.0

Source: Figures have been taken from Indian Tourism Statistics, 2020 published by Marketing research division, Ministry of tourism, Govt. of India

It is evident that tourism is a growth-oriented industry. It has never looked back since it started in the early fifties.

India's Share in World Tourism

India being a big country has everything to offer to everybody. Visiting India is an enthralling and memorable experience to one and all. India is a tourist paradise and has all unique features of modernity and traditional hospitality.

India has been a late starter in tourism. Understandably, after independence in 1947, the attention of the government and people was focused on key areas like agriculture, irrigation, industry, power and the infrastructure. Education literacy, health care, social reform occupied canter stage in government and political thinking and so-called "luxury" activities like tourism were left to their own devises. Tourism thus grew on its own (Ranga, 2000).

The international tourist arrivals in India were only 16,829 in 1951. Arrivals jumped to about 1.3 million or thirteen lakhs in 1990 – not including the citizens of Bangladesh and Pakistan. Visitors from Pakistan and Bangladesh were another four lakh.

Tourism has now become a significant industry in India. It is an emerging employment generator, a significant source of foreign exchange for the country. India in the year 2019 received 10.93 million of foreign tourists and foreign exchange earnings were 30.058 billion. Similarly in the year 2019 approximately 2321.98 million of domestic tourist visited on tourism in different states of India. International tourist arrivals in India are expected to reach 30.5 million by the year 2028. India's share in world tourism in the year 2019 is just 1.23 per cent. Share in receipts is 2.03 per cent. (Indian Tourism Statistics, 2019).

Components of Tourism

In order to travel to a particular area there must be a reason, for example a person may travel for leisure, business, visiting friends and relatives, health, education etc. He/She select a

Table - II
The growth pattern of tourists in India may be seen in the following table

Years	*Domestic (in million)*	*Foreigners (in million)*
2000	220.11	2.54
2005	392.04	3.92
2010	747.70	5.78
2015	1431.97	8.03
2016	1615.39	8.80
2017	1657.55	10.04
2018	1854.93	10.58
2019	2321.98	10.93

Source: figures have been taken from Indian Tourism Statistics, 2020 published by Marketing research division, Ministry of tourism, Govt. of India

Table - III
Share of India in the World Tourism Receipts

Year	*Per cent Share of India in World Tourism Arrivals*	*Per cent Share of India in World Tourism Receipts*
1996	0.40	0.65
2000	0.39	0.73
2005	0.49	1.10
2010	0.61	1.56
2015	1.15	1.73
2016	1.21	1.84
2017	1.26	2.03
2018	1.24	1.97
2019	1.23	2.03

Source: figures have been taken from Indian Tourism Statistics, 2020 published by Marketing research division, Ministry of tourism, Govt. of India

destination for one or the other reason. Transport is necessary to travel and hotels to stay at the destinations for one or the other reasons. So tourism industry has various components: A) Attractions, B) Accommodation C) Transport D) Shopping

Attractions: Attraction is the most important as these are the base of tourism. Unless these are there, tourist will be inspired to go and enjoy to a particular destination. Attractions are natural and man-made

Transport: Connectivity is very important for tourism development. This could be possible only if adequate transportation infrastructure and access to destination is efficient, comfortable and inexpensive. A tourist in order to get his destination therefore, needs some mode of transport. This mode of transport may be air, rail, road, sea.

Accommodation: This is an important part of the tourism infrastructure because any traveller will need a bed to sleep at the end of the day. Accommodation comes in many forms like hotels, motels, lodges, guest houses, furnished apartments, camps, resorts etc.

Shopping: Tourists love to buy gifts, mementos, jewellery and other items form the tourist spots as are typically associated with these spots. Shopping in the context of tourism administration has become a roaring business nowadays. All the products to be sold in shops or bazaars of tourist spots are the resources of shop owners. Further products, eatables, cold drinks, etc. sold at beaches, lakes, parks, etc. are also resources of the vendor of such items. Finally, the shops and buildings in which, these products are sold are also the resources of those vendors who own such shops and buildings. (Jayapalan, 2001)

Special Interest Tourism

In spite, India having great tourism potential for its unique cultural heritage, historical past and natural attraction is unable to attract foreign tourist due to the poor perception among

European countries because developed countries particularly Britishers who ruled over India for 200 years projected India as a land of poverty, heat and dust. By introducing "Special Interest Tourism" (Variety in tourism products) to visitors, so the main aim is to change the existing perception of India. When travel is centred around a special interest of tourist like eco, cultural, adventure, sports, religion, architecture, museums, photography, Buddhism, cuisine, shopping, museum, golf and many more is referred as Special Interest Tourism, which has been a practice for long in many developed countries.

To increase tourist traffic (especially of foreigners), to change existing perception about India and to popularize India as a tourist destination is the basic objective or goal of special interest tourism. It not only boosts tourist traffic to India from other countries but also generates curiosity to see the country itself and have the experience at first hand, appealing for India as a travel destination.

As shopping is a basic ingredient of tourism and considered as Special Interest Tourism. Special interest tourism is always motivated by particular interest of the tourists that act as a main inspiration for travel.

Special interest tourism appears to be a type of tourism that can offer multiple opportunities and can therefore be developed more or less in tune with the preferences of the tourists opting for special interest tourism because it provides:

- The interest component in Special Interest Tourism.
- The total experience to the tourist.
- The decision to visit a destination again and again. (Andrew, 2007)

Shopping and Tourism

Tourism and shopping are inextricably linked and countries with substantial turnover of tourists have taken full advantage of this phenomenon. Whenever tourists visit these places, one of the objectives of the visit is shopping. Tourists' plan weekend trips to Hong Kong, Paris, London and Singapore primarily for shopping. The price advantage, the well laid out infrastructure, the attractive and alluring display of merchandise in shopping malls and departmental stores - these are the factors which motivates tourists to go on a shopping, when they visit these places.

The launch of Suraj Kund Craft Mela in Haryana close to Delhi in the year 1986 was aimed as showcasing India's rich heritage of handicrafts and handlooms for tourists in the month of February every year. The shilpagram at Udaipur (Rajasthan) is yet another attempt towards promotion of Indian Handicrafts. Similarly, tourism department of Uttar Pradesh has been organizing, Taj Mahotsav in Agra every year in the month of March only to promote Indian handicrafts. The main objectives of these fairs among tourists were to project the traditional rural ambience of a typical village, to highlight the finest handicraft and handlooms traditions of the country with lot of cultural and entertainment programmes which makes these events memorable for tourists.

Similarly to promote tourism, Delhi Administration has done a commendable job in setting up Delhi Haat - which is a year round exposition of country's crafts and cuisine. Maharashtra Tourism Development Corporation has been running a craft fair in Mumbai's art district, Kala Goda in the month of January. The Corporation provides a platform for artisans, street performers, musicians and dancers from various parts of India to show their talents. In order to make India a shopping hub among tourists, there is need to set up more crafts fair (melas) at important touristic events like Pushkar Fair, Desert Festival (Jaisalmer), Kite Festival (Ahmedabad) and Sonepur Fair in Bihar.

The state emporia, run by various State Governments, can display a vital role in promoting and marketing our handicrafts. Central Cottage Industry Emporium in the national capital and State Emporia are doing a great job in the promotion of handicrafts. There is need to attract private entrepreneurship in this sector. The setting up of a shopping complex known as 'Village' in Hauz Khas, Delhi, has been a welcome step. The establishment of 'Santushti' by Air Force officers' wives in New Delhi has been another imaginative step.

In Kolkatta, a complex known as Swa Bhumi has come up through private enterprise and initiatives to sale of handicrafts/ handlooms. 'Vaishala' in Ahmedabad which has a unique museum of 'untensils' along with village-like atmosphere, replete with entertainment and excellent eating facilities, has been another bold and imaginative effort at showcasing rural India. Another similar complex 'Chaukhi Dhani' near Jaipur has become quite popular with the tourists.

There is need to have such complexes in other metropolitan cities and touristic places. Simultaneously, we need to decongest and spruce up traditional shopping centres like 'Chandni Chowk' in Delhi, 'Hazarat Ganj in Lucknow, 'Char Minar' in Hyderabad and Chowranghee in Kolkata where the tourists can find shopping and exciting and exotic experience. (Goswami, 2003)

Impact on the economy

All major countries of the world depend on the motive force of tourism industry to boost their economies. According to the Tourism Statistics, (2019), published by marketing research division, Ministry of tourism, Govt. of India, footprint of foreign tourists increased from 2.54 million in the year 2000 to 10.93 million in 2019. The foreign exchange earnings of USD 30.058 billion, or 9.2% of the country's GDP, placed India seventh in the global ranking. International tourist arrivals in India were expected to reach 30.5 million by the year 2028. As the impact of COVID-19 pandemic is unpredictable now, this estimate could change substantially. Domestic tourism during the same period, increased from 220.11 to 2123.00 million. Globally, tourism accounted for 319 million jobs, or 10% of the total employment and 10.4% of the total GDP, in 2018. Travel and tourism employ more than 42 million people in India, which is approximately 8.1% of the total employment opportunities. Last year, it contributed 9.3% to India's GDP, which can accelerate to 9-10% annual growth and add millions of high-quality jobs each year. Given that 72% of India's population is below 32 years of age, tourism is the perfect fit for generating jobs for the coming generations (Bhandari, 2018). Increasing tourist arrivals, both international and domestic, have created jobs in remote areas like Ladakh, interior parts of Himachal Pradesh, Madhya Pradesh and the North East of India. Pristine beauty of these places, rich ethnic culture, mouth-watering cuisine and colourful fairs and festivals, contribute a lot to the national earnings and creation of new job opportunities.

Societal development

All round developments due to tourism lead to financial stability and better standards of living, health care and education. Local societies develop broader perspective by interacting with tourists. Younger generations stand to gain a lot because their horizons expand and the urge to do something new and bold is evoked. In order to reach the benefits of tourism to the marginalised and vulnerable people, tourism industry is increasingly popularising the products of rural India. Many remote places specialize in handicrafts such as textiles, articles of decoration, furniture, toys, foot wear, stationery, paintings

& drawings, which are liked by both, foreign and local tourists. Some exquisite creations come even from the physically handicapped people and their incomes increase. Wonderful creativity of many obscure sculptures and architects does not escape the discerning tourists and that opens new vistas for their talent to flourish. These creations contribute greatly to promote the art & culture of far flung destinations.

Tourism Concern on Covid-19 pandemic

The current Covid-19 pandemic has added an unprecedented dimension of road blocks. It is likely to take at leasta couple of years for the tourism industry and handicraft world to recover from this rude shock. Production for business came to a complete standstill. Many of the art lovers and stores have not only pulled back due to financial uncertainty but also galleries have shut doors and events such as crafts fairs have been cancelled. If there is no support and revival package from the government there could be job cuts in the textile sector, which has been severely hit by the on-going pandemic.

This new challenge can be tackled with the willing cooperation of the government by the introduction of "Atmanirbhar Bharat Abhiyan". The aim of this Abhiyan is to make country independent by empowering the poor, labourers, migrants working in handicraft sector and to make India a global hub for tourism and to strengthen our domestic tourism.

Domestic tourists who play an important role in developing tourism. There will be a fall in the flow of foreign tourists in India due to on-going Covid-19 pandemic in the coming years. But it will be our domestic tourism that will bail out during this crisis. India is the second largest populated country in the world. So promotion of domestic tourism is the call of the time. To come out of this crisis even Prime Minister of India urging each citizen to visit 15 tourist destination in India by 2022, so that tourism industry can be put back to the business.

Solutions for the Revival of Handicraft sector in India

The on-going coronavirus pandemic has impacted all the industries across the globe but the worst affected industry has been the art and handicraft world like cancellation of orders, pending of payments, shipment on hold or struck in transit etc. were some of the difficulties faced by both artisans and craft enterprises during phases 1 and 2 of the countrywide lockdown. Production for business came to a complete standstill. There is an urgent need to transform the landscape of handicraft manufacturing. Some of the steps that can be taken to improve the situation include:

- The entry of many e-commerce players and conducting online melas in order to revive the industry and generating income for the weavers have raised hopes of empowering artisans across the country, giving them once again the privilege of selling their artefacts in the unprecedented times when the expenditure on such items has gone minimal.
- India's crafts and textiles are considered as the pride of the nation. Patterns and techniques of weaving changes very fast and we need to preserve the Indian weaves at any cost so that these ancient techniques don't get lost. For this, the younger generation have to be encouraged by the government and local authorities to take up weaving as a sustainable earning avenue and create opportunities for the limited infrastructure up grade.
- Various organisations and NGOs need to step up to expand skills of weavers and artisans. The textile and handicraft partners working in this sector should

help artisans to shift their business to PPE model, generating some income opportunity for them. It is also essential to work on long term concerns like building resilience beyond wages so that they can sustain themselves in the world during and post-Covid. Resilience can be built by focusing on expanding the skills of the artisans and working on developing other less intricate products that are in need at that particular period of time. They should learn to do most of the services in-house like dyeing of fabrics to become more self-sufficient.

- During the on-going Covid-19 period, in order to keep the artisans and weavers spirits high, it is important to build trust with the artisans. Artisans and weavers should be counselled regularly so that they can share their concerns. More such meetings should be organised on whats-app calls with them.
- In order to revive the handicraft sector during Covid-19 period, government can create a supporting environment that is favourable for handicrafts manufacturers and artisans, with faster response against foreign dumping and competing imports. Apart from entrepreneurs, investors can also channel their money to select those companies, which benefit local manufacturers, giving the war-cry of 'Make in India' a financial boost and vocalising the local goods.

Conclusion

Tourism and shopping are inextricably linked and countries with substantial turnover of tourists have taken full advantage of this phenomenon. Shopping is a well-organised activity and the literature (brochure etc.) brought out by – tourism boards,

Municipal Corporations, traders associations and others local bodies-highlight this vital aspect of tourism.

Handlooms are the second largest employment generating sector in the country, next only to agriculture. Handlooms and handicrafts are a source of livelihood for millions of people. If handloom weavers and artisans have to overcome this situation, the government has to immediately announce an economic package or financial bailout by the Ministry of Textiles, Govt. of India for them as part of the Atma Nirbhar Bharat Abhiyan. The Handloom and Handicraft Boards have to be immediately revived and put back into action. Instead of filling these with political appointments who have little awareness about the sectors, capable persons who have rich experience in the field must be appointed as Board members, which alone reflects the government's commitment towards the cause of handlooms and handicrafts.

The Boards have to function as the facilitators between the weavers and artisans, their representatives and the government and prepare as well as implement plans for supply of raw material, providing credit support and market linkages, and enable weavers and artisans to access various welfare measures announced by the government. The present GST on handlooms and handicrafts should be abolished, tax relief, subsidized raw materials and adequate funds must be allocated in the plan budgets.

The development of handicraft industry should be left to the initiatives of the government and private sector. The government should concentrate on planning broad strategies of handicraft development, provision of fiscal and monetary incentives to catalyse private sector investment and devising an effective regulatory and supervisory mechanism to protect the interest of the industry.

In fact other part of the world may learn many things from India. Indians might be poor from pocket but the wealth what they have in their behaviour is matchless in the world. Shopping in tourism can be very helpful for regional development and employment. Thus tourism brings buyers to the producers' doorstep as the artisans at work, lend an authentic flavour to the tour package.

References

Andrew, S, (2007), Introduction to Tourism & Hospitality Industry, Tata McGraw Hill Co. Ltd, New Delhi, pp. 20-21.

Bhandari, A. 2018. How Tourism can be an employment generator?, Hindustan Times, New Delhi, 19 June, ht education, pp.2.

Goswami, B.K., Raveendran, G, (2003), A Textbook of Indian Tourism, Har-Anand Publications, pp. 68-72.

Indian Tourism Statistics, Ministry of Tourism, Government of India, 2020.

Jayaplan, N, (2001), An Introduction to Tourism, Atlantic Publisher and Distributors, New Delhi, pp.107-113.

Negi, JM, (1996). Tourism and Travel Concepts and Principles, Gitanjali Publishing House, New Delhi, pp. 15-17.

Ranga M, (2000), Tourism Potential in India, Abhijeet Publications, pp. 7.

Seth, PN, & Bhatt, SS, (2003), An Introduction to Travel & Tourism, Sterling Publisher, New Delhi, pp. 15-16.

Declaration

I, Dr. Brijesh Kumar, declare that the Paper entitled "Revival of Handicraft Sector in Tourism in India through Atmanirbhar Bharat Abhiyan" is neither published and not under consideration for publication any elsewhere.

Chapter – 4

पंडित दीनदयाल उपाध्याय के स्वदेशी चिंतन भारतीय अर्थव्यवस्था एवं वर्तमान संवैधानिक उपबंध

चन्दन कुमार

सम्पूर्ण आलेख (FULL PAPER) : संविधान से तात्पर्य ऐसे दस्तावेज से है जिसकी एक विशिष्ट विधिक पवित्रता होती है जो राज्य सरकार के अंगों (कार्यपालिका, विधायिका और न्यायपालिका) के ढाँचे को और उनके प्रमुख कार्यों को निर्दिष्ट करता है और उन अंगों के संचालन के लिए मार्गदर्शक सिद्धांतों को विहित करता है। संवैधानिक विधि की कोई निश्चित परिभाषा नहीं है। सामान्यतः इस शब्द का प्रयोग ऐसे नियमों के लिए किया जाता है जो सरकार के प्रमुख अंगों की संरचना, उनके पारस्परिक सम्बन्धों और प्रमुख कार्यों को विनियमित करते हैं। विधिक अर्थ में ये नियम दोनों प्रकार के होते हैं– कठोर विधि नियम और प्रथाएँ जिन्हें सामान्यतः अभिमत कहा जाता है जो अनिनियमित नहीं होती हैं किन्तु सरकार से संबंधित सभी व्यक्तियों पर बाध्यकारी होती हैं। ये ऐसे अनेक नियम और प्रथाएँ हैं जिनके अनुसार हमारी सरकार की प्रणाली का संचालन किया जाता है। इस अर्थ में विधि का भाग नहीं होती हैं कि उनके उल्लंघन के लिए न्यायालय में कार्यवाही की जा सकती है। यद्यपि एक संवैधानिक विधि का अधिवक्ता सरकार के विधिक पहलुओं से ही सरोकार रखता है फिर भी उसे संवैधानिक विधि के इतिहास और राजनीतिक संस्थाओं के संचालन के लिए उपर्युक्त प्रथाओं और अभिमतों का ज्ञान रखना आवश्यक होता है।

किसी भी देश का संविधान एक दिन की उपज नहीं होता है। संविधान एक ऐतिहासिक विकास का परिणाम होता है। अतएव भारतीय संविधान के आधुनिक विकसित रूप को समझने के लिए उसकी ऐतिहासिक पृष्ठभूमि का भी सम्यक् ज्ञान आवश्यक है। ऐतिहासिक प्रक्रिया के सम्यक् ज्ञान के बिना हम संविधान को भलीभाँति नहीं समझ सकते हैं। किन्तु इसके लिए हमें अंग्रेजों के भारत–आगमन काल से पहले नहीं जाना होगा, क्योंकि भारत में सांविधानिक परम्परा का विकास अंग्रेजों के भारत में आगमन के समय से ही प्रारंभ हुआ। आधुनिक राजनीतिक संस्थाओं का उद्भव एवं विकास इसी काल में हुआ। भारतीय संविधान के ऐतिहासिक विकास का काल सन् 1600 ई0 से प्रारम्भ होता है। इसी वर्ष इंग्लैण्ड में ईस्ट इण्डिया कम्पनी की स्थापना की गयी थी।

पंडित दीनदयाल जी ने राष्ट्र व संविधान परिषद विश्लेषण किया व इस विषय पर अत्यधिक संतूलित विचार व्यक्त किये।

राष्ट्र की एकात्मता को क्षीण करने वाले प्रत्येक विचार को, वह किसी भी क्षेत्र से संबंधित क्यों न हो, पं. दीनदयाल जी ने सदैव घातक एवं त्याज्य ही माना था। उसमें निहित संकट को वे तुरंत ही राष्ट्र के ध्यान में लाने की चेष्टा किया करते थे। एक राजनीतिक दल के नेता होते हुए भी उनकी राष्ट्रहित दक्ष मेधा केवल लोक–रंजन की सतही नारेबाजी के व्यामोह में कभी नहीं पड़ती थी। इस संदर्भ में दो महत्वपूर्ण प्रश्नों का उल्लेख समीचीन होगा, पहला है हमारे संविधान का और दूसरा आनुषंगिक राज्यरचना का।

पंडित जी ने ''भारतीय संविधान पर एक दृष्टि'' शीर्षक एक लेख लिखा था, जिसमें उन्होंने पर्याप्त आशावादी दृष्टिकोण रखा सा लगता है। उस लेख में उन्होंने लिखा है– कि देश की बदलती राजनीतिक, आर्थिक एवं सामाजिक परिस्थिति के कारण संविधान सभा और उसके सदस्यों की मानसिकता में जैसे–जैसे परिवर्तन होता जा रहा है, वैसे–वैसे संविधान का स्वरूप भी बदलता जा रहा है। यह स्वाभाविक भी है, क्योंकि स्वतंत्रता–प्राप्ति के बाद हमारा देश धीरे–धीरे अपने स्वाभाविक स्परूप को पहचान रहा है। अपना स्वरूप क्या है और आत्मा क्या है, इसके ज्ञान का उदय हो रहा है। परतंत्रता के काल में आयी विकृति दूर होकर हमारी अपनी प्रकृति प्रबल होती दिखाई दे रही है। अतः स्वाभाविक है कि इस

प्रकृति की अभिव्यक्ति जीवन के सभी क्षेत्रों में होगी और उसका प्रभाव इन क्षेत्रों का नियंत्रण करने वाले हमारे संविधान पर भी पड़ेगा।''

1919 के अधिनियम द्वारा स्थापित दोहरी शासन–प्रणाली पूर्ण असफल रही, क्योंकि वह भारत में एक उत्तरदायित्वपूर्ण सरकार की स्थापना न कर सकी। भारत की जनता को शीघ्र ही पता चल गया कि अंग्रेजों से आजादी हासिल करना आसान नहीं था। परिणामस्वरूप भारतवायिों ने नये उत्साह और नयी प्रेरणा से अपने स्वतंत्रता–संग्राम को आगे बढ़ाया।

सन् 1935 का भारत सरकार अधिनियम भारत में उत्तरदायित्वपूर्ण शासन की स्थापना के मार्ग में सन् 1919 के भारत सरकार अधिनियम के बाद दूसरा महत्वपूर्ण कदम था। यह एक बहुत लम्बा और जटिल अधिनियम था। इसमें 321 अनुच्छेद तथा 10 अनुसूचियाँ थी। भारत का वर्तमान संवैधानिक ढाँचा बहुत कुछ सन् 1935 के अधिनियम पर आधारित है।

1935 के अधिनियम ने सर्वप्रथम भारत में संघात्मक सरकार की स्थापना की। पिछले सभी अधिनियमों के अन्तर्गत स्थापित सरकारों का स्वरूप एकात्मक था। यह संघ ब्रिटिश भारतीय प्रान्तों तथा कुछ भारतीय रियासतों को, जो संघ में शामिल होने को सहमत थीं, मिलाकर बनाया जाता था। इस प्रकार संघ की सदस्यता राज्यों की इच्छा पर निर्भर थी और जब तक राज्यों ने इस संघ में शामिल होने की सहमति न दे दी हो, उक्त संघ की स्थापना सम्भव नहीं थी। अधिनियम के अन्तर्गत संघ में शामिल होते समय रियासतों के शासकों को एक प्रवेश–प्रलेख पर हस्ताक्षर करना पड़ता था, जिसके द्वारा केन्द्रीय सरकार को समर्पित प्राधिकार की सीमा को उल्लेख किया गया था। अन्य विषयों के बारे में इकाइयों को पूर्ण स्वतंत्रता थी, किन्तु प्रान्तों के शासकों ने संघ में शामिल होने की कभी सहमति नहीं दी और इस प्रकार 1935 के अधिनियम द्वारा परिकल्पित अखिल भारतीय संघ की स्थापना न हो सकी।

सन् 1935 के अधिनियम द्वारा प्रान्तों के दोहरे शासन को समाप्त करके उसे केन्द्र में लागू किया गया। केन्द्रीय सरकार की कार्यकारिणी शक्ति गवर्नर जनरल में निहित थी। संघ के अन्तर्गत प्रशासन के विषय दो भागों में विभक्त थे– (1) रक्षित, और (2) हस्तान्तरित। रक्षित विषयों के अन्तर्गत प्रतिरक्षा, विदेशी मामले, धार्मिक विषय और जनजाति क्षेत्र आदि

सम्मिलित थे। इन विषयों का प्रशासन गवर्नर जनरल अपनी परिषद् की सहायता से करता था। अपनी परिषद् की सलाह मानने के लिए वह बाध्य नहीं था और अधिकतर वह अपनी शक्तियों का प्रयोग विकानुसार करता था। हस्तांतरित विषयों का प्रशासन गवर्नर जनरल अपनी मंत्रिपरिषद की सलाह से करता था जो विधानसभा के प्रति उत्तरदायी है।

सन् 1935 के अधिनियम की सबसे अधिक महत्वपूर्ण विशिष्टता थी– प्रान्तों में स्वायत्त शासन की स्थापना। सन् 1919 के अधिनियम द्वारा वह एक निश्चित प्रगति थी। विधि बनाने की दृष्टि से विषयों को दो भागों में विभाजित किया गया था– (10) प्रान्तीय, और (2) केन्द्रीय। प्रान्तीय विषयों पर विधि बनाने का आत्यन्तिक अधिकार प्रान्तों को दिया गया था। इन विषयों पर से केन्द्र का नियंत्रण समाप्त कर दिया गया। यद्यपि राज्यों के संघ में सम्मिलित न होने से अखिल भारतीय संघ की स्थापना न हो सकी। किन्तु जहाँ तक विधि बनाने की शक्ति का प्रश्न था, इस अधिनियम के अन्तर्गत केन्द्रीय सरकार एक प्रकार से संघात्मक सरकार की तरह कार्य करती थी।

इस विषय पर उन्होंने कई बार मत व्यक्त किया कि हमारे संविधान में राष्ट्र की स्वभावगत विशेषताओं को प्रतिबिंबित् नहीं किया जा सका है। विदेशी, विशेषतः अमरीका के लिखित और ब्रिटेन के अलिखित संविधानों में से बहुत सी बातें हमने उधार उठायी हैं। यही नहीं, 1935 के उस विधान की, जिसने स्वराज्य की एक किश्त प्रांतीय स्वायत्तता के रूप में दी थी, की छाया हमारे संविधान पर पडी है। इस विधान द्वारा ब्रिटिश संसद द्वारा यहां के लोगों को दिये गये अधिकारों में 'फूट डालो और मारो' वाली कुटिल नीति प्रतिबिंबित हुई है। किन्तु ब्रिटिशों द्वारा दिये गये अधिकारों की गहन समीक्षा करते हुए अनिष्ट बातों को अस्वीकार करने का समुचित प्रयास हमारी संविधान सभा ने नहीं किया। राजनीतिक शीघ्रता के कारण अनेक विभेदकारी प्रावधान ज्यों के त्यों बनाये रखे गये। राष्ट्र को एकात्मता की दिशा में ले जाने के लिए आवश्यक चिंतन नहीं हुआ। सावधानी नहीं बरती गयी। भारतीय प्राचीन परंपरा का भी ग्रह्माग्राह्मता की दृष्टि से अध्ययन नहीं किया गया। पं. दीनदयाल जी ने इस परानुकरण के दोष को राष्ट्र के लिए हानिकारक माना था।

पं. दीनदयाल जी का सबसे बड़ा आक्षेप गलत शब्दप्रयोगों के

बारे में था। वे कहा करते थे कि अमरीकी ढंग से हमने अपने यहां के प्रांतो–प्रदेशों को राज्य (स्टेट्स) कहा फिर, भारत एक अनेक राज्यों का संघ (फेडरेशन) है, यह गलत धारणा हमने बोयी। यह ठीक है कि प्रत्येक राज्य का अपना स्वतंत्र संविधान नहीं है और राष्ट्र की नागरिकता एक ही है, किन्तु हमारे स्वीकृत संविधान में ही विघटन के बीजों को दीनदयाल जी ने बराबर देखा था। उनका आग्रह था कि भारत की प्रकृति एकात्मक शासन (यूनीटरी फार्म ऑफ गवर्नमेंट) की है। इसीलिए आवश्यक था कि भारत के संविधान के प्रथम परिच्छेद में ही स्पष्ट निर्देश होता कि 'भारत एक एकात्मक राज्य होगा।' काश, ऐसा हो पाता तो बात भारत की स्वाभाविक, आकांक्षाओं के अनुरूप होती। पं. दीनदयाल जी ने कहा था कि 'यूनियन' में पारस्परिक सुविधाओं या स्वार्थ के लिए सहयोग करने की भावना होती है। एकात्मता में राष्ट्रशरीर एक है और प्रांत उसके विभिन्न अवयव हैं, यह भाव प्रकट होता है। इस भावना के साथ सत्ता का विकेन्द्रीकरण किया, तो संपूर्ण शरीर को उससे बल प्राप्त होता है। राज्यों के बारे में दीनदयाल जी द्वारा व्यक्त भय बाद के काल में यथार्थ सिद्ध हुआ है। विशेषतः भाषिक राज्यरचना के लिए हुए आंदोलन, उसमें प्रयुक्त असहिष्णु भाषा, राज्यों की स्वयत्तता की बढ़ती मांग, और उसकी बाद की अनेक घटनाओं ने दिखा दिया है कि देश में राष्ट्र और राज्य की धारणाओं को मिला दिया जा रहा है। प्रादेशिक देशभक्ति की भावनाओं को भड़का कर चुनाव जीतने, उसके लिए प्रादेशिक हितसंबंधों पर आधारित राजनीतिक दलों का निर्माण करने, अन्य राज्यों के बारे में असहिष्णु और परायेपन का व्यवहार करने, नये–नये राज्यों की मांग करने, राज्यों को भाषिक राष्ट्रीयताएं (लिंग्विस्टिक नेशनलिटीज) बताने, एवं प्रत्येक प्रदेश की संस्कृति भिन्न होने की भाषा प्रयुक्त करने की प्रवृतियाँ बढ़ती ही जाती दिखाई देती है। अकाली केशधारियों के आंदोलन जैसे कुछ आंदोलनों में तो विदेश–व्यवहार, प्रतिरक्षा एवं परिवहन के अतिरिक्त अन्य विषयों में केन्द्र के हाथों में कोई सत्ता न हो, यह मांग भी की जा रही है।

संविधान में भारत के प्रभुत्वसम्पन्न लोकतांत्रिक गणराज्य को 'राज्यों का संघ'' घोषित किया गया है। विभाजन के पश्चात् सुदृढ़ केन्द्रयुक्त परिसंघ की स्थापना का उद्देश्य राजनीतिक का प्रशासनिक दोनों ही रहा है, फिर भी संविधान को पूर्णरूपेण परिसंघात्मक नहीं बनाया जा

सका। संविधान सभा के अनुसार संघ को 'परिसंघ' कहना आवश्यक नहीं था। संविधान का प्ररूप प्रस्तुत करते हुए प्ररूप समिति के अध्यक्ष डॉ0 अम्बेडकर ने कहा था कि "यद्यपि यह संविधान संरचना की दृष्टि से फेडरल हो सकता है, किन्तु कुछ निश्चित उद्देश्यों से समिति ने इसे 'संघ' कहा है।

जैसा कि संविधान सभा में कहा गया था, ये उद्देश्य दो तथ्यों की ओर संकेत करते हैं– (अ) अमेरिकी संघवाद की भाँति भारत का संघवाद संघ की इकाइयों के बीच परस्पर करार का परिणाम नहीं है, (ब) राज्यों को स्वेच्छानुसार परिसंघ से पृथक् होने का अधिकार नहीं दिया गया है। डा0 अम्बेदकर ने संघ शब्द का आशय इस प्रकार व्यक्त किया है– "यद्यपि भारत को एक फेडरेशन होना था, लेकिन यह फेडरेशन राज्यों के बीच हुए करार का परिणाम न था ओर न किसी राज्य को फेडरेशन से पृथक् होने का अधिकार ही दिया गया है। फेडरेशन एक संघ है, क्योंकि यह कभी समाप्त नहीं होगा। यद्यपि प्रशासन की सुविधा के लिये सम्पूर्ण देश और इसके निवासी एक ही स्त्रोत से उद्भूत सर्वोच्य शक्ति के अधीन रहने वाले व्यक्ति हैं। "राज्यों को इस संघ से पृथक् होने का कोई अधिकार नहीं है।" इसको स्थापित करने के लिये अमीरकियों को एक गृहयुद्ध का सामना करना पड़ा था तब जाकर कहीं उनका फेडरेशन अविनाशी बन सका। संविधान–निर्माताओं ने इसे प्रारम्भ से ही स्पष्ट कर देना उचित समझा है।"

संघ का नाम 'इंडिया' अथवा 'भारत' है। प्रथम अनुसूची में विनिर्दिष्ट इसके सदस्यों को राज्य कहा जाता है।

अनुसार यदि कोई राजनीतिक दल का सदस्य स्वेच्छा से दल छोड़ता है या पार्टी के निर्देश के विरूद्ध सदन में मतदान करता है या नामजद सदस्य निर्वाचन के 6 माह के भीतर किसी राजनीतिक दल में सम्मिलित हो जाता है तो उसकी सदन की सदस्यता समाप्त हो जायेगी। उक्त नियम का एक अपवाद भी है जिसके अनुसार यदि 1/3 सदस्य मूल दल छोड़कर पृथक दल गठित कर लेते हैं या मूल राजनीतिक दल के सदस्यों का अन्य दल में विलय हो जाता है और उनकी संख्या 2/3 है तो इसे एक नया राजनीतिक दल या समूह माना जायेगा और उसे दल–बदल नहीं माना जायेगा। दुर्भाग्यवश बेईमान राजनीतिज्ञों के लिए

उक्त प्रावधान एक वरदान साबित हुआ जिन्होंने तात्कालिक राजनीतिक लाभ के लिए इसका दुरूपयोग किया। फलतः इन सत्तालोलुप राजनीतिज्ञों द्वारा अनेक राज्य सरकारों का पतन हुआ। 1989 में इस बीमारी का प्रभाव केन्द्र सरकार पर पड़ा और श्री वी0 पी0 सिंह की जनता दल की सरकार का उस समय पतन हो गया जब श्री चन्द्रशेखर के दल ने सरकार बनाया जो केवल चार माह तक सत्ता में रही और कांग्रेस के समर्थन वापस लेने के कारण गिर गई। 1991 के संसदीय चुनाव में किसी दल को अपेक्षित बहुमत नहीं मिला। किन्तु राष्ट्रपति ने सबसे बड़े दल कांग्रेस को सरकार बनाने का निमंत्रण दिया। श्री पी. वी. नरसिंह राव के नेतृत्व में अल्पमत सरकार सत्ता में आई। किन्तु झारखण्ड मुक्ति मोर्चा (सिवूसरन) के चार सदस्यों को मिलाकर उन्होंने संसद में अपना बहुमत सिद्ध कर दिया। आगे चलकर जनता दल से श्री अजीत सिंह 20 सदस्यों के साथ अलग हो गये और कांग्रेस में सम्मिलित हो गये। इस प्रकार उनकी सरकार को लोकसभा में बहुमत प्राप्त हो गया। इसी परिणाम–परम्परा में देश में प्रादेशिक दलों के उदय का परिणाम आज देश में पर्याप्त चिंता का विषय बन गया है। दक्षिण में आंध्रप्रदेश में री नंदमूरि तारक रामाराव के तेलगू देशम दल ने कांग्रेस (आई) समेत सभी राष्ट्रीय दलों को धूल चटाकर बहुत बड़ी विजय प्राप्त की है। तमिलनाडु में द्रविड़ मुन्नेत्र कषगम और अन्ना द्र.मु.क. दोनों प्रादेशिक दलों की जनमानस पर पकड़ विगत पन्द्रह वर्ष में विकट रही है। अन्य किसी भी राष्ट्रीय कहलाने वाले दल की दाल वहां नहीं गलती। अकाली दल पंजाब का प्रादेशिक दल ही है। आज यह सत्ता में आ गया है। सत्ता का लालच उसमें इतना प्रबल है कि उसका एक धड़ा आतंकवादी हो गया है और सिखों को हिंदू नहीं मानता। सिखों के लिए स्वतंत्र 'खालिस्थान' के निर्माण की बात करने तक उसका साहस बढ़ गया है। उसी ने पंजाब में हिंसा का नंगा नाच प्रारंभ कर दिया है। काश्मीर और पश्चिम बंगाल भी प्रादेशिक दलों की सत्ता के अधीन हो गये हैं। प्रादेशिक दलों की यह महामारी कहां कितनी फैलेगी, केन्द्र–राज्य संबंधों में कितना तनाव बढ़ेगा, और परिणामतः राष्ट्रीय एकात्मता को कितने और कैसे–कैसे आघात सहने पड़ेंगे, कोई नहीं कह सकता। पं. दीनदयाल जी ने इन परिणामों के भय को पहले से ही पहचान लिया था। इस भय से मुक्त होने के कुछ उपाय भी उन्होंने सुझाये थे, यह बात

ध्यान में लेना नितांत आवश्यक है। हमारे यहां राजनीतिक दलप्रणाली की परिकल्पना प्रमुखतः इंग्लैंड में प्रचलित लोकतंत्र के स्वरूप के अनुसार हमारे संविधान में की गयी है। किन्तु भारत जैसी अनपढ़ जनता में इस प्रणाली के कारण तुरंत ही कौन सी अनिष्ट प्रवृतियां बढ़ जायेगी, किसी ने ठीक से सोचा ही नही। कहना पड़ता है कि पाश्चात्य लोकतंत्र–प्रणाली का सूक्ष्म मूल्यमापन कर लेने का धारासभा के विचारकों ने ध्यान नहीं रखा। इसी में लोगों के सिर पर तानाशाही शासन सवार होने की परिस्थिति निर्मित हो सकती है, इस अनुभव की उपेक्षा की गयी। अनिष्ट दल–अभिनिवेश समाजजीवन के निचले स्तर तक रिसता चला जाये तो जाति, पंथ, पैसा आदि के आधार पर हमारा समाज कितना कलह जर्जर हो जायेगा, इसका भी कोई विचार नहीं किया गया।

वर्तमान में राष्ट्रीय स्तर के राजनीतिक दलों में एकता तथा अनुशासन में कमी आई है और दल के विभिन्न वगों के आचरण के फलस्वरूप दल का नेता जो प्रधानमंत्री बनता है उसकी शक्ति एवं प्राधिकार में भी कमी आई है। कांग्रेस पार्टी जो देश की एक सबसे बड़ी पार्टी है वह इससे काफी प्रभावित हुई है। यह देखा गया कि प्रधानमंत्री को अपने दल के भतरी विवादों को निपटाने में बहुत अधिक समय लगता है और देश के कार्यों में व्यवधान होता है। उसे अपने दल के विभिन्न वर्गों को मंत्रीमंडल में स्थान देकर संतुष्ट करना पड़ता है। 1976 तक कांग्रेस पार्टी में एकता एवं अनुशासन था क्योंकि उसमें नेहरू और श्रीमती इंदिरा गांधी जैसे नेता थे। इसके पश्चात् संयुक्त दल की सरकारें कई राज्यों में बनीं किनतु असफल रहीं। कांग्रेस पार्टी में भी एकता तथा अनुशासन का अभाव हो गया। 1991 के चुनाव के पश्चात् प्रधानमंत्री श्री राव को कर्नाटक में 3 और आन्ध्र प्रदेश में 2 मुख्य मंत्रियों को बदलना पड़ा। 1993 में कई राज्यों में चुनाव के पश्चात् कांग्रेस पार्टी में नेता के चुनाव में पर्याप्त कठिनाई हुई थी जैसे हिमाचल प्रदेश और मध्य प्रदेश। इन राज्यों में पूर्ण बहुमत होने के पश्चात् भी नेता के चुनाव में 10 दिन का समय लगा गया, क्योंकि इसके कई दावेदार थे।

प्रशासकीय घटकों (एडमिनिस्ट्रेटिव यूनिट) का निर्माण करते समय ध्यान में रखने के लिए एक निकष भाषा अवश्य है। किन्तु वह एकमात्र निकष नहीं है। इस बात का ध्यान हमारे यहां नहीं रखा गया। संविधान

में निर्धारित 15 वर्ष की अवधि 1965 में बीत जाने के बाद भी हिन्दी को सम्पर्क–भाषा के रूप में लागू करने में भारत सरकार ने जो उपेक्षा की, उसकी दीनदयाल जी ने प्रखर आलोचना की है। सरकार ने उचित भूमिका ली होती तो प्रश्न की जटिलता में नये–नये आयाम न जुड़ते और न ही दक्षिण में विरोध खड़ा होकर अंग्रेजी के सखी भाषा के रूप में सदा के लिए मत्थे पड़ने का कोई कारण होता। दीनदयाल जी का मानना था कि राष्ट्रीय आत्मा की अभिव्यक्ति राष्ट्र की अपनी भाषा में ही उत्तम प्रकार से सहज में हो सकती है। उनका विचार था संविधानसभा का सारा कामकाज चूंकि अंग्रेजी में हुआ था, अतः संविधान पर भी उसका प्रभाव पड़ा है। संविधान का विचार हिंदी में किया जाता तो उसमें अधिक भारतीयता आयी होती, ऐसा उन्होंने एक लेख में लिखा है। भाषा के अनुषंग में संविधान के बारे में उन्होंने कहा है– "आज हमारे विद्वान लोग पश्चिम से मुँह फेरकर सोच ही नहीं सकते। मुँह फेरना तो दूर रहा, वे केवल पश्चिम के आधार पर ही चिार कर सकते है। संविधान का विचार उन्होंने अंग्रेजी भाषा के माध्यम से ही किया। हिन्दी का अंगीकार उन्होंने राजभाषा के रूप में किया तो है और तदनुसार संविधान का अनुवाद भी हिन्दी में किया जायेगा, किन्तु संविधान की अंग्रेजी प्रति ही अधिकृत मानी जायेगी। संविधान का प्रारूप मूलतः हिन्दी या अन्य किसी भारतीय भाषा में किया गया होता तो आज जैसी अभारतीयता उसमें प्रबलता से नहीं पायी जाती, क्योंकि भाषा तब केवल विचाराभिव्यक्ति का माध्यम नहीं अपितु विचारों की दिशा निर्धारित करने वाली वस्तु होती, हिन्दी शब्दावली, उन शब्दों के अर्थ एवं व्यक्त होने वाले भाव, सबमें भारतीय जीवन की ही अभिव्यक्ति होती और उसके विकास की दिशा क्या हो, इसकी भी प्रेरणा प्राप्त होती। किन्तु अंग्रेजी भाषा के प्रयोग के कारण भारतीय भावनाओं की अपेक्षा अंग्रेजों की भावनाओं की ही अभिव्यक्ति उसमें हुई है। अतः हमारा संविधान भारत में जन्मे अंग्रेजी बालक की भाँति 'एंगलो–इण्डियन बन गया है, भारतीय नहीं।

प्रोफेसर ह्यिर के अनुसार परिसंघीय सिद्धांत के अन्तर्गत संघ और इकाइयों में शक्तियों का विभाजन होता है और यह विभाजन ऐसी रीति से किया जाता है जिससे प्रत्येक अपने क्षेत्र में पूर्णतया 'स्वतंत्र' हों और साथ ही साथ एक–दूसरे के सहयोगी भी हों, न कि एक–दूसरे के अधीन हों।

अमेरिका के संविधान को सर्वसम्मति से एक परिसंघात्मक संविधान माना जाता है। यह संघीय और प्रान्तीय दो सरकारों की स्थापना करता है। इसमें दोनों सरकारों की शक्तियों का विभाजन है जो अपने–अपने क्षेत्र में सार्वभौम हैं। इस प्रकार परिसंघीय सिद्धांत का सार है– स्वतंत्रता एवं समन्वयकारिता। प्रोफेसर ह्वियर अपनी उपर्युक्त परिभाषा देने के पश्चात् संसार के विभन्न संविधानों को स्वयं इस कसौटी पर जाँचते हैं वे कहते हैं कि क्या हमें संविधान के उन रूपों तक सीमित रहना चाहिये जिनमें परिसंघीय सिद्धांत पूर्णरूप से एवं बिना किसी अपवाद के लागू होते हैं? ऐसा कहना तर्क–संगत नहीं होगा। स्वयं अमेरिका के मूल संविधान में संघीय सिद्धांत का एक महत्वपूर्ण अपवाद निहित था। सीनेट का गठन प्रान्तीय विधानमंडलों द्वारा चुने हुए प्रतिनिधियों द्वारा होता था। इस प्रकार संघ सरकार कुछ हद तक प्रान्तीय सरकारों पर आश्रित था।

भारत की स्वाभाविक आंतरिक एकात्मता को बिना कोई बाधा पहुंचाये प्रशासकीय इकाइयों का निर्माण कैसे किया जाय, इस प्रश्नका विशुद्ध स्वदेशी उतर पं. दीनदयाल जी ने एकात्म प्रशासन का पक्ष लेते हुए दिया है। उनका कहना है कि ऐसा करने से आज हमारे संविधान में पायी जाने वाली 'फेडरल' और 'यूनिटरी' की अस्वभाविक खींचतान नहीं रहेगी। उनका मत है कि एकात्म भारत को साकार करने वाली पद्धति और प्रक्रिया से ही एकात्म प्रशासन में राष्ट्रीय एकात्मता को पुष्ट किया जा सकेगा और विभिन्न राष्ट्र–घटकों की विशेषताओं को भी संजोया जा सकेगा। इस व्यवस्था में केन्द्र एक रहेगा, किन्तु सत्ता का केन्द्रीकरण उसमें न होकर समाज–जीवन के निचले धरातल तक सत्ता का विकेन्द्रीकरण होता जायेगा। इस योजना में उन्होंने 'जनपद' की स्वदेशी परिकल्पना को आधारभूत माना है। जहां एक ही भाषा बोली जाती है, आंतरिक एकता की सुंदर अभिव्यक्ति दिखाई देती है, ऐसे क्षेत्रों को ही हमारे यहां 'जनपद' कहा गया हे। ब्रज, अवध, भोजपुर, मगध, मिथिला, कोशल, कलिंग, विदर्भ, कान्हदेश, मालवा, कोंकण, मालाबार आदि सारे जनपद ही थे। इन जनपदों में किसी विशिष्ट भारतीय भाषा का प्रभाव होता है। उसी भाषा में साहित्य–सृजन होता है और उस भाषा के प्रभाव में जनपद परस्पर पूरक होते हैं। इसी प्रक्रिया से देश में महाराष्ट्र, गुजरात, तमिलनाडु, बंगाल आदि प्रांतों का निर्माण हुआ दिखाई देता है।

इन सबका समेकित विचार करते हुए राष्ट्रजीवन के विकास का मार्ग कया हो, यह निश्चित करना भारतीय इतिहास के साथ सुसंगत होगा। इस भूमिका का पक्ष लेते हुए पं. दीनदयाल जी ने कहा है कि प्रांतरचना काविचार करते समय जनपद–जीवन की पूर्णतः उपेक्षा कर दी गयी है। तुलसी–रामायण की भाषा की उपेक्षा होने पर अवध जनपद अशांत अवश्य होगा। खनदेशी का अर्थ कोंकणी नहीं है। इन्हीं बातों को ध्यान में लेकर एकात्म भारत के लिए पं. दीनदयाल जी द्वारा एकात्म विधान के निर्माण हेतु सुझायी रचना इस प्रकार हैः–

प्राथमिक प्रशासन ग्रामीण अंचल में ग्राम पंचायत के अधीन रहे। जनपद पर आधारित जनपद सभाएं स्थापित की जायें। आज की नगर–परिषदों (म्युनिसिपैलिटियों) से अधिक, किन्तु विधान सभाओं से कम अधिकार उन्हें रहें। संसद सार्वभौम हो। जनपद सभा और संसद के बीच वाली सभी सत्ताओं को समाप्त किया जाय। प्रशासन की सुविधा के लिए कुछ जनपद सभाओं का समूह बनाते हुए प्रांतों का निर्माण किया जाय, राज्यों का नहीं। इन प्रांतों के लिए केन्द्रीय नियंत्रणाधीन प्रमुख नियुक्त कर उन्हें पर्याप्त प्रशासकीय अधिकार दिये जायें ताकि आज के प्रांतवाद का राष्ट्रीय एकता की भावना पर अतिक्रमण रूके।

लगभग 30 वर्ष पूर्व पं. दीनदयाल जी ने क्रांतदर्शिता से लिखा था 'आज प्रांतवाद निश्चय ही सिर उठा रहा है। केन्द्र और प्रांतों में संघर्ष खड़ा होने की संभावना स्पष्ट दिखाई दे रही है। अतः राष्ट्रीय शक्ति को सुसंगठित करना परिस्थिति की नितांत आवश्यकता है। सत्ता की सुविधा के लिए आवश्यक सत्ता का विकेन्द्रीकरण केवल जनपदीय स्तर पर ही हो। आज की प्रांतीय विधानसभाएं सत्ता के विकेन्द्रीकरण को अनुभव ही नहीं कर पा रही है। प्रत्युत उन्हें लगता है कि उन्होंने अपने अधिकार केन्द्र को सौंप दिये हैं। इसीलिए आज का विकेन्द्रीकरण एक ओर जहां राष्ट्रीय एकता के मूल पर प्रहार कर रहा है, वहीं दूसरी ओर जनपदों का जीवन भी पैरों तले रौंदा जा रहा है।

विद्यमान परिस्थति की पृष्ठभूमि में इस सारे चिंतन में राष्ट्रीय आत्मा का बोध एवं स्वदेशी परिभाषा में उसे व्यक्त करने की पंडित जी की अनुपम शैली का परिचत मिलता है। आज के विकेन्द्रीकरण में जिलों और जिला–परिषदों की एक सीढ़ी है। किन्तु जीवनकाल की दृष्टि में

पंडित जी द्वारा दर्शाये गये जनपदों के स्थान के साथ जिला प्रशासन का कोई संबंध ही नहीं आता। प्रत्युत असंतुष्टों को नष्ट करते हुए सत्ताधारी राजनीतिक दल के लिए समर्थन जुटाने का साधन बनाकर जिलों को तोड़ा या बनाया जाता है। केरल में एक जिला केवल मुसलमानों के आग्रह के कारण बनाया गया। अब ईसाइयों का अनुनय करने के लिए एक और जिला बनाया जा रहा है। प्रांतों या राज्यों के बारे में भी यही स्थिति रही है। राज्यों की संख्या में लगातार वृद्धि होती जा रही है। गोआ या पांडिचेरी जैसे प्रदेशों का व्ययसाध्य और अनावश्यक अस्तित्व उनकी विधानसभाओं सहित बनाये रखा गया है। ईशान (उत्तरपूर्वांचल) में जनजातियों के लिए उदयाचल नामक एक अलग राज्य बना देने का वचन दिवंगत प्रधनमंत्री श्रीमती इंदिरा गांधी ने असम चुनाव–प्रचार में दिखाया था। राष्ट्रीय एकता, भारत की एकात्मता, राज्यशासन के सिद्ध ांतों और भारत की जीनव–विषयक विशेषताओं का परस्परानुकूल संवर्द्धन करने के लिए, वास्तव में आवश्यक व्यवस्था का निर्माण करने के स्थान पर सरकार एवं सत्ताधारी दल द्वारा भारत में भवितव्य के साथ किये जाने वाले खिलवाड़ के विरूद्ध पं. दीनदयाल जी ने देश को सावधानी की चेतावनी दी। संविधान के बारे में पंडित जी का चिंतन कुछ प्रासंगिक लेखों में ही व्यक्त हुआ है। उस चिंतन को सम्पूर्ण एवं सुसंगत रूप में ग्रंथबद्ध करने का उन्हें अवकाश नहीं मिल पाया। 1975 से लगाये गये आपातकाल में संविधान का जो गुड़ गोबरकर दिया गया, उसे देखने के लिए पंडित जी जीवित नहीं थे। भारत में आधुनिक काल में संविधान और शासनप्रणाली कैसी हो, इसका केवल सूचक उल्लेख उकने यहां–वहां लिखे गये लेखों में ही हमारे लिए उपलब्ध है। अतः कोई कह सकता है कि ये विचार पर्याप्त स्पष्ट एवं समग्र नहीं है। काल ने दीनदयाल जी को पर्याप्त समय ही नहीं दिया, परिणामतः उनका कितना सारा चिंतन तो अधूरा एवं अप्रकट ही रह गया है। किन्तु उनके द्वारा हार्दिकता से किये गये मार्गदर्शन की ओर से समुचित ध्यान दिये बिना ही उनके सारे चिंतन की उपेक्षा की गयी, उसे तिरस्कृत किया गया। 1950 के बाद आज तक संविधान में बीसियों संशोधन किये गये। प्रांत बनाये और तोड़े गये। यह सब कुछ केवल राजनीतिक सुविधा के लिए ही किया गया। दीनदयाल जी संविधान और प्रशासन में जिस भारतीय आत्मा को लाना

चाहते थे, वह उनमें लाया ही न जा सका। संविधान में उतना लचीलापन है भी नहीं। दीनदयाल जी ने कहा था कि राष्ट्र की जनता जाग्रत और स्वत्व सम्पन्न हो जायेगी तो शायद वह विदेशी रंगरूप के संविधान को अस्वीकार कर देगी और भारतीय तो शायद आदर्शों एवं प्रकृति को प्रकट करने वाला नया संविधान तैयार करेगी। भविष्य के गर्भ में क्या है, कौन बता सकता है?

संदर्भ ग्रंथ सूची

1. उपाध्याय, दीनदयाल, पोलिटिकल डायरी, सुरूचि प्रकाशन, नई दिल्ली।
2. सिंह अमरजीत, मैं दीनदयाल उपाध्याय बोल रहा हूँ, प्रभात प्रकाशन, नई दिल्ली।
3. भिषीकर, चन्द्रशेखर परमानंद, पं. दीनदयाल उपाध्याय, विचार दर्शन–खण्ड–5 (राष्ट्र की अवधारणा, सुरूची प्रकाशन, नई दिल्ली।
4. उपाध्याय जय–जय राम, भारत का संविधान, सेन्ट्रल लॉ एजेन्सी, इलाहाबाद।
5. पाण्डेय, जय नारायण– भारत का संविधान, सेन्ट्रल लॉ एजेन्सी, इलाहाबाद।
6. वसु, दूर्गादास– भारत का संविधान, एक परिचय, लेक्सिस–नेक्सिस, नई दिल्ली।

Chapter - 5

"Vision of Atmanirbhar Bharat : Role and Significance of MSMEs"

I. K. Mathad and B.V.V. Sangha's

Abstract: The present paper aims to explore the changing role of MSMEs (Micro, Small and Medium Enterprises) in making India 'Atmanirbhar'. The said research paper proposes list of certain measures to be taken by the government to include and encourage MSMEs in making the mission of 'Atmanirbhar Bharat' realistically achievable. In this context the authorities must address key inputs such as access to financial equity, technical workforce and building market competitiveness and soon.

Design/Methodology: The study is based on secondary source of information collected from various sources such as published articles, Government and other websites, news, etc.

Findings: Research paper findings indicate that a systematic framework is required to include MSMEs in making the 'Atmanirbhar Bharat' a reality. It may be advised that there is a need to understand our strengths and accordingly to bring up and support the industry. There is no point in getting driven by the 'anti-china' sentiments. It may be suggested to start with creation of agro based MSMEs as agriculture is Inida's strength and is the largest employment generating industry; Artisans and Craftsmen are using natural resources for making their products. Providing training and technology to artisans and craftsmen will definitely enhance their business prospects. Another sector is healthcare which will offer opportunity for MSMEs to provide a range of products and services for the masses. Later other sectors may be thought such as manufacturing (healthcare, consumerelectronics, power equipment, etc) and lastly technology based industry such as products and services making use of AI (Artificial Intelligence).

Originality: This paper attempts to offer some of the options that may be considered or implemented in the context of strengthening of MSMEs. With significant contribution from the MSME sector in the country's GDP and employment generation, their employment will certainly help in achieving the vision of 'Atmanirbhar Bharat'. Agriculture based manufacturing activity will definitely provide boost to MSMEs and will result in employment generations.

Introduction: Changing Face of Indian Economy andtheBackground

It may be interesting to take a note of the journey embarked by the country from becoming a vision towards becoming 'Atmanirbhar'. Let us review some of the certain important reforms:

In 1991: Prime Minister Narasimha Rao and Minister of Finance Manmohan Singh, from June1991 to May 1996 are credited with completing monetary change programs. These developments initiated by the Indian government in1991 are focused on fast and generous mix of the Indian economy with the worldwide economy in a blended way. Accordingly, the industrial policy in the poster form period mainly aimed at de-licensing, privatization, FDI promotion and trade liberalization in the manufacturing sector (Ahluwalia, 2005).

In 2016: The year 2016 checked 25 years of financial advancement in India. A fourth of a century has since passed, and the economy has seen different ages of changes in various circles of monetary undertaking; some succeeded, while others didn't. In November 2016, the Government of India announced demonetization policy' that may have adverse effects on some sectors, but it has helped digital payments to post good growth. (PIB, 2017) [2].There is an increased acceptance of debit card in the market is observed thereafter.

Here it may be stated that India has been a visionary country taking measures to improve the economy and the governance. This has been indicated by the annual growth rate of Gross Domestic Product (GDP), as provided by The World Bank.(See Exhibit 1 below)

Exhibit 1: GDP Growth (Annual%) -India

GDP Growth (AnnualIn %)	*1995*	*2000*	*2005*	*2010*	*2015*
	7.5%	3.8%	7.9%	8.5%	8%

Source: The World Bank Data[WB,2019][3]

Vision and Mission of Atmanirbhar India (OI, 2020), (HT, 2020), (ET, 2020), (IE, 2020)

Atmanirbhar Bharat, which means 'independent India', is the vision of the Prime Minister of India Narendra Modi (with a mission of) making India "a greater and more significant aspect of the worldwide economy". This will be accomplished by seeking after arrangements that are effective, serious and strong, and acting naturally supporting and self-creating.

'Atmanirbhar Bharat Abhiyan' upholds Indian economy in battling against Covid-19. The clarion call give by the Hon'ble Prime Minister to utilize these difficult occasions to become Atmanirbhar(confident) has been very generally welcomed to empower the resurgence of the Indian economy (Govt. 2020). It rests on five components viz. the Economy, Infrastructure, System, Vibrant Demography and Demand. As one of the elements of 'Atmanirbhar Bharat', Micro, Small and Medium Enterprise(MSME) area in India can assume a significant function by standing, vigorous on all the five a spects, in this manner accomplishing the vision of confident

India(Sood,2020)[9]. In view of this, strengthening of the MSMEs is the key to realize the vision of 'Atmanirbhar Bharat Abhiyan'.

Significance of MSMEs (Sood, 2020)

It may be noted that the role of MSME sector has been changing over the years. Earlier it is to provide the support to the economy. Now with this atmanirbhar mind set, MSME will become the backbone of the economy as conveyed by our Hon'ble Prime Minister by promoting the concept 'vocal for local'. Therefore, as mentioned earlier the concept 'vocal for local' calls from strengthening of the industry sectors and in particular the MSME sector. This will ensure making of required goods and services within the country making itself-sufficient country. It might be noticed that after farming, MSME is the second-biggest sector in India.

Industry Sectors suitable to MSMEs

When we look at the import export list of items for India, the import export balance is not uniform and is heavily skewed towards imports. Imports are dominating the exports. This needs to be changed to become 'Self Reliant' or 'Atmanirbhar Bharat' in reality.

India's economy posted its steepest contraction on record in the April-June quarter of the current fiscal year (2020-2021). This is mainly due to the fact that the strict lockdown imposed to prevent the spread of Covid infection has halted all kinds of economic activity, shutdown consumption and investment, and lead to job and income losses. (Gupta, 2020). (See Exhibit 2).

It is observed that except agriculture, which grew at 3.4% all other sectors saw a sharp fall in output Q1 2020 (April to June). Sectors for restructuring of loans for the banks it has

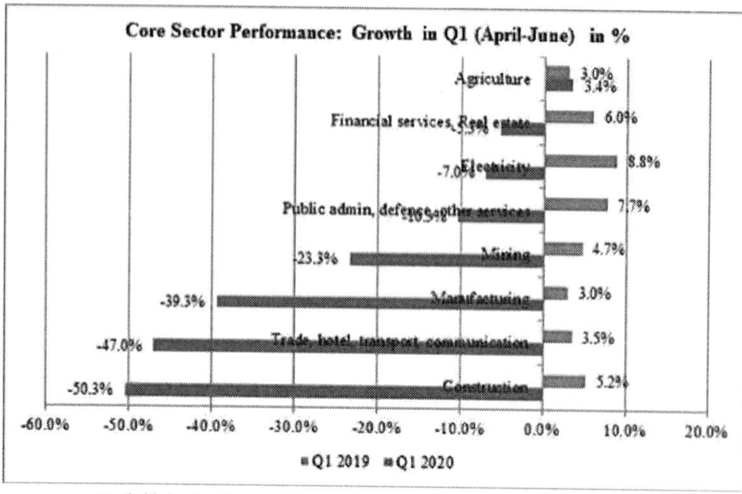

Exhibit 2: Core Sector Performance: Q1 Growth

Source: (Gupta, 2020

mentioned that sectors such as agriculture, food processing and pharmaceuticals how no impact during pre and post Covid period (Checklist, 2020).

It may be observed that India was two diversity in agricultural produce, fruits and vegetables and related farm produce that is consumed in domestic market. Presenting or offering this form produce innovatively (in the domestic market) through agro based enterprises or agro based business MSMEs will be advantageous for both the farmers and rural entrepreneurs this will create more business opportunities.

Apart from the farm produce, eco-friendly crafts are in demand. It may be observed that India also has diversity in skills in the form of a presence of artisans and craftsmen across different regions in the country. These artisans and craftsmen use agricultural products and natural resources to produce different types of products. Providing training or technology to these people will certainly enhance their business prospects. Involvement of MSMEs from the rural areas may provide more business opportunities and employment generation. Making announcement of becoming' self reliant' and making actual efforts for the same are two different things. Agriculture will certainly help India in becoming Atmanirbharta. Agro-based MSMEs will become key drivers in this process. Use of locally available resources will provide boost to domestic market. To summarize, agriculture is of prime importance in terms of employment generation and may lead to establishment of agro-based MSMEs. Food processing is sub-set of agriculture and offers good potential for employment as well as for domestic consumption.

It is required to strengthen the MSMEs by fixing the various issues that they are facing since last two decades (Sood, 2020).These are man power, finance and support for promotion. If India as a country, looking to become a dollar 5 trillion economy, it will not happen without a healthy, vibrant MSME sector, and a lot of entrepreneurship. This will not only enhance manufacturing activity but also create employment opportunities.

It may be suggested that following industry sectors may be seen as a potential for MSMEs in achieving reality of becoming' Atmanirbhar Bharat'. Some of these agriculture, healthcare, low cost goods/ every day use goods, festive occasion goods and so on. Other factors that may be considered for manufacturing (in a phased manner) are consumer electronics, organic chemicals, machinery, apparel, solar power equipments, telecom, AI based products and **services**, etc.(Srivastava, 2020) ,Rama Rao and Ranjan,2020), (Sengupta and Katragaadda, 2020).

Steps to Follow: Inclusion of MSMEs in Building Atmanirbhar Bharat

In his Independence Day speech, Prime Minister Narendra Modi repositioned the 'Make in India' agendas 'Make in India for the world'. This signifies India's aspiration to be powerful trading nation on the back of quality products, competitive manufacturing, and integration into the world economy (Srivastava, 2020).

It is required to strengthen the MSMEs by fixing the various issues that they are facing since last two decades. These are critical aspects for the success of MSMEs (Sood, 2020) [9] and are as listed below:

- Quality Workforce/Manpower.
- Access to Financial Credit.
- Branding and Promotion.

It is obvious that growth of manufacturing sector results in employment. As elaborated earlier, the MSME area has been supporting economy as industry sector that is contributing to both the GDP and exports. With the conversations gaining momentum, it is an opportunity for the MSME sector to capitalize on the' Make in India' bandwagon and catch on with zeal. There is ample scope for the MSME sector to identify areas for local production of goods right from raw material to the finished product(Varaganti,2020).

In this context, India can plan to promote its manufacturing and trade with the help of MSMEs. According to (Srivastava, 2020) [12], there could be followings ways to encourage the MSMEs:

- Providing assurance of quality workforce.
- Making Financial Credit easily accessible so as to have financial stability.
- Providing Branding and Promotion support to enhance the market visibility of MSME's and their products in domestic markets.
- Good reforms towards'reduction in input costs' will benefit MSMEs and make Indian attractive place to

do business. This will ensure domestic value addition which will make MSMEs attractive and competitive.

- With 'Make in India' agenda, support MSMEs and create a good infrastructure for them. Let the MSMEs get access to such resources such as design studios, innovation labs, and strengthening of standards and quality infrastructure.
- It may be noted that the steps or approaches when systematically implemented will benefit the industry and in turn the country in long terms. Of course a word of caution is stated here that in this context much will depend on the seriousness of implementation and monitoring by all the respective agencies, including coordination from state authorities.

With this elaborate discussion, this paper has attempted to illustrate the fact that MSMEs can become the backbone of the economy if supported with suitable policy measures. They can be enough competitive to produce the required goods within the country and part of Atmanirbhar Bharat in a more significant way provided that the government offers them able support.

Note: The illustrations, names of the organizations, and brand names used in this research paper are provided as examples. They are used for representation purposes only.

References

Ahluwalia Montek S. (2005). Lessons from India's Economic Reforms published in the book titled 'Development Challenges in the1990s'-Leading Policy makers Speak from Experience; aco-publication of the World Bank and Oxford University Press, March 2005.

PIB. (2017). A year after demonetization. Press Information Bureau (PIB). Available from: *https://pibindia.wordpress.com/2017/11/07/a-year-after-emonetization/#more17460*

WB.(2019). GDP Growth (Annual%)-India Data. The World Bank. Available from: *https://data.worldbank.org/indicator/NY.GDP.MKTP.KD.ZG?locations=IN.*

4) OI. (2020). Aatmanirbhar Bharat not self-containment: PM assures global investors". Outlook India. 9 July 2020.

5) HT.(2020). To spur growth: Nirmala Sitharaman on PM Modi's Atamanirbhar Bharat Abhiyan. Hindustan Times. 13 May 2020.

ET. (2020). Bennett University Webinar: Need to tap Artificial Intelligence to fight Covid, says IT minister Ravi Shankar Prasad. The Economic Times, 26 May 2020.

IE. (2020). PM Modi's self-reliant India Mission economic package: Here is the fine print. The Indian Express. Misra, Udit(13May2020).

Govt.(2020). Building Atmanirbhar Bharat & Overcoming COVID-19. Available from: *https://www.india.gov.in/spotlight/building-atmanirbhar-bharat-overcoming-covid-19*

Sood Prateek. (2020). How Can MSMEs Play A Significant Role To Achieve The Vision of Atmanirbhar Bharat? Article in Business World, July 2020. Available from: *http://www.businessworld.in/article/How-Can-MSMEs-Play-A-Significant-Role-To-Achieve-The-Vision-Of-Atma-Nirbhar-Bharat-/03-07-2020-293664/#*

Gupta Surojit. (2020). GDP Collapses 23.9% in Q1,worst among big economies. Article appeared in Times of India, Pune edition dated September 1, 2020.

Chapter - 6

Digitalization in India

DR. INDU SINGH

Abstract: India is currently the most linguistically varied country in the world. In this paper, we focus on how India is on its way to become one of the leading cosmopolitan country in the world in terms of digitalization. Digitalization is the strategy of adopting recent technologies in IT to make the most of the digital resources available in the enterprise. Also, we have mentioned various fields where digitalization has highly marked its importance like digital India, digital culture, digital camera, digital computer, digital education, etc.

Keywords: DII, DE, DM and DC.

Introduction

'Digitization' and 'digitalization' are two conceptual terms that are closely associated and often used interchangeably in a broad range of literatures.

Digitization refers to "the action or process of digitizing; the conversion of analogue data (esp. in later use images, video, and text) into digital form." Digitalization, by contrast, refers to "the adoption or increase in use of digital or computer technology by an organization, industry, country, etc."

"Digitalization includes Digitization"
"Digitization is the first step to realize digitalization"

Without digital information, No Big data based solution possible" Digitalization is the use of digital technologies to change a business model and provide new revenue and value-producing opportunities; it is the process of moving to a digital business.

Representation of digital economy

The time is right for Indian companies to pursue digitalization-whereby digitized resources, such as cloud-based software and machines equipped with digital sensors, are transformed into new sources of profitable revenue. In just the next few years, various components of the digital ecosystem in India- including the digitized consumer, generation of digital data volumes, e-commerce and tech-savvy talent pools – are expected to mature. The survey of more than 100 senior executives to find their readiness to make the most of fast-maturing opportunity. It was found that very high levels of awareness amongst executives on digital technologies of the present and future, such as Internet Of Things. Executives that were surveyed also agree that digitalization is a strategic growth-imperative.

Many of the survey participants believe that high costs are preventing them from taking full advantage of digital technologies. Moreover, a large number are seeing the gains they have made from digital adoption hit a plateau.

Application Areas of Digitalization

Digitalization goes beyond the technical process of digitization. In digitalization, innovation comes not only from the digitization of phone, cars, or books. It is a much broader change of organizing logic in multiple industries and marketplaces that become connected through a common digital infrastructure. Some of the areas where digitalization is concerned in alarming rates are-

Digital India

The Digital India programme is a flagship programme of the Government of India with a vision to transform India into a digitally empowered society and knowledge economy.

Vision Areas of Digital India. The Digital India programme is centered on three key vision areas. They are listed below as-

Digital Infrastructue as a Utility To Every Citizen. A well connected nation is a prerequisite to a well served nation. Once the remotest of the Indian villagers are digitally connected through broadband and high speed internet, then delivery of electronic government services to every citizen, targeted social benefits, and financial inclusion can be achieved in reality. One of the key areas on which the vision of Digital India is centered is "digital infrastructure as a utility to every citizen".

A key component under this vision is high speed internet as a core utility to facilitate online delivery of various services.

Governance And Services On Demand. Over the years, a large number of initiatives have been undertaken by various State Government and Central Ministries to usher in an era of e-governance. Sustained efforts have been made at multiple levels to improve the delivery of public services and simplify the process of accessing them. E-governance in India has steadily evolved from computerization of Government Departments to initiatives that encapsulate the finer points of Governance, such as citizen centricity, service orientation and transparency.

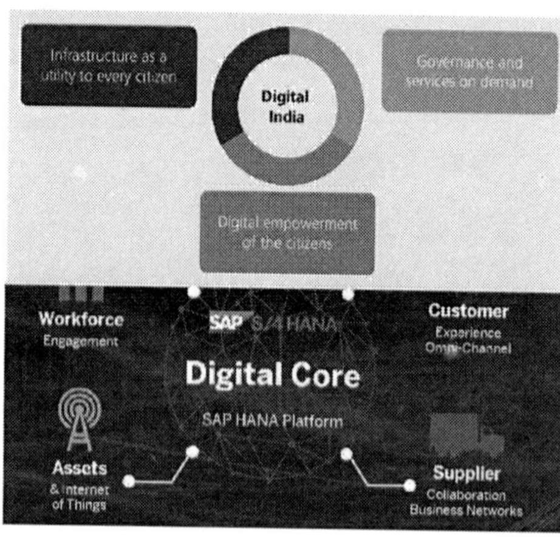

Digital empowerment of citizens. Digital connectivity is a great leveller. Cutting across demographic and socio-economic segments, Indians are incredibly connecting and communicating with each other through mobile phones and computer riding on digital networks. The Digital India programme itself promises to transform India into a digitally empowered society by focusing on digital literacy, digital resources, and collaborative digital platforms. This also places emphasis on universal digital literacy and availability of digital resources/services in Indian languages.

Digital Culture

Exploring the intersections of technology, knowledge, and culture in a digital age!!

Digital culture is many things and applicable to multiple topics — but it all boils down to one: the relationship between humans and technology. These ideas are often overlooked as technology becomes a second nature to us.

Digital Culture Program supports activities that examine the role of technology in social science research, in the circulation and distribution of information, and in the shaping of cultural and political systems, serving the organization's core aims to deepen and democratize knowledge.

Digital Camera

Since the 1990s, digital cameras have become more and more common—and also more affordable. Because of this, it's now easier than ever to get started with photography. Luckily, you don't need to buy a professional-level camera to get good results. The most important factor is the **skill of the photographer**. In this tutorial, we'll show you how to use **lighting**, **composition**, and your camera's **settings** to take better digital photos—no matter what kind of camera you have.

Most cameras can be grouped into four main types: **digital SLR (or DSLR), point-and-shoot**, **bridge cameras**, and **camera phones**.

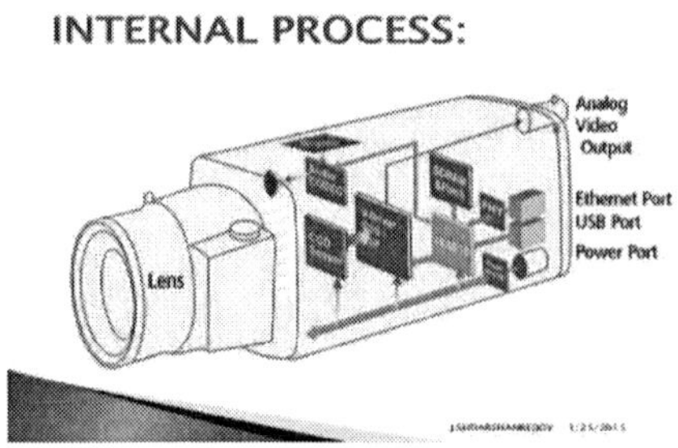

Digital Computer

A computer that represents discrete(digital) information by numerical (binary) digits is called a digital computer.

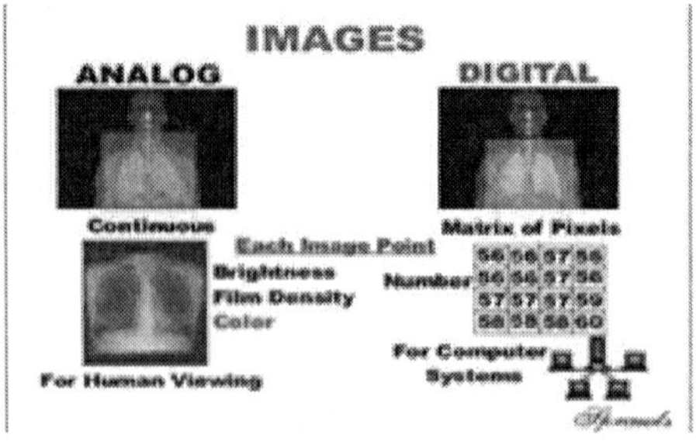

Generally it uses binary number system and thus it can understand only 0 and 1.

Digital Economy

The digital economy is the new productivity platform that some experts regard as the third industrial revolution. Digital revolution, also known as 'The Internet Economy' or Internet of Everything (IoE), is expected to generate new market growth opportunities, jobs and become the biggest business opportunity of mankind in the next 30 to 40 years.

The digital economy is the worldwide network of economic activities enabled by information and communications technologies (ICT). It can also be defined more simply as an economy based on digital technologies. Multiple definitions for the term exist, with variations in what should be included in this new economic paradigm.

Components of Digital Economy. The three main components of the 'Digital Economy' concept can be identified as:

(a) e-business infrastructure (hardware, software, telecoms, networks, human capital, etc.).

(b) e-business (how business is conducted, any process that an organization conducts over computer-mediated networks).

(c) e-commerce (transfer of goods, for example when a book is sold online).

However, the digital economy is not simply about moving business transactions from face to face to online. The digital economy is about transforming the many facets of business interactions and transactions and also enabling economic innovations. For example, the digital economy both is enabled by and has given rise to the advent of new digital currencies and payment processes (i.e., Bitcoin and the digital wallet).

Digital Economics

For several years now digital has been an appendage to "business as usual." But recently, digital transformations have reached the tipping point where digital has become "business as usual"; the tail has become the dog. Digital is not just part of the economy — it is the economy.

It's an economy of limitless opportunities for some and disruption and displacement for others. Many firms — such has Kodak, Blockbuster, Sears, and Blackberry — were unable to adapt, while others are thriving. According to MIT Sloan research, the companies that are adapting to a digital world are 26% more profitable than their industry peers.

The 4 Things It Takes to Succeed in the Digital Economy

Customer expectations. Digital technologies enable companies to better engage with their customers and offer superior experiences at affordable costs. But providing outstanding experiences to increasingly savvy, and fickle, customers is getting harder. Customer expectations go beyond ease of use; they're now expecting proactive experiences.

Product enhancements. Thriving companies are also integrating related products and services into sophisticated industry solutions, while extending and restructuring industry boundaries, essentially creating whole new industries. Michael Nilles, recently promoted to Schindler's chief digital officer, offers a great example. Schindler has expanded its business beyond its elevator and escalator products to become a mobility solutions company, offering its technology in a variety of industries including health care, hotels, offices, malls and retail outlets, and sports arenas and expos. A major enabler in this evolution was the development of smart elevators and escalators that constantly collect sensor data and transmit it over the internet to Schindler's back-end systems, where the data is analyzed, generating maintenance notifications long before an actual breakdown. These notifications, enriched with expert repair advice, are then dispatched in real time to Schindler's service applications, where technicians are scheduled as appropriate.

Collaborative innovations. Companies must become more innovative to better respond to the highly competitive, global business environment. Collaboration is indispensable for innovation, both within the company's own boundaries and beyond, with customers, partners, startups, universities, and research communities. Thriving companies are harnessing collaborative digital networks to build ecosystems, such as Amazon, PayPal, Fidelity, Aetna, Apple, and Microsoft.

Organizational leadership. Companies must rethink their structures and culture to better deal with new market environments and business models. The hierarchic organization that prevailed in the 20th century's production-oriented industrial economy will not work in the more global and fast-changing digital economy. The companies that are most successfully adapting are making a cultural shift from "Mad Men" to "Math Men," where decision making is increasingly based on data rather than on the frequently wrong opinions of senior executives. These companies are adding data scientists to enhance organizational learning. They've made some decisions faster by relying on algorithms, and they are introducing artificial intelligence, robotics, and other advanced technologies as appropriate.

Digital Media

Digital Media is a blend of technology and content, and building digital media products requires teams of professionals with diverse skills, including technical skills, artistic skills, analytical and production coordination skills.

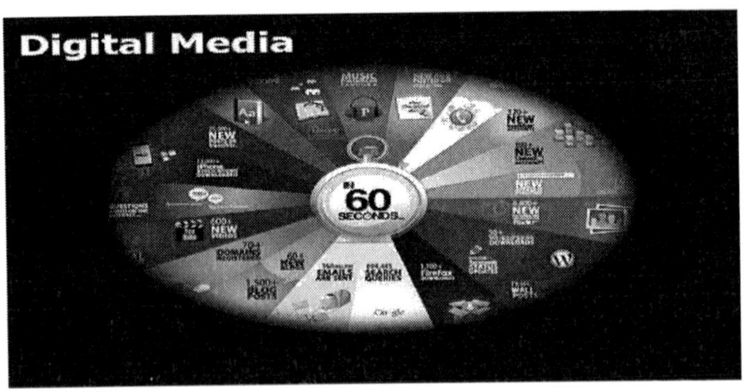

All of these skills need to be balanced on a team, with all team members focused on creating the best user experience.

Digital media products can be found in:

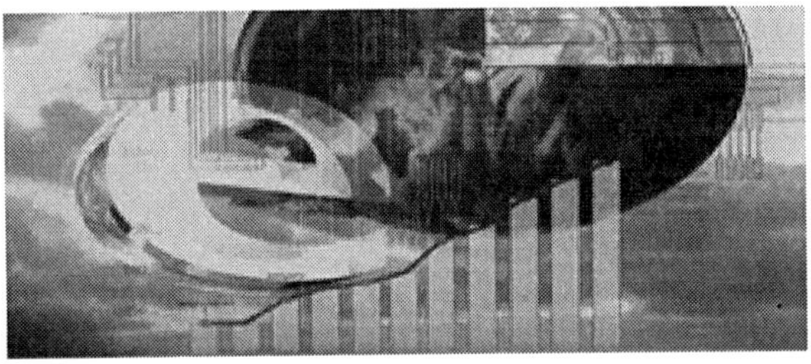

- E-Commerce
- Games – console, online and mobile
- Websites and mobile applications
- Animation
- Social media
- Video
- Augmented reality
- Virtual reality
- Data visualization
- Location-based services
- Interactive Storytelling

Digital media can include these industries: Entertainment, Technology, E-Commerce, Non- Profit, Health, Education, Marketing and advertising, Government, Sports, Environment, Television, Publishing.

Digital Versus Film Photography

The digital revolution has caught up to film in many regards, killing many of the arguments for film being better than its technological counterpart. However, the most notable reason to shoot analog may be the resolution obtained from medium format cameras. Not all explanations can be laid within technical comparisons though. Many will argue that shooting analog is a more personal and enjoyable experience – that decision, is completely up to you.

Digital Education

The role of every learning individual is thousand-fold when it comes to economy. A child who is studying today is an asset for the nation tomorrow, hence what he is been taught and his sources are to be taken into deep consideration. That is when the world of internet, computers and *swagger* comes into picture!!

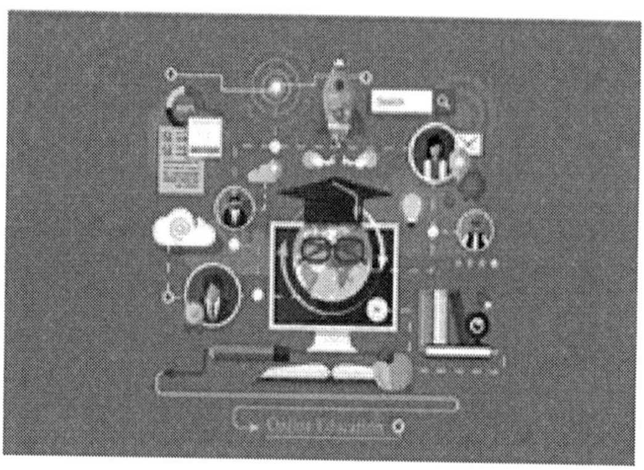

A new era of defining characteristic civilization has now arrived. So has digitalization in education.

Conclusion

To help companies embrace digitalization systematically, we have defined a framework for achieving efficient as well as profitable digitalization. To develop this framework, we analyzed the experiences of firms that have begun finding their feet in this effort.The proposed framework comprises three steps:

Step 1) Create awareness and ownership around digitalization: Help people throughout the organization understand what digitalization is and what advantages it offers, and foster a sense of ownership around digitalization at the highest level.

Step 2) Design a digitalization roadmap: Putting customers at the center of the roadmap, design a digital business value tree and a digital operating model mapping the technology and skills required to harness the true power of digital assets.

Step 3) Digitalize business model: Make the right choices about your customer value proposition, resources, profit formula and performance metrics and nurture the capabilities and culture needed to support your business model.

We believe that by mastering this three-step process, companies based in India can accelerate their transition into becoming truly digitalized powerhouses capable of profiting from such material opportunities the nation has to offer.

References

http://play.google.com/store/apps/details?id=com.incognisys.digitalindia

https://petapixel.com/2015/05/26film-vs-digital-a-comparison-of-the-advantages-and-disadvantages/

http://culturedigitally.org/2014/09/digitalization- and-digitization/

http://www.dighist.org/wp-content/uploads/2011/03/DigitizationBannerFinal1.png

https://acloudin.wordpress.com/2016/04/09impact-of-digitalization-of-education-in-india/

https://digitalculturist.com/what-is-digital-culture- 5cbe91bfad1b#.mlprjfl4z

https://hbr.org/2016/03/the-4-things-it-takes-to-succeed-in-the-digital-economy 9

https://googleweblight.com/i?u=https://www.accenture. com/in-en/insight-india-path- digitalization&grqid=QSFlAXkz&hl=en-IN

Chapter - 7

Sustainable Agriculture: Need for Paradigm Shift

Mr. Krishan Dahiya* & Ms. Khushbu Dahiya**

Introduction

If India has to achieve the goal of sustainable development, it has to develop, its agriculture. The reasons are many. Agriculture being mainstay and livelihood of almost 60% of rural population, it still contributes 16-17% of GDP, a source of continuous consumption and hence aggregate demand (food and food processing items) to accelerate production, basics of trade (intra-regional and international), a source of economic empowerment and it also carries a sense of social prestige and political power in rural India. Presently importance of agriculture becomes more in other sense i.e. govt. can fulfill its requirement of food through procurement by FCI and distribute it under TPDS (Targeted Public Distribution Scheme), as an obligation under National Food Security Act, to 190 million poor Indian masses. Therefore, keeping in view the objective of Atmanirbhar Bharat, govt. has announced a package of 20 lakh crore on 12 May 2020, for revival of Indian Economy which is suffering from COVID-19 pandemic, to its recovery in 2021. Mainly, Atmanirbhar Bharat Abhiyaan comprises of five pillars: 1. Economic revival 2. Infrastructure development 3. System i.e. economic system for production

4. Demographic dividend (provision for job to skilled migrant population) 5. Demand creation, as catalyst for capacity utilization and absorption. Now this financial package for 20 lakh crore being 10% of GDP require a vibrant ecosystem in agriculture by boosting aggregate demand on one hand and creation of supply chain as well as value addition on the other hand, as a boost for income output and employment, which is a necessary condition for economic recovery. Let us discuss, some basic requirement for sustainable agriculture, through this paper.

Objectives of the Study

1. Whether farmer, as an entrepreneur and agriculture as a primary economic enterprise, be left out on market forces of demand and supply (laissez faire policy) or it should be provided grants, subsidies, income and price support, etc.
2. What form of paradigm shift is required to transform traditional subsistence agriculture to sustainable agriculture as a goal for Atmanirbhar Bharat?

Research Methodology

The topic sustainable agriculture, is more descriptive conceptually and analytical in nature hence effort is made to provide logical explanation keeping in view of its objective. Information for this research paper is based on various journals, periodicals, books and literature available from time to time.

Review of Literature

W.A. Lewis (1955) in his book "*Theory of Economic Growth*" expressed that enhancing agriculture productivity helps in industrial expansion in three ways i.e. 1. Providing wage goods at suitable price 2. Mobilization of savings for capital formation 3. Agriculture to transfer surplus manpower for capital formation in industrial sector.[1]

R. Nurkse emphasized the role of surplus labour in agriculture for capital formation in under developed countries.[2]

K. Mandelbaum (1947) in his book "*Industrialization in Backward Areas*" also emphasized the benefits of diversion of surplus labour from agriculture to non agriculture projects.

Economists like Schultz, Viner, Coale and Hoover (1958) in his book "*Population Growth and Economic Development in Low-Income Countries*" also favoured increase in food supply in agriculture sector be given highest priorities.[3]

Economists like *Higgins,* Kurihara (1958), Leibenstein and Hrishman favours raising agricultural productivity by giving priority to Big Push type industrialization.[4]

Higgins in his book "*Economic development*" observes that during second plan, India's foreign exchange crisis was due to unplanned food imports.[5]

E. Staley in his book "*The Future of Under Developed Countries*" explained that industrialization is encouraged by enhancing agricultural productivity.[6]

Subrata Ghatak *(1984)* emphasized labor intensive technique and less machinery due to cheap labour in agriculture.[7]

T.N. Schultz emphasized in his book "*Transforming Traditional Agriculture*" that agriculture development require technology process.[8]

J.W. Mellor (1966) explained in his book "*Economics of Agriculture Development*" that land reform is an important development in agriculture.[9]

A.M. Khusro (1973) in his book "*Economics of Land Reform and Farm Size in India*" favours ceilings on land holdings.[10]

F. R. Frankel (1971) P.R. Bardhan (1974), G. R. Saini (1976) explained that Green Revolution in India mainly helped rich farmers.[11]

J. R. Westley (1983), Usha Nagpal (1979), George Blyn (1983) explains that Green Revolution benefitted small farmers. It also reduced income inequality as well.[12]

After going through the review of literature and keeping in view the present state of Indian economy, it is amply clear that green revolution, technological upgradation, soil, water and crop management has benefitted resourceful farmers more, due to access to credit, marketing, insurance and government support rather than small and marginal farmers constituting 86% of farming, which still awaits, the fruits of development. Small & marginal farmers lags behind, in adoption of necessary skills enterprise, training, technology, credit and market access. Although government has promised doubling the farmer's income by 2022 through various measures especially income support of Rs 6000 per annum per farmer, along with agriculture reform program to enhance soil fertility, water management and technological support. Zero based natural farming coupled with digital agriculture i.e. Artificial Intelligence, Cloud Computing, Internet of Things and Precision agriculture can be the game changer for small farmers if implemented in an honest, vigorous, transparent and impartial manner.

Now let us discuss the problem with sustainable agriculture through this paper.

Problems in Indian Agriculture

With mechanization, especially after green revolution of 1966, there is definite increase in agricultural production in productivity. Government schemes from time to time like Integrated Rural Development Program, Intensive Agriculture Development Program, Dryland Farming, Rain-fed Agriculture has accelerated agricultural development. Presently, government has initiated many schemes for reforms in agriculture i.e. Soil Health Card , Neem Coated Urea, Pradhan Mantri Krishi Sinchai Yojana, Jal Jeevan Mission, Per Drop More Crop, Har Khet Mein Paani for water management, Pradhan

Mantri Fasal Bima Yojana for insurance cover , E-NAM (One Nation One Market) for marketing management, Zero based Natural Organic Farming to reduce economic cost for small and marginal farmers, income support through PM Kissan Sammaan and lastly promise of doubling farmer's income by 2022, on the recommendation of Ashok Dalwai Committee, implementation of MS Swaminathan report, purchase on MSP and now agriculture farm laws to reform agriculture through private contract farming, for a better barrier-free domestic and international trade. Efforts are being made for sustainable agriculture through creation of National Infrastructure Fund of rupees one lakh crore, encouraging FPO/VPO for farmers in a favourable, competitive environment, at national and international level, but there are some genuine concerns which require proper attention by all stake-holders, connecting with farming for practical analysis, policy making, and its sincere implementation.

The first question to be probed is that there cannot be a single model for agricultural transformation in India. Here, the answer is logical and simple. Farming is a production activity where farmer, being producer and an entrepreneur has to take some rational decisions. For a producer, rational and logical decision is profit maximization. If he is a small and marginal farmer, then his rational behaviour for decision making, as an entrepreneur is quite different form a big farmer. Let us assume that a small and marginal farmer has to take some decisions like – What to produce? How to produce? When to produce? For whom to produce (for self consumption, or for market). These rational decisions depend upon, his access to capital, skill, technology, marketing, pest, insurance and government support. Now, if he has no resources available with him except his own land (one or two acre), his family savings if any (when no access to credit due to one reason or other) as capital and his own enterprise. Now all his rational decision of What, When, How and for Whom to produce is taken, keeping in view, the profit maximization. Now his profit depends upon either to increase total revenue (either by higher price or by higher productivity or both) or to reduce total cost (more of implicit cost and less of explicit cost). Now there is second case of a farmer having 5 or 10 acres of land. He has to take rational decision as an entrepreneur for profit maximization (increasing total revenue and reducing total cost with less of implicit cost and more of explicit cost) regarding what, how, when and for whom to produce. Both the farmer's (small and big) getting price, income, credit and market support by the government, but their strategy for profit maximization will be different because small farmers cannot bear loss in case of adverse natural conditions, cannot think for crop rotation, diversification and decision regarding, what to produce (traditional, organic, commercial, horticulture and vegetable crops, if prevailing market price and market conditions is not in its favour. But in case of a big farmer he can bear risk, diversify agriculture, go for commercial farming and can take risky decision and survive, in case of prevailing market price and imperfections because of assets and resources available, with government support regarding price, market and insurance cover. Therefore, the model for agricultural transformation cannot be same for big, small & marginal farmers due to economic viability of cost and benefit and assets (tools, machinery, implements) available to them, in the prevailing agriculture market conditions.

The second most important aspect, which requires attention is, whether farmer be left on economic forces of demand and supply with government support or without support? Here the farmer's income, irrespective of a small or a rich farmer depends upon access to land, labour, technology, seed, soil, and water and pest management. But here also, small farmer lags behind as an access to resources, skill, training, knowledge, technology credit and market support and even access to local bureaucracy or other governmental agencies, providing services to the farmer due to one reason or other. In a welfare state, government role becomes prominent as a promoter, facilitator and regulator in case of new farming laws and initiating contract farming. In contract farming, a service provider i.e. contractor has also to take rational decision for profit maximization i.e. provision of seeds, machinery, technology, pests, grading, packaging, transportation and marketing for regional and international trade in a consistent, stable, certain and investment friendly government policies. In case of contract farming (a contractor or service provider), the price of produce given to a farmer is his economic cost but it is the income to a farmer. So, there is a trade-off between the farmer and contractor (benefit of one party is loss to the other party). Therefore, a mutual negotiation is required on both sides which depends upon the bargaining strength of VPO/ FPO and service provider (a private company). Naturally the bargaining strength of MNC or private company is greater than farmer or VPO (village producer organization)/ FPO. Moreover, there is again a rider, for example what is the composition of FPO? Whether it constitutes small farmer or big farmer or both? Or what type of produce traditional/ commercial? What type of services provided (pre harvest – seed, machine, implements and pests; or post harvests – marketing, transportation, storage, etc). Prices at which the service is provided? The type of contract (seasonal, annual or bi-annual) entry and exit conditions of farmer in FPO/VPO in case of breach of contract or adversity. Here, the whole exercise becomes more complex, in case of volatile demand and supply conditions which usually prevails in agriculture due to imperfections, distortions and speculations. To meet the objective of all the stakeholders, consistency and enabling environment is not only essential as a policy tool by government but government has also to be the voice of millions of farmers for assured returns in a welfare state, otherwise the whole exercise of agricultural reforms would become futile. If it is to be left for market forces, without govt. support, regulation and monitoring a monopsony or oligopoly type cartel situation may occur in agriculture, benefitting private companies and harming millions of farmers. Government to make contract farming a success, have to provide counter guarantee of MSP to all the farmers for assured returns, only then apprehension, fear and mistrust would be reduced. So, either government must ensure regulated contract farming with rider or old model of government APMC market with MSP to the farmers.

The last argument is that, a paradigm shift is needed for new agricultural reform. The new paradigm shift, should be cluster based (Growth pole and Growth centre) in rural and sub-urban areas, innovating agriculture, based on geo-climatic and area specific approach such as paddy, wheat, sugarcane production in western India, fruits and horticulture in hilly areas in J&K, Himachal Pradesh and Uttarakhand, pulses, edible oil in MP and central India, cotton or sugarcane in Gujarat and Maharashtra, growth of fisheries and aquaculture in coastal India, bamboo and plantation crops in North-east. Amul, Vita and Verka can be the leading example for dairy farming and processing for rural upliftment to follow. These area specific growth pole and growth centre for whole of India can best utilize the enabling business environment of trade, commerce and transport as an infrastructure. Moreover, entry of sufficient firms is essentially needed to cater the demand and supply of these growth pole and growth centers to avoid exploitation and speculative practices by the trader. So, if it is left unbridled, monopsony or oligopoly type cartel may occur in future which may lead to imperfections in market. So, to protect the millions of consumers and farmer interests, due to unfavorable and distorting trade, government intervention is necessary. Moreover, the government cannot serve as a watchdog but has to play the role of promoter, facilitator, regulator and monitor, to make this agricultural reform a success. If capital market has SEBI as regulator, insurance market has IRDA and PFRDA as regulator, banks has RBI as regulator, why not have a regulator for farmers i.e. Farmer's Commission and Grievance Redressal Mechanism at block, district, state and national level to redress the grievances of all the stake holders. The government as a facilitator and regulator is also urgent and expedient in a federal polity having government of different parties at centre and state level, having dissenting priorities and programs to build a common consensus for policy implementation. Moreover, water, market and agriculture are in the state list, while MSP or assured return for supplementing farmers income is central objective as a precedent, therefore a better coordination of centre, state and regulating agencies for farmer, is necessary, for agricultural reform in India to meet the objective of self-sufficient and sustainable agriculture.

Conclusion

All the efforts made by the government for sustainable agriculture through soil, crop, water, pest, marketing, insurance, credit and infrastructure support are praiseworthy as a policy measure. But the real question is how and in what manner they should be sincerely implemented across farmers, across regions, across all the stakeholders, in a transparent, impartial and purposive manner in the sustainable ecosystem. All this require a strong vigour and commitment by FPO, private investors and government agencies in particular, as a promoter, facilitator and regulator coupled with committed, rural responsive and responsible bureaucracy, right from ground level to the top, so that desired objective may be achieved as per target, set by the government for Atmanirbhar Bharat and Sustainable Agriculture.

Notes

1. B.N GHOSH: *Economics Development and Planning*, pp. 126-127.
2. Lewis, W. A. (2013). *Theory of economic growth*. Routledge.
3. Petersen, W. (1959). Coale and Hoover, Population Growth and Economic Development (Book Review). *Journal of Asian Studies*, *18*(4), 524.
4. Kurihara: "Theoretical Objections to Agricultural-Biased Economic Development", *Indian Journal of Economics,* Oct. 1958, pp. 163-169.
5. Higgins: *Economic Development*, pp. 717-719.
6. Staley, E. (1961). future of underdeveloped countries.
7. Subrata Ghatak and Ken Ingersent, *Agriculture and Economic Development (New Delhi, 1984),* p.69.
8. T. W. Schultz, *Transforming Indian Agriculture*, p. VII.
9. Mellor, J. W. (1966). The economics of agricultural development. *The economics of agricultural development,* p. 251.
10. Khusro, A. M. (1973). Economics of land reform and farm size in India, p.XIV.
11. Misra, S. K., & Puri, V. K. (2011). *Indian economy* (p. 174). Himalaya Publishing House.
12. J. R. Westley, Agriculture and Economic Growth: The case of Punjab-Haryana, Ph.D. Dissertation submitted to the American University, Washington, D.C., 1983.

References

Lewis, W. A. (2013). *Theory of economic growth*. Routledge.

Nurkse, R. (1966). Problems of capital formation in underdeveloped countries.

Higgins, B. : Economic Development, Problems, Principles and Policies.

Mandelbaum, K. (1945). *Industrialisation of backward areas.* Basil Blackwell, Oxford.

Misra, S. K., & Puri, V. K. (2011). *Indian economy* (p. 174). Himalaya Publishing House.

Staley, E. (1961). The Future of underdeveloped countries.

Ghosh, B.N : *Economic Development and Planning.*

Frankel, F. R. (2015). *India's green revolution: Economic gains and political costs.* Princeton University Press.

Bardhan, P. K. (1974). Inequality of farm incomes: a study of four districts. *Economic and Political Weekly*, 301-307.

Blyn, G. (1983). The green revolution revisited. *Economic Development and Cultural Change, 31*(4), 705-725.

Chapter - 8

Achieving Self-Reliance Through Prime Minister's Employment Generation Programme

Ms. Namita

Abstract: Entrepreneurship is a powerful mechanism for economic and social development, generating incomes and jobs, and creating self-employment opportunities. MSMEs plays a pivotal role in developing the entrepreneurial cultural in India, and is a major force in providing self-employment and livelihood. Making India self-reliant is one of the major goals of the MSMEs through promoting self-opportunities for the young generation. India implemented policies aimed at reducing transaction costs, supporting MSMEs, enhancing competition, fostering employment creation and securing sustenance through the Aatmanirbhar Bharat Abhiyan. This study is an attempt to explore the performance of various schemes being implemented by the MSMEs for employment generation, entrepreneurship development programs being organized by the ministry for promoting entrepreneurial culture. The data were collected from the secondary sources such as annual reports and publication of MSMEs and KVIC to analyze the performance of schemes over the years. PMEGP scheme of MSMEs has substantially contributed towards the growth of the Indian economy by way of generating self-employment opportunities. The role of women in entrepreneurial has increased over the years. There is a need for improvement in current policies and schemes to make women more aware and active in entrepreneurial activities.

Keywords: MSME, Entrepreneurship, Indian Economy, KVIC, PMEGP.

Introduction

India implemented policies aimed at reducing transaction costs, supporting Micro Small and Medium Enterprises (MSMEs), enhancing competition, fostering employment creation and securing sustenance through the Aatmanirbhar Bharat campaign (self-reliant). A strong industrial sector is a sine quo non for an Aatmanirbhar Bharat. This campaign was launched by government of India with the aim of making the country independent against the tough competition in the global supply chain and to help in empowering the poor, who have been adversely affected by pandemic. Hon'ble Prime Minister Shri Narender Modi said that when India is moving to become Aatmanirbhar the Indian diaspora has an important role in strengthening the identity of brand India. He urged people to use Make-in-India products more and more.

With Aatmanirbhar Bharat campaign, the focus now has been shifted to MSMEs sector. MSME sector in India is a key economic driver, and the Indian government has long relied on it to fulfil its socio-economic objectives. MSMEs not only providing self-employment and livelihood but they are generating numerous opportunities for the others. MSMEs have played crucial role in generating huge employment opportunities at comparatively lower capital/investment cost than large industries. Moreover, they have helped in industrialization of rural and backward areas, thereby, reducing regional imbalances, assuring more equitable distribution of national income and wealth.

Role of Micro Small Medium Enterprise in promoting Entrepreneurship and Economic development

Entrepreneurship is one of the important inputs in the economic development of a country. The growth of an economy is based on various indicators and one of the main indicators in the recent times is the entrepreneurship. Entrepreneurship is a powerful mechanism for economic and social development, generating incomes and jobs. It can be explained as initiating and running an enterprise, mainly beginning as a small enterprise, by utilizing the entrepreneurial skills and abilities and offering the products and services to the society based on innovative ideas, and the individuals who do all these activities are recognized as "entrepreneurs". MSMEs are not only providing livelihood to the owners; rather, they are generating employment opportunities to others also. India aims at decentralized industrial structure to militate the regional, economic and social imbalances in levels of economic development, small-scale entrepreneurship in such industrial structure plays an important role to achieve balanced regional development. MSMEs sector have contributed immensely to the country's socio-economic development. It not only generates employment opportunities but also works hand-in-hand towards the development of the nation's backward and rural areas. The Indian MSMEs sector contributes about 29% towards the GDP through its national and international trade.

The Ministry of MSME runs numerous schemes targeted at providing credit and financial assistances, skill development training, infrastructure development, marketing assistance, technological and quality upgradation and other Services for the MSMEs across the country.

MSMEs aims to enhance competitiveness, technology improvement, adoption of best manufacturing practices, marketing of products, employment generation for building women entrepreneur. The government provides several schemes to women entrepreneur such as Trade Related Entrepreneurship Assistance and development scheme for women (TREAD), Micro & Small Enterprises

Cluster Development Programme (MSE – CDP), Credit Guarantee Fund Scheme, Entrepreneurship Development Programme (EDPs), Technology Up gradation and Marketing development Export promotion, PMEGP. Entrepreneurship and Skill Development Programme (ESDP), a Central Sector Scheme meant for creating awareness about entrepreneurship among the youth aspiring for building their career and hand holding them to create their small business ventures. The scheme also envisages capacity building of existing MSME for implementing good management practices in their units for improving productivity and product quality etc. **Prime Minister Employment Generation Programme (PMEGP)** is one the major schemes being implemented by the MSMEs to promote entrepreneurship among youth. Implementation of PMEGP was a step towards encouraging young entrepreneurs to set up their own enterprises and generating employment via those organizations.

Objectives of the study

- To explore the role and objectives of PMEGP scheme.
- To examine the performance of PMEGP over the past five years from 2015 to 2019.
- To analyse the role of PMEGP scheme in promoting women entrepreneurship.

Research Methodology

The study is based on secondary sources of data which was gathered from annual reports and publications of the MSME's and KVIC. Performance is analysed using percentages and CAGR.

Where CAGR is = [(Ending Value ÷ Beginning Value) 1/n] – 1

Analysis

Objective 1: To explore the role and objectives of PMEGP

Overview of Prime Minister Employment Generation Programme (PMEGP): India holds a vast potential for staggering economic growth involving every individual in the country. However, most individuals are stopped on their tracks to financial prosperity due to a lack of funds which further fosters a disparity in income rather than inclusive growth, ironically typical for a varied economy.

To address this disparity as well as cultivate entrepreneurship potential in individuals from both the urban and rural regions, the government of India introduced PMEGP in 2008. PMEGP was introduced by converging two existing government initiatives, namely Pradhan Mantri Rozgar Yojana (PMRY) and Rural Employment Generation Programme (REGP). PMEGP was introduced by the Govt. of India in September, 2008 for rural industrialization as well as to provide continuous and sustainable employment generation in rural and urban areas. PMEGP is a credit linked subsidy scheme aims to generate employment opportunities in both rural and urban areas for the MSMEs through setting up of new self-employment projects in the country. The ministry of MSME, govt. of India has nominated Khadi and Village Industries Commission (KVIC) as the national nodal agency with the active participation of the state khadi and village industries boards (KVIBs), district industries centres (DICs) working under the jurisdiction of the respective state governments and banks at the state and districts level. The subsidy has to be given through the designated banks for eventual disbursal to the beneficiaries or entrepreneurs directly into their bank accounts. The maximum cost of the project eligible for financing under PMEGP is Rs.25 lakhs in manufacturing sector and Rs.10 lakhs in service sector.

Table I
Beneficiaries contribution and rate of subsidy under PMEGP

Categories of beneficiaries under PMEGP	*Beneficiary's own contribution to project cost*	*Rate of subsidy (on project cost)*	
Area (location of the project /unit)		Urban	Rural
General category	10%	15%	25%
Special category (including SC/ ST/OBC/Minorities/ Women/ Ex. Servicemen /Physically handicapped/ NER, Hill and Border areas, etc.)	05%	25%	35%

Source: KVIC annual report

Objectives of the PMEGP Scheme

- Generate employment opportunities in rural as well as urban areas of the country, through setting up of new self-employment ventures/projects/ micro enterprises.
- Bring together widely dispersed traditional artisans/rural & urban unemployed youth and give them self-employment opportunities to the extent possible, at their place.
- Provide continuous and sustainable employment to rural and urban unemployed youth in the country, for better livelihood and also to arrest the distressful migration of rural youth to urban areas.
- Increase the earning capacity of artisans/workers and contribute to increase in the growth rate of rural and urban employment.
- Facilitate participation of the financial institutions/banks for higher credit flow to micro enterprises.

Entrepreneurs Development Programme (EDP)

EDP programme under PMEGP is implemented through departmental training centres of KVIC, KVIBs, central and state govt. agencies, Rural Self Employment Training Institutes (RSETI) and Rural Development and Self Employment Training Institute (RUDSETIs) centres. However, to speed up the EDP training flow, EDP to be conducted through utilizing the available infrastructure with Departmental Training Centers, KVIC and Khadi Institution, if the same is not available then RSETI & RUDSETIs. The objective of EDP is to provide orientation and awareness pertaining to various managerial and operational functions like Finance, production, marketing, enterprise management, banking formalities, bookkeeping etc.

Table II
EDP Duration under PMEGP

Manufacturing/ service sector projects up-to an inclusive of Rs.5 lakh project cost	*6 working days*
Manufacturing/service sector projects with project cost more than Rs.5 lakh to Rs.25 lakh	10 working days

Major Industries Under Which Enterprises Have Been Set Up by PMEGP beneficiaries

- Service and Textile Industry
- Agro Based and Food Processing Industry Rural Engineering and Bio Technology
- Mineral Based Industry
- Polymer and Chemical Based Industry
- Forest Based Industry
- Hand-made Paper and Fiber industries

Objective 2: To Examine the Performance of Pmegp

The comparative analysis of number of projects to be assisted, margin money to be issued and number of employment opportunities generated under PMEGP from 2014-15 to

2018-19 is reported in table I. During the year 2014-15 to 2018-19, number of projects actually assisted has increased from 48,168 to 73,427 with CAGR of 11.12%. The margin money actually issued the same time period has increased from Rs. 11.22 billion to Rs. 20.7 billion registering the CAGR of 16.53%. Regarding employment, the number of employments generated has increased from 87,056 to 5,87,416 with CAGR of 61.17% (during 2014-15 to 2018-19).

Table III
Performance under PMEGP

	TARGET			*ACHEIVEMENT*		
Years	*No. of projects*	*Margin Money (Rs. in billion)*	*Employ-ment*	*No. of projects*	*Margin Money (Rs. in billion)*	*Employ-ment*
2014-15	87,924	10.93	7,03,492	48,168	11.22	87,056
2015-16	64,529	12.86	5,16,232	44,340	10.2	3,23,362
2016-17	54,345	10.83	4,34,760	52,912	12.81	4,07,840
2017-18	58,750	11.7	4,70,000	48,398	13.12	3,87,184
2018-19	72,381	20.69	5,79,048	73,427	20.7	5,87,416
CAGR	-4.75%	17.29%	-4.75%	11.12%	16.53%	**61.17%**

Source: KVIC annual reports

Table IV reveals zone-wise performance under PMEGP during 2018-19 in terms of number of projects supported, employment opportunities generated, production and sales value under various industries being setup by PMEGP beneficiaries/entrepreneurs. From the table IV it can be seen that, south zone has assisted highest number of projects and generated highest employment opportunities during the year followed by north zone. In central zone 13,044 projects are assisted and 1,04,352 employment opportunities are created. In east zone 10,812 projects are assisted and 86,496 employment opportunities are created. In terms of production and sales, west zone has reported highest production value of Rs. 22.1 billion. Regarding sales, south zone has reported highest sales of Rs. 31.75 billion during the year. Lowest production and sales are reported in north east zone with production value of Rs. 5.02 billion and Rs. 8.85 billion during the year.

Table IV
Zone-wise Performance under PMEGP scheme during 2018-19

Sr. No.	*Name of Zone*	*No. of Projects*	*No. of Employment*	*Production (Rs. in billion)*	*Sales (Rs. in billion)*
1.	North Zone	15,413	1,23,304	14.97	24.60
2.	North East Zone	9,263	74,104	5.02	8.85
3.	East Zone	10,812	86,496	14.92	21.27
4.	Central Zone	13,044	1,04,352	18.66	27.73
5.	West Zone	9,220	73,760	22.10	29.69
6.	South Zone	15,675	1,25,400	21.26	31.75
	Total	73,427	5,87,416	9,693	**143.89**

Source: KVIC annual reports

OBJECTIVE 3: To analyse the role of women beneficiaries under PMEGP since inception (2008-09 to 2018-19)

Women are taking a stronger and more robust role in some economies, though they still lag significantly behind men in others. The status of women in developing economies has immensely improved, and MSMEs are instrumental in promoting women empowerment though not equal to men's representation, yet still achieved some significant milestones. The role of women beneficiaries is shown in figure where it can be seen the women entrepreneurs has increased from 4930 in year 2008-09 to 25399 in 2018-19 with CAGR of 17.81%.

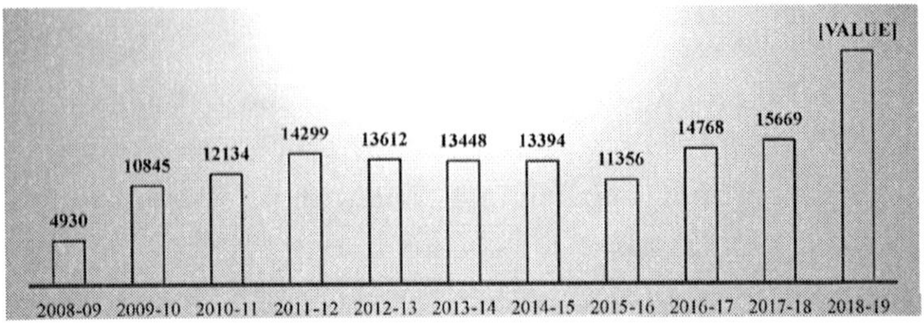

Chart I: Women Entrepreneurs/Beneficiaries under PMEGP

Source: KVIC annual reports

Conclusion and Suggestion

Medium, Small, and Micro Enterprise (MSME) sector in India is a key economic driver, and the Indian government has long relied on it to fulfil its socio-economic objectives. MSMEs not only providing self-employment and livelihood but they are generating numerous opportunities for the others. PMEGP is such programme of MSMEs, which has the potential to solve the problem of Indian economy especially rural and backward India. Under PMEGP (during 2014-15 to 2018-19) number of projects actually assisted has increased from 48,168 to 73,427 with CAGR of 11.12%. The margin money actually issued during the same time period has increased from Rs. 11.22 billion to Rs. 20.70 billion registering the CAGR of 16.53%. Regarding employment, the number of employments generated has increased from 87,056 to 5,87,416 with CAGR of 61.17% (during 2014-15 to 2018-19). The status of women in developing economies has immensely improved, and MSMEs are instrumental in promoting women empowerment though not equal to men's representation, yet still achieved some significant milestones. Women beneficiaries/entrepreneurs has increased from 4,930 to 25,399 with CAGR of 17.81% (during 2008-09 – 2018-19). Women are taking a stronger and more robust role in some economies, though they still lag significantly behind men in others. Various schemes and programs have been implemented by MSMEs to promote entrepreneurial culture in India. In order to become self-reliant, India must focus on micro enterprises. PMEGP is one of the major schemes of MSMEs which has potential to create employment opportunities, self-empowerment and self-employment opportunities. It will also create employment opportunities for others. Number of projects assisted, margin money disbursed and employment opportunities created has increased during the study period. But in order to become self-reliant Bharat, government needs to increase the margin money to be disbursed under this scheme. People applying for PMEGP loan scheme needs to be innovative so that they can have higher chances of loan approval. Projects are rejected because they lack innovativeness are creativity. Government needs to increase the number of EDPs training in order to make aspiring entrepreneurs competitive, skilled and innovative.

In the ever-changing business environment, heavily influenced by accelerated technological progress, government need to focus on these changes and make micro enterprises competitive. In order to survive in this changing environment entrepreneurs needs training, support and up-dation in technology. Instead of opposing these changes government must ensure that the beneficiaries/entrepreneurs get proper support in terms of everything. During the pandemic, government of India introduced various relief programs and packages for MSMEs. We need to encourage young generation as they are future aspirants of any nation, and with the help of them, we change the world in a positive way.

References

Govt. of India, Khadi and village Industries commission (2011). Annual Report 2014-15.

Govt. of India, Khadi and village Industries commission (2011). Annual Report 2015-16.

Govt. of India, Khadi and village Industries commission (2011). Annual Report 2016-17.

Govt. of India, Khadi and village Industries commission (2011). Annual Report 2017-18.

Govt. of India, Khadi and village Industries commission (2011). Annual Report 2018-19.

Chapter – 9

Sustainable Economic Developments

Nikita Chhatriya

Abstract: India has the largest youth population in the world, it is also one of the biggest advantages we have over other countries. Our economy is greatly dependent on the youth and especially youth entrepreneurship. Especially after COVID-19 and India-China conflict, our country needs more and more products to be Designed and manufactured in India. At this time it is beyond important to focus not just on economic and financial development but sustainable economic development. Every effort to uplift the Economy whether it is through Agriculture & Food Processing, Automobile, Manufacturing, Infrastructure

Industries or Vocal for locals come with a lot of pressure on the environment. So, it is extremely important to focus on sustainability at the same time because if not done it can cause more harm than good. Our future depends on the youth and we need to teach youth the importance of entrepreneurs that focus on sustainability.

The COVID-19 pandemic has bought a major downfall of India's Economy. Thousands of people lost their jobs, around 53 percent of businesses were affected and the fiscal deposit went down by 3.1 percent when led to a loss of trillions of dollars. Solutions are needed to be found so that the economy of our country can grow and recover from all the impact that COVID-19 pandemic has brought, but not at the expense of public good. Our environmental quality is a scarce resource which needs to be treated fairly and protected by every business whether it is manufacturing, agriculture or so on and so forth.

Objectives

- To gauge the role and contribution of global economies in Self-relevant India.
- To know about the importance of Youth Entrepreneurs in the Country.
- To appraise the international-Relations and Global collaboration in Atma Nirbhar Bharat mostly focused on Sustainable economic development.
- To examine the financial packages and funds appropriation by the government of India for Degitelixed Independent India.
- To assess the upcoming prospects of Entrepreneurship for the youngsters in terms of skills, digitelizations, health and employability in post COVID phase.
- To access the opportunities for making India better for our coming generations.

Manuscript

In order to learn abouts sustainable economic development especially in the context of Atma Nirbhar Bharat post covid. First it is really important to learn about Sustainable economic developments in general. It will be much easier if we move step-by-step because it is a somewhat large and complex topic to deal with in the first place.

So, what is sustainable economic development? In broad terms, sustainable development is a process that aims for human well-being and economic development is, whilst ensuring that ecological systems are in balance. To successfully achieve this necessary and challenging change, it is vitally important for everyone to take responsibility and do what is possible from their perspective.

"Sustainable development is development that meets the needs of the present without compromising the ability of future generations to meet their own needs"

—The Brundtland Commission definition from 1987

People + Planet + Business = Sustainable Development

Entrepreneurs do not need to become experts in environmental and social issues to make a difference. A basic awareness and understanding of these areas, however, increases their ability to do the right thing from the beginning. If we consider the examples from today's world there are a lot of big and small companies working towards sustainability who might not be very well educated about that but they still try their best to make a change in the world.Eg. Nestle, Unilever, tesla. The goal can be achieved in any field , FMCG, Manufacturing and what not. Ever heard of schools made from plastic residue. That is creativity and knowledge.

Entrepreneurs must decide which policies, programs, and investments are most likely to help drive sustainable economic growth. Public resources may be invested in a variety of inputs, including human capital development through health care and education, as well as physical infrastructure in the form of roads, electrification and technology as a whole.

Entrepreneurs should not consider education and infrastructure a binary choice. The fact is that human capital development is fundamentally dependent on infrastructure. A solid foundation of economic growth requires a combination of these investments. But with limited resources we must determine where in the spectrum of human capital development to concentrate investments to get the best overall return and build the necessary supporting infrastructure. Especially after the whole COVID - 19 pandemic our country's economy had faced a major downfall and we must use our resources as carefully as possible. Another interesting change we saw in the economy and in regards to big and small businessmen is that small business owners suffered loss and some even closed their businesses. On the other hand big business owners saw it as an opportunity and in turn gained more money. You may ask why? Well, because it all depends on how carefully one uses available resources.

You might listen to people talking about how they cannot fulfill the needs their business has by available funds and how they need more. Which is fine because every business needs extra money to grow but you should also know how to make money fast by using what you have and still taking good care of the environment.

Covid-19 Impact

Earlier I talked a little bit about the COVID-19 impact Moving forward but now it's time to dive deep because it is by now probably the biggest economic recession in the history of World. It is even bigger than the 2008 recession. Although India's economy is consistently growing from past several decades, it still faced a downfall during this Global pandemic which affected many likes, businesses, the environment and probably our future generations and well. It's our time to contribute to society and try to get everything back to normal as soon as possible. Currently India has the biggest youth populations in the world which is a really big thing. Nowadays youth have all the information available on their fingertips and they can make a permanent impact on the country through their knowledge, skills, creativity, education and how I like to call it attention to the surroundings.

While India Inc has already made the green switch for electricity, households and smaller businesses have also started following the path. "Awareness in India has caught on, and despite the widespread cost-sensitivity, customers are willing to pay for quality as they look at the long-term cost-benefit analysis," says Ritu Lal, head of institutional relations at Amplus Solar, whose B2C rooftop business, started in 2019, has been their fastest growing segment.

"A lot of the action against climate change will require collaboration and cooperation to save ourselves," says Anirban Ghosh, chief sustainability officer, Mahindra Group.

Beyond environmental protection, sustainability is also about ensuring people here continue to have jobs, and that Singapore society remains inclusive and liveable.

American economist Jeffrey Sachs noted that "*while sustainable development was initially a concept that centred on how development should not threaten the needs of present and future generations, it has evolved.*"

The COVID-19 pandemic has forced us to confront critical questions and decisions concerning our future and the role of cultural heritage in it. Looking ahead, the post COVID-19 phase provides an opportunity to 'build back better' by rethinking and further strengthening the role of heritage in sustainable development, in. Nevertheless, this will require the Youth of our country to reconsider its position and proactively take concrete steps to advance social, environmental, and economic sustainability. The webinar will address this issue, with particular focus on museums and their collections.

With all this technology it's very easy to connect with people around the world and if we use it for good things we can learn a lot from these people and their achievement and then implement the same .

References

Wikipedia

Economist

Harvard Business Review

Economic times

Forbes

Chapter - 10

Sustainable Agricultural Development: A Perspective of Aatma-Nirbhar Bharat

Dr. Niraj Kumar Singh

Abstract: Atmanirbhar Bharat, which is self-reliant India is a Hindi phrase used by Hon'ble Prime Minister Narendra Modi on 12th May 2020. He announced the special economic package of Rs. 20 lakh crore which was about 10 percent of GDP of India as a booster to economic development during and after the COVID-19 pandemic. Presently, the COVID-19 pandemic and its effects has created hinderance in Global supply chain. The Atmanirbhar Bharat Mission is basically focused to sort-out these anomalies and also to realise the potential that Indian economy has sufficient capacity to move in this direction. Qualitative improvement in agrarian sector / rural economy is the key to realise the potential of maintaining and sustaining the domestic as well as global supply chain. The Government has announced governance and administrative reforms along with infrastructure development capacities and logistics under Atmanirbhar Bharat Mission. The intent of Government is laudable as they are committed for doubling the farmers income by 2022.

Introduction:

The concept of Atmanirbhar Bharat is basically Self-dependent India which has a bigger and significant role in global economy and global supply chain. It does not mean a closed economy, self-containment, import substitution based or being protectionist. The ultimate goal of this exercise is to increase the share of Indian Economy in Global economy. Indian economy should not be self-centered rather than it should increase its trade share in Global supply chain. The Atmanirbhar Bharat approach is based on Human Centric Globalization rather than Economic Centric Globalization. The concept of Human Centric Globalization is based on philosophical understanding of '*Vasudhaiva Kuṭumbakam*' that is basically an ancient Indian doctrines which means 'The world is a family' (Karekatti,2013). It also focuses on the need to reform the global multilateral system to enhance its relevance and to improve its effectiveness to make it the basis for a new type of human-centric globalisation. The mindset of free India should be 'Vocal for Local'. We should appreciate our local products, if we don't do this then our products will not get the opportunity to do better and will not get encouraged. It is also stressed that our products should not only be 'Make in India' but the promotion of those products should also take place so that these products could be made competitive to global brands (Raj Saikia et.al, 2020). Amul Managing Director RS Sodhi explained that the phrase 'Vocal for Local' refers to the products to be made competitive vis-a-vis global brands and that it did not mean that one must only buy products that have a logo 'Make in India' on it. An extension of this slogan is 'Local for Global' that local products in India should have global appeal and reach (Sharma,2020).

Five pillars of Atmanirbhar Bharat have been announced by government and it is evident that a self-reliant India would stand on five pillars. Firstly, economy which requires to brings in quantum jump and not incremental change. Secondly, infrastructure, a world class infrastructure setup which should become the identity of India. Third, system should be based on 21st century technology driven arrangements. Fourth, vibrant demography, demographic dividend which is our source of energy for a self-reliant India, and fifth one is demand, whereby the strength of our demand and supply chain should be utilized to full capacity (Chakraborty,2020).

Agricultural Stimulus Package

Government of India has announced agricultural stimulus package to boost the agriculture sector. Agrarian economy has been suffering from many years and response of stimulus is long awaited since Green Revolution. Under the Atmanirbhar Bharat Mission package eleven measures have been suggested by finance Minister Nirmala Sitharaman. Out of those eleven measures eight were for infrastructure enhancement capacities and logistics while three were for governance and administrative reforms (Balajee, et.al 2020).

Agricultural Infrastructure Fund for farm-gate infrastructure to be setup

A Rs. One lakh crore fund has been announced for Agri-infrastructure fund for farm-gate infrastructure. The financing facility will be provided for funding Infrastructure Projects at farm-gate & aggregation points (Primary Agricultural Cooperative Societies, Farmers Producer Organisations, Agriculture entrepreneurs, Start-ups, etc. The fund is expected to improve the number of adequate cold chain and post-harvest management infrastructure in the vicinity of farm-gate causing gaps in value chains

Formalisation of Micro Food Enterprises (MFE) scheme

The government of India will launch a scheme to help 2 lakh Micro Food Enterprises (MFE) to install technical process and attain FSSAI food standards, build brands and marketing. This scheme promotes the vision of PM 'Vocal for local with Global Outreach. It will be implemented in cluster-based approach (for example, Mango in Uttar Pradesh, kesar in Jammu and Kashmir, bamboo shoots in North-East, Chili in Andhra Pradesh and Tapioca in Tamil Nadu) as Rs. 10000 crores have been allocated to facilitate the Micro Food Enterprises. The expected outcomes of this scheme would be improved health and safety standards, integration with retail markets and it will also improve the supply chain and enable the exporters to access the unexploited export areas.

Pradhan Mantri Matsya Sampada Yojana for Fishermen

Government will launch the PMMSY for integrated, sustainable, inclusive development of marine and in land fisheries and to fill critical gaps in the fisheries value chain. Rs 11,000 crore will be allocated for activities in marine, inland fisheries and aquaculture. Rs.9000 crore for strengthening infrastructure – fishing harbours, cold chain, markets etc. This initiative will lead additional fish production of 70 lakh tonnes over 5 years and provide employment to over 55 lakh persons, also doubling the exports to Rs 1,00,000 crore.

National Animal Disease Control Programme

National Animal Disease Control Programme for Foot and Mouth Disease (FMD) & Brucellosis launched with total outlay of Rs. 13,343 crores. It will ensure that 100 percent vaccination of cattle, buffalo, sheep, goat and pig population (total 53 crore animals) for the above-mentioned diseases.

Animal Husbandry Infrastructure Development Fund to be setup

Government announces an Animal Husbandry Infrastructure Development Fund worth Rs. 15,000 crores. The fund aims to support private investment in Dairy Processing, value addition and cattle feed infrastructure. Incentives to be given for establishing plants for export of niche products.

Promotion of Herbal Cultivation

The National Medicinal Plants Board (NMPB) will support cultivation of herbal medicinal plants leading to income generation for farmers. NMPB will support cultivation of medicinal plants in 10,00,000 hectares in the next two years with outlay of Rs. 4,000 crores. A network of regional Mandis for Medicinal Plants will be established. The board will bring 800-hectare area by developing a corridor of medicinal plants along the banks of Ganga.

Support for Beekeeping initiatives

Government will implement a scheme for infrastructure development related to integrated beekeeping development centres, collection, marketing and storage centres, post-harvest & value addition facilities etc. These initiatives will lead to increase in income for 2 lakh beekeepers and quality honey to consumers.

Operation Greens- Top to Total

Operation Greens run by Ministry of Food Processing Industries (MOFPI) will be extended from Tomatoes, Onion and Potatoes (TOP) to all fruit and vegetables (TOTAL). The Scheme would provide 50 percent subsidy on transportation from surplus to deficient markets, 50 percent subsidy on storage, including cold storages. the scheme to be launched as pilot project for the next 6 months and will be extended and expanded. The expected outcomes of these measures will lead to better price realisation to farmers, reduced wastages & affordability of products for consumers.

Amendments to Essential Commodities

The Essential Commodities Act, 1955 will be amended to enable better price realisation for farmers and make agriculture sector competitive. Agriculture food stuffs including cereals, edible oils, oilseeds, pulses, onions and potato shall be deregulated. Stock limit to be imposed under very exceptional circumstances like national calamities, famine with surge in prices.

Agriculture Marketing Reforms

A Central law will be formulated to provide adequate choices to the farmer to sell their produce at remunerative price, promote barrier free Inter-State Trade and a framework for e-trading of agriculture produce.

Agriculture Produce Pricing and Quality Assurance

A facilitative legal framework will be created by the government to enable farmers to engage with processors, aggregators, large retailers, exporters etc. in a fair and transparent manner. The integral part of the framework is Risk mitigation for farmers, assured returns and quality standardization.

Major Challenges to Rural Development

Agriculture is major source of livelihood in rural India. India's two third population and seventy percent workforce living in rural India. However, rural economy constitutes 46 per cent of national income (NITI Aayog, 2017). Mahatma Gandhi once said that real progress did not mean simply the growth and expansion of industrial centres and output but primarily the development of Rural India. Rural development is a comprehensive term which principally focuses on overall development of Rural India. The purposes of rural development are related to productivity enhancement of agricultural sector. Formations of alternative means of livelihood are significant for rural development. The expansion of health, education and sanitation facilities in rural areas is fundamental requisite of rural development. These facilities have played an important role in women's empowerment and inculcated a sense of social and distributive justice in rural India.

The agriculture sector in India has been suffering since Independence from policy paralysis because most of governments from states to centre have been remained hesitant to the reforms in agriculture sector. Primarily, governments had been cautious because of huge economic costs involved in it and absence of strong political will power, the agricultural reform could never see the light of day. Policy makers since Green Revolutions have predominantly focused on raising the agricultural output and improving food security rather than recognising the needs to increase the farmers income.

The average land holding size has been drastically reduced and total numbers of Small and Marginal farmers have increased enormously primarily due to division of ancestral property and defragmentation of agricultural land. Small land holdings have been uneconomic because cost of production is too high with limited out-put (Imai, et.al 2010). Agricultural sector has been victims of broken and fragmented supply chains. There was largely absence of storage facilities, cold chains, marketing infrastructure and inadequate connectivity in rural setup. The lack of credit accessibility and awareness has limited the scope of farm mechanisation. The shortage of irrigation facilities and high cost and less accessibility to high yielding variety (HYV) seeds have made Indian agriculture un-economic and un-productive. Therefore, younger generations are least fascinated in farming and losing their interests in rural areas and migrating towards urban centres. The changing global scenario and distress agriculture have burdened the farmers so much that country has witness a sharp increase in number of farmer suicide in last decade.

Agricultural Produce Market Committee (APMC) Act has many discrepancies that have not been addressed since long time. Last Model APMC Act was introduced in 2003 and it was first attempt to bring reforms in agriculture marketing (Mohanty & Singh, 2014). Despite of all the efforts, Governments could not reduce the deficiencies of the agriculture market and it created long chain of middle man between agriculture produce and market. The overall scenario was so deplorable that it could create an adverse impact on food security of country. Agricultural reforms were the only hope to sort out all these problems, however, it was also necessary for doubling the farmers income by 2022.

Governance and Administrative reforms under Atmanirbhar Bharat Mission

To achieve the above-mentioned objectives central government have passed three agriculture acts from parliament. These three measures were parts of governance and administrative reforms under Atmanirbhar Bharat Mission package announced by Finance Minister (Sahoo, et.al, 2020).

The Farmers' Produce Trade and Commerce (Promotion and Facilitation) Act 2020 or The Market Place Law

As per new market place law, it empowers the farmers, and they can sell their produce anywhere not just in the APMC approved mandis or market places. The formers can sell their produce inside the state, outside the state, or if they wish they can also sell it online. It promotes barrier free inter and intra state trade of agriculture produce. The new law was design to create an ecosystem where traders and farmers enjoy the complete freedom to purchase and sell farm produce outside the APMC approved mandis.

The Farmers (Empowerment and Protection) Agreement on Price Assurance and Farm Services Act 2020 or The Contract Farming Law

Farmers can enter into contact with agribusiness firms, wholesalers, exporters or large retailers for sale of upcoming agricultural produce at a pre agreed price. In other words, companies can have contracts with farmers and buy their produce. They could be able to set the price, the standards and qualities for the produce and other legalities can be mentioned previously. It will reduce the risk of market volatility from farmers to sponsors. It would also enable the farmers to access modern tech and get better inputs and reduce the burden of marketing and will boost the farmer's income. Farmers can also involve in direct marketing by removing mediators for full price realisation of their produce.

The Essential Commodities Act 2020 or Essential Commodities Amendment

The Essential Commodities Act was introduced in 1955. The objective of this act was to controls the production, supply and the distribution of certain food commodities. The new law has removed commodities like cereals, pulses, oilseeds, onion and potatoes from the list of essential commodities. Which means unless there is a disastrous condition like a war does not exist, the government will not impose any restriction on stockholding of food items. This provision will attract private sector/FDI into agriculture sector as it will remove fears of private investors of excessive regulatory interference in business operations. It will bring investment for agricultural infrastructure like cold storages, cold chain and modernise food supply chain. This law will also help in bringing price stability for both farmers and consumers.

Disagreements / Apprehensions

States will lose revenue as they won't be able to collect 'mandi fees' if farmers sell their produce outside registered APMC markets. The future of commission agents in APMC mandis are at stake if entire farm trade moves out of mandis. It may eventually end the MSP-based procurement system although Government gave assurance in Parliament that MSP shall be continue. Contract farming agreements clause could also create problems to farmers because they won't be able to negotiate about their terms and conditions. The large private players, exporters, wholesalers and processors, the sponsors will have an edge in terms of disputes with farmers. The provisions of disputes settlement mechanism are doubtful and could create problems for small and marginal farmers. Large companies will have the freedom to stock commodities- it means they will dictate terms to farmers which may lead to less prices for the cultivators. the recent decision on export ban on onion creates doubt on its implementation. The poor implementation of this acts will not only affect the farmers but consumers will also be affected as private players will always try to maximise its profits.

Conclusions

The new agricultural laws have been part of the much-needed and long-awaited reforms in the agriculture sector and it will improve the lives of million farmers in the long run. The government is also ready to make modifications to address the genuine concerns of the farmers. Several experts think that the farm laws are a step forward in the right direction. Noted agricultural economist Ashok Gulati, who was a member of Prime Minister's Economic Advisory Council from 1999 to 2001, says the three farm laws will benefit the farmers. Government is firm and adamant about the agricultural reforms. The three agricultural reform should not be seen in isolation as these reforms are the parts of eleven farm measures announced under Atmanirbhar Bharat Mission package by Finance Minister. Other eight measures have been announced to boost cultivation related infrastructure in rural India. The better implementation of these agricultural reforms can be done only if there is already an infrastructural development at the farm level. Private players will only participate in the agriculture sector if they are facilitated with better infrastructural facilities. Private sector primary focus always been more towards profit maximization. Since, Government approach is in right direction as they have rightly understood the problems of farm sector. So that, they have announced governance and administrative reforms along with infrastructure development capacities and logistics under Atmanirbhar Bharat Mission. The intent of Government is praiseworthy and they are committed for doubling the farmers income by 2022. The results of these reforms will be visible in next few year. The implementation of agrarian policies is the fundamental for the sustainable development of agricultural in India.

References

Aayog, N. I. T. I. (2017). Changing structure of rural economy of India implications for employment and growth. *National Institution for Transforming India, Government of India.*

Balajee, A., Tomar, S., & Udupa, G. (2020). Fiscal Situation of India in the Time of COVID-19. *Available at SSRN 3571103.*

Chakraborty, U. K. (2020). Opportunities for Tribal Entrepreneurship Development in Jharkhand to Combat Post COVID-19 Challenges. *Parikalpana: KIIT Journal of Management, 16.*

Economic Survey (2020-21) Volume 1, Government of India, Ministry of Finance, Department of Economic Affairs, Economic Division, New Delhi-110001

Garg, S. (2020). Reinventing Higher Education post pandemic: New Realities and Vision. *University News*, *58*, 49.

Imai, K. S., Arun, T., & Annim, S. K. (2010). Microfinance and household poverty reduction: New evidence from India. *World Development*, *38*(12), 1760-1774.

Joshi, V., Panigrahi, C. M. A., & Pitke, M. (2020). Vision of 'Atma Nirbhar Bharat'Role and Significance of MSME. *The Management Accountant*, *55*(12).

Karekatti, T. (2013). The Idea of 'Vasudhaiva Kutumbakam'and Modern Indian Writers: A Study of Raja Rao, Chaman Nahal and Datta Bhagat. *Critical Space*, 52.

Kumar, P., Singh, S. S., Pandey, A. K., Singh, R. K., Srivastava, P. K., Kumar, M., ... & Drews, M. (2021). Multi-level impacts of the COVID-19 lockdown on agricultural systems in India: The case of Uttar Pradesh. *Agricultural Systems*, *187*, 103027.

Massand, A., Lodi, M. K., & Ambreen, L. (2020). Atmanirbhar Bharat: Economic, Legal, and Social Aspects. *International Journal of Management (IJM)*, *11*(6).

Mittal, V., & Kumar, M. (2021). Hara Bhara Atmanirbhar Bharat. *European Journal of Molecular & Clinical Medicine*, *7*(11), 6553-6572.

Mohanty, S. S., & Singh, A. (2014). Agricultural produce market committee (APMC) act in Uttarakhand and its impact on agribusiness. *International Journal of Marketing and Technology*, *4*(4), 189-203.

Patel, G. R., Christian, B. M., Patel, H. C., & Pawar, N. B. (2020). Gobar Bank: The Pace towards "Atmanirbhar BHARAT". *Biotica Research Today*, *2*(10), 1088-1091.

Patil, M. L. Impact Of Covid 19 On Different Sector Of Indian Economy. *War Against COVID-19: An Alarm to Mankind (A Multidisciplinary Approach)*, 61.

Raj Saikia, C., Nath, P. K., & Deka, H. (2020). Assessing the Vulnerability and Resiliency of Indian Agriculture: A COVID-19 Perspective. *International Journal of Management*, *11*(10).

Roy, A., & Bhusan, B. (2020). Impact Of Covid-19 On Goods And Services Tax (GST) With Respect To Micro Small And Medium

Enterprises (MSME) Sector. *PalArch's Journal of Archaeology of Egypt/Egyptology, 17*(9), 4792-4799.

Sahoo, J. P., Samal, K. C., & Behera, D. (2020). Impact of India's New Farm Act, 2020 on Farmers and Markets. *Biotica Research Today, 2*(10), 985-987.

Sharma, S. (2020). Viswa Vision for Atmanirbhar Bharat. *Available at SSRN 3705150.*

Singh, K. (2009). *Rural development: Principles, Policies and Management.* SAGE Publications India.

Vijayalakshmi, G. M. Impact of the COVID-19 on Indian Economy. *COVID-19 on Indian Economy*, 116.

Chapter - 11

Atmanirbhar Bharat and Women Empowerment

POONAM

Atmanirbhar Bharat, which means 'independent India' or 'independent India', is a term utilized by the Prime Minister of India Narendra Modi according to financial improvement in the country. Today's ladies are re-planning the world. Lady is not, at this point a simple item or an individual in subjugation yet an equivalent accomplice. Ladies have consistently had the option to flawlessly deal with different duties and challenges and worked adequately to keep their homes, families, networks and society very much incorporated and efficient. The strengthening and self-rule of ladies and the improvement of their political, social, monetary and wellbeing status is an exceptionally significant end in itself.

Inferable from common socio-social and monetary standards where guys are praised as providers and ladies' great duty is taking care of the family unit obligations, ladies in India are now attempting to have something reasonable in the economy. The current COVID-19 flare-up is taking steps to subvert India's accomplishment in shutting the sexual orientation gap. The current setting demonstrates there is work to be done before we reach there. Gender gap unemployment has expanded. Ladies joining the labour force have dropped from 32.2 percent in 2005 to 23.4 percent in 2019. The scene glances grimmer in the current COVID situation with work misfortune for ladies remaining at 26.3 percent while the equivalent for men is at 23.3 percent.

We should remember that for a general public to become Atmanirbhar, it is crucial to saddle the Iccha Shakti, Gyan Shakti and Karma Shakti of ladies. The 'Shakti' (force) of the ladies has been hailed from days of yore, alongside a profoundly situated bias. Gopal Ganesh Agarkar, a nineteenth century scholarly and mastermind, enthusiastically needed to eliminate the bias and required an extreme change for ladies' empowerment. The sanity of the emphasis on youth and ladies is commenced on the job this fragment plays in pushing the country's plan for reasonable improvement by 2030 and its aspiration of a $5 trillion GDP by 2025.Women, specifically, can possibly produce 150–170 million positions by 2030 and add $700 billion to the GDP by 2025 through labour force support.

Innumerable ladies' stalwarts like Savitribai Phule, Sarojini Naidu, Sushma Swaraj, Saina Nehwal, Dr Rakhamabai, Lakshmi Sahgal, M. S. Subbulakshmi, and the rundown goes on. Commitment of ladies in the development history is very obvious, in any case, as a general public, we have neglected to keep up the poise of a lady. Our antiquated sacred texts and culture show how we should put confidence, keep up pride and regard ladies as we regard Goddess Lakshmi, Durga, and the sky's the limit from there. Ladies drive improvement will make ready for independent Bharat from a genuine perspective. We ought not fail to remember that half the populace has a place with our ladies.

Ladies in India do 9.8 times as much neglected consideration and homegrown work as men when contrasted with the worldwide normal of 2.6 times. This restricts their possibilities for monetary advancement. They experience gender pay gaps as well as face a danger of viciousness including lewd behaviour at public, private and working environments and now progressively in computerized spaces. The current government is passing on us to free our insight and point of view from the reliance on momentary material increase or misfortune and spotlight on the drawn-out progression of the country. Independence implies non-passionate reliance or all in all our inward joy not subject to our outer accomplishments.

Furthermore, it is fundamental for the accomplishment of economical turn of events. Ladies are the foundation of the general public and have consistently assumed a positive part in forming our general public. Financial strengthening of ladies is the most suitable answer for incorporating ladies to the formative objectives of the country and Atma Nirbhar Bharat. Monetary education, innovation mindfulness, advanced proficiency and sustaining of a pioneering attitude are key zones of help for all classes of women entrepreneurs. In the event that endeavours are made to empower development and are planned to change necessities of the section, it can support the development direction of India.

The Government of India has taken activities to expand ladies' support in the labour force at various degrees of associations. Beginning from notices eliminating limitations on ladies' entitlement to work around evening time in production lines, in underground mines, arrangements as load up individuals to far reaching maternity advantages and assurance from inappropriate behaviour at the working environment, reformist laws and approaches have been set up to change the actual texture of business tasks including making worksites ok for ladies and young ladies. Ladies' monetary strengthening is acquiring footing with bigger private establishments and worldwide organizations showing an interest in advancing sexual orientation correspondence through their strategies and practices.

Ladies driven advancement will prepare for independent Bharat from a genuine perspective. We ought not fail to remember that half the populace has a place with our ladies. The flexibility, energy and responsibility for family, society and nation have appeared at changed timeframes for various segments, as to save the pride of ladies, opportunity battle, initiative, political development, online media advertising news coverage and battling against indecencies in the public arena.

In the hurly-bite of the exceptional creation of a seething pandemic and limping economy, the public authority of India has ignored a critical part of development which could place a spoke in the wheels of Atma Nirbhar Bharat i.e., the lady's residents.

Apparently, ladies as a financial specialist neglected to make the cut in the independence Indian development. Atmanirbhar Bharat Abhiyan is tied in with making the country financially energetic, in any case, within the sight of such glaring imbalances, the mission will crash and burn in the event that it neglects to make exceptional instruments for empowering ladies' monetary investment.

A few accomplishments so far through Atmanirbhar Bharat

i. The PPE (Personal Protective Equipment) industry in India has become a Rs 7,000 crore in two months, the second biggest after China. It develops from zero creation before March, to 1,50,000 pieces per day by the start of May.
ii. Mukesh Ambani reported in mid-July that Jio has made a total 5G arrangement utilizing 100% local advancements and arrangements. It will empower India to dispatch a top notch 5G assistance.

iii. In July 2020, Apple reported to make one of their top-notch iPhone models in India interestingly.

iv. The biggest asset in the country worth Rs 21,000 crore was arrangement by the IIT Alumni Council with the point of supporting the mission towards independence.

The five columns

i. Economy: Quantum bounces and not gradual changes: Focusing on instruction and mindfulness for rustic ladies on Cyberspace.

ii. Framework: One that addresses current India - gave our foundation.

iii. Framework: Technology-driven-Motivating and tutoring an ever-increasing number of ladies in tech and digital areas.

iv. Demography: Vibrant demography of the biggest majority rules system – Change the Security story from Survival to Strength.

v. Request: Full use of the force of interest and supply-Capacity working to meet the tremendous ability hole in the internet by engaging and instructing ladies.

Placing cash in the possession of ladies is a spirit promoter. Cash gives them the self-sufficiency of financial dynamic and buying power. Given that ladies are drivers of 70% of buyer buy choices, it has a falling impact on the bigger economy. However, the compensation hole has proceeded. As indicated by an enrolment warning firm, the sex pay hole in India remained at 19% in the man's kindness. Heartbreakingly, the hole just gets complemented as one ascent up the range of abilities and experience stepping stool. This dissimilarity won even in ladies driven areas like medical services and social work. In provincial territories, in a gauge, a male salaried representative acquired almost 1.4 to 1.7 occasions a female salaried worker.

India's female workforce interest remains at around 20%, which is one of the most reduced on the planet. It has been declining over the long haul, notwithstanding rising female training levels and falling ripeness.

This doesn't indicate towards a promising circumstance around ladies' admittance to financial freedoms. Significantly, more than 90% of ladies work in the casual or sloppy area and in particular sorts of occupations and areas that are untalented and pay less with practically no execution of work laws.

The significance of ladies' liberation can't be restricted to simple hypocrisy on a solitary day. Consistently ought to be a ladies' day for stopping such a separation and accomplishing sex-based balance and ladies' liberation.

For this, there is supreme requirement for change in the attitude of individuals, especially men. Tragically even 69 years after Independence, we are as yet talking as far as finishing sexual orientation separation and the detestable act of female foeticide. The new episode in which 19 cut short female embryos were found in Sangli locale of Maharashtra has stunned the still, small voices of right-thinking individuals. Schooling, strengthening, qualification and liberation are needed to introduce a general public where ladies are treated as obvious equivalents taking all things together circles of life.

While 33% booking for ladies in neighbourhood bodies is being executed, now is the ideal opportunity to broaden reservation for ladies in congregations and Parliament. Some ideological groups are against the reformist Women's Reservation Bill on the presumptive ground that holding 33% seats for ladies in neighbourhood bodies didn't fill its need as the spouses of ladies chose through such seats were administering as a substitute. This might be valid in disengaged cases yet it doesn't mirror the truth. We need to receive a more receptive methodology on the issue.

Likewise, the opportunity has arrived to stop victimization ladies for the sake of religion, custom or individual laws as on account of triple talaq.

In 2020, India leads the diagrams as far as female pilots on the planet with generally 12.4% of Indian pilots being female when contrasted with other created countries, for example, UK which had 4.7% of female pilots, France which had 7.6%, Japan which had 5.6% and the USA with just 5.1%. India is likewise the world's quickest developing aeronautics market; our homegrown air traffic is filling in twofold digits, in this manner not just bringing about an expanded interest for pilots, yet in addition making occupations in numerous different administrations inside the flight business. There is a chance and hope of a flood in the quantity of ladies' business visionaries in India, from being simply 14% or 8.5 million to being an astounding 58 million; and for them to develop from miniature, little to medium and enormous occupation making business visionaries.

India is a place that is known for customs, custom and practices which have been created through hundreds of years to hundreds of years. These traditions, custom and practices become the cognizance of our general public. We love female Goddesses, give significance and regard to our moms, little girls, sisters, spouses, friends, etc. And yet, we can't overlook the male centric arrangement of our general public and male prevalence. Indeed, standards of sexual orientation balance are cherished in our Constitution. The Constitution of India awards balance to ladies as well as enables the State to embrace proportions of positive segregation for ladies.

The worldwide pandemic shows us the advantages of 'Be Indian and Buy Indian'. We have now gotten basically mindful of our own store network. We realize that depending on different nations for basic things will at last put you at their leniency. To evade such difficulty for ourselves, it is a higher priority than at any other time that we become independent and lessen our reliance on different nations. The pandemic has shown the significance of neighbourhood fabricating, nearby market and neighbourhood inventory network. Accentuation of 'vocal for nearby' affirms that it is about 'made in India' and is to promote Indian items to turn out to be sufficiently enormous to become worldwide brands. Thus, for the incorporation of ladies, it is required to comprehend the current circumstances and difficulties confronting ladies; and likewise make proper moves, proposals and answers for each lady at the grassroots level. Indeed, obvious independence will not come from persevering industrialization, however just from confinement and decentralization, as being shown by sure on surprising accounts of empowered rural communities.

Bibliography

https://m.dailyhunt.in/news/india/english/the+sentinel-epaper-senteng/the+role+of+women+in+atmanirbhar+bharat-newsid-n210549584

http://epao.net/epSubPageExtractor.asp?src=features.Spotlight_On_Women.Role_of_Women_in_Atmanirbhar_Bharat_Self_reliant_India_By_Meinam_Binota

https://www.linkedin.com/pulse/role-women-atmanirbhar-bharat-sailaja-vadlamudi?trk=public_profile_article_view

https://www.magzter.com/stories/Business/SME-World/Empowering-Women-Critical-to-Achieving-Goal-of-Atmanirbhar-Bharat

https://www.thehindubusinessline.com/opinion/theres-no-progress-if-women-lag-behind/article9575999.ece

https://www.cxotoday.com/press-release/women-entrepreneurs-the-key-for-unlocking-indias-true-potential/

https://www.sentinelassam.com/editorial/the-role-of-women-in-atmanirbhar-bharat-498378

https://timesofindia.indiatimes.com/readersblog/youth2020/atmanirbhar-bharat-and-women-empowerment-26777/

Chapter - 12

Vocal for Local: A Step Towards Sustainable Economic Development of India

S. S. CHARANTIMATH AND S. M. KHOT

Abstract: Sustainability is mostly perceived as the combination of environmental, social and economic performance; while still remain difficulties in defining sustainable economic development. Today, the human needs of many people are not met, and by the same time the ability of future generations to meet their needs is being compromised. It is because this that sustainable development has raised as a concept, affected by the need to offer people a kind of development which can meet the needs of the present without compromising the capacity of future generations to meet theirs. Economic growth may result in an improvement in the standard of living related to a small proportion of the population whilst the majority of the population remains poor. It is how the economic growth is distributed amongst the population that determines the level of development. The concept of sustainable development has become a widely recognized goal for human society of the 21st century. Prime Minister Narendra Modi said the mindset of free India should be 'vocal for local'. Which means we should appreciate our local products, if we don't do this then our products will not get the opportunity to do better and will not get encouraged. In India, people should support 'Make in India' and become self-dependent, try to minimize imports and maximize exports. It will helps India to be one of those countries on which the world depends and that will be a beautiful sight to watch. In this research it is analyzed how the concept of 'Vocal for Local' will helps for sustainable development in India and how should it really be conceptualized and what should be done in order to achieve it.

Keywords: Economics, Sustainable Development, 'Vocal for Local', 'Make in India'

Introduction

Former Prime Minister PV Narasimha Rao had unleashed the India growth story and Atal Bihari Vajpayee gave the country the infrastructure push. Though Vajpayee lost the 2004 election, his 'Shinning India' campaign created the much-needed optics for the India growth story vis-à-vis China. Prime Minister Narendra Modi's latest slogan 'Be vocal about local' is built on both the reform agenda of Narasimha Rao and Vajpayee's infrastructure focus to address a serious weakness in the India growth story — low share of manufacturing in the country's GDP vis-à-vis China. The weakness is crucial. All the big talk of consumption- and service-led growth of the previous decade ended in creating low value-addition potential. Despite high growth numbers, India created fewer job opportunities. The situation was perfectly summed up as "jobless growth". Ever since Modi assumed power in 2014, he wanted to correct it by tapping new value-added opportunities (Digital India), promoting entrepreneurship (Stand-up India and Start-up India), and paving the way for domestic manufacturing (Make in India). While the start-up ecosystem definitely improved in India, the drive to give a push to manufacturing witnessed limited success.

How Vocal for Local help in Sustainable Economic Development of India

Last week, the Indian Prime Minister Narendra Modi addressed the nation about the importance of local manufacturing and supply chains amid the COVID-19 crisis. Coining the phrase,

"Vocal for Local", he asserted that it is the need of the hour for the nation to come together to encourage local businesses and products.

"It is time to be vocal about local. We have to make local our motto. Global brands began locally. But when their people started marketing and branding, they became global. Every Indian should be vocal for local." he said.

Shedding light on the importance of using products that are made in India and 'Atma-Nirbharta' (self-reliance), he asserted that the country needs a boost to its economy that can also simultaneously transform local businesses. He also said that the khadi and village industries had successfully transitioned from local to global and could be a case study for all other local industries and enterprises.

What does all this mean to you, you ask? If you're wondering how to be more 'vocal for local', read on to learn more about the best ways you can make your business go local too!

Benefits of Vocal for Local

1. It strengthens the economy
2. It increases employment
3. It also increases the national income of the country
4. Increases efficiency
5. Quality goods are made
6. People grow
7. Inflation is less
8. The spirit of patriotism will awaken in the minds of people
9. People will become self-sufficient
10. Business will increase
11. Demand for foreign goods will decrease
12. People will use goods produced from their own country
13. Resources will develop
14. Foreign tax will decrease

Rise of Swadeshi Movement in India

While 'Vocal for Local' has become the most trending phrase in the last two days, it is nothing but an extension of the 'Swadeshi Movement' idea conceived by some great freedom fighters of the country, including the Father of the Nation, Mahatma Gandhi. The movement, which started in the early 1900s, called for the use of locally-made products. The trend lasted for some years before Economic Liberalisation began in the wake of the 1991 economic crisis, which led to a steady rise in FDI with the entry of global brands into the country. This phenomenon led to stiff competition between the home-grown players and foreign players as the latter offered better quality products at competitive prices. Unable to compete, many small Indian players got acquired by big multinational companies. Except for few diversified conglomerates such Tatas, Godrej, Reliance, and Raymonds, to name a few, many smaller brands fell by the wayside.

The Prime Minister's 'Vocal for Local' clarion call is to help in expanding the startup ecosystem by multi-folds, thereby aiding the country's aim to become a $5 trillion economy by 2025. The idea is to create more local brands and take those to the global arena. It is only possible with a focus on technology-based companies that can be scaled-up faster.

The Prime Minister's vision to focus on home-grown companies would encourage investors to look for enterprises and other consumer brands as the idea is to not only increase domestic consumption but also intensify the export activities and rely less on imported products.

Finance Minister Nirmala Sitharaman has announced some measures and sops for the MSMEs and for micro food processing units that would help create smaller ventures. The change in the definition of MSMEs also, in a way, helps the startup ecosystem as many of these startups fall under the revenue bracket mentioned under the new definition. Under the new definition, these companies can grow to a specific size without losing their MSME tag and benefit.

Best Ways to Go Vocal for Local in Your Business

For an economically independent India, we need to rise to the occasion and support our local businesses. We need to create products and services that are made in India, made for India and also made for the world. We also need to refocus our strategies from being profit-driven to becoming more people-centric.

Don't Just Buy, but Promote

here needs to be a greater focus on supporting local products. Homegrown products shouldn't just be purchased but also actively promoted and marketed. We need to encourage local manufacturing to improve supply chains across the country and boost the economy. When Prime Minister Narendra Modi addressed the nation this week, he spoke about the strengths of the nation when it comes to stepping up in times of distress.

Made by Indians, For the World

Creating a self-reliant India means having to be completely self-sufficient and producing and supporting local businesses and services. It is very different from the earlier isolationist and protectionist movements around the world. A few other measures include trying to discourage imports and the procuring of domestic goods. Import substitution, an objective that drove nationalist economic policies in the 20th century, is back.

We need to revive local industries that were previously taken for granted. It is time to usher in economic policies that produce sustainable incomes, aid in job creation and re-energize the local economy. With apps like Yelo, you can create your own online marketplace to serve the needs of citizens across the country. Tookan lets you deliver services to even the most remote areas via contactless delivery to ensure complete safety during the COVID-19 times.

Make in India

This is partly due to domestic reasons—like poor infrastructure, archaic legal ecosystem leading to low ease of doing business in majority of States, and constraints in availability of land which became highly complicated following the 2013 amendment in the Land Acquisition Act, among others.

To top it, the prevailing global trade and investment architecture foiled India's attempts to promote manufacturing.

For example, India had undertaken the rapid solar capacity addition programme with an eye on domestic manufacturing. However, a 2016 WTO ruling went against Indian interests. Though India finally won the case in 2019, Chinese gear makers made good use of the time in grabbing majority share of the Indian market.

In private, Indian policymakers, industry and experts in global consulting firms often blamed it on the opaque financing systems in China that leaves scope for disguised State subsidies.

However, there was no way they could speak of it in the open. This was either due to lack of proof or due to the muscle power of China.

Over the last few years, India tried to break open this Chinese defence by taking advantage of the trade war unleashed by the US, simmering tensions between China and its economically powerful neighbours, and growing concern among global businesses about the flipside of putting all eggs in one basket.

The effort was partly successful. For example, a high duty wall reduced the import of finished electronic goods, including mobile phones, drastically. But the gains were limited to the extent of shifting assembling jobs to India. Many or most components are still imported from China. Imposing barriers on import of goods from China is not enough either. China preempted such moves and acquired capacities directly or indirectly in countries, which enjoy trade advantage in the WTO regime.

Corona Opportunity

In his address on May 12, the Prime Minister made it clear that he is committed to remove all domestic hurdles before manufacturing and attract a share of the global value chain (which is now concentrated in China).

While liquidity issues are separately handled by the Reserve Bank of India, Modi promised "bold reforms" in removing obstacles in the areas of labour, land and law. He has also promised to create world-class infrastructure.

The reasons are apparent. There is a consensus across the world against concentration of the value chain in China. This is both due to business risks as is made evident by Covid-19 as well as due to strategic reasons.

The US may have access to technology in pharmaceuticals but 80 per cent of its API comes from China. For India, the average is 65-70 per cent. To reduce this dependence, India is setting up eight bulk drugs parks. The pandemic may make it easier to implement this plan.

Significantly, the Prime Minister didn't make any mention of China or issues other than those which are domestic in nature. However, he stoked nationalism (a tool used by China to the maximum degree) in giving a call to promote local industry.

It would, however, be naive to assume that Modi is merely taking his chances in view of the current controversy and disruption in global value chain. It is also immature to assume that the Prime Minister's call for self-reliance is built on the anti-globalisation narrative.

Also, China has been quick to restart the economy and a simple tweak in the exchange rate of RMB may see many companies drop their relocation plans for higher profits. After all, relocation is not an easy affair, and China, having built a critical mass, offers a better ecosystem for industry.

A Calculated Move

Actually, Covid-19 gave the entire world a godsend opportunity to carry out changes which they have been aspiring to do. India is trying to make the best of this opportunity. As a politician, Modi has three distinct qualities — his ability to identify future trends, appetite to take risks, and the ability to make common Indians believe in his dreams. No one believed that 137 crore Indians would voluntarily go under house arrest for months at the call of the Prime Minister. But they did.

Over the last six years, when he struck a strategic military pact with the US and made every attempt to improve India's influence in the region, Modi made the world believe that New Delhi was ready to shoulder the responsibility of maintaining a power balance in the region, provided they stand by India.

However, he was careful to avoid taking any confrontationist stance against China. This was most evident in India's careful handling of the QUAD (Quadrilateral Security Dialogue). On the contrary, the Prime Minister always stressed on the importance of India-China cooperation. The underlying agenda was a claim for equal stake.

By claiming a stake in the global value chain, the Prime Minister brought out the agenda in the open. He is not interested in taking India back to the closed economy days.

He is giving a perfect excuse to the power houses of the day to enforce a change in the global architecture governed by either the UN or the WTO. The ultimate aim is to find a place for India in the global power order.

Conclusion

We should support local businesses and create our own local venture. The ongoing pandemic situation has forced companies and businesses to rethink their operational strategies. Many businesses used this opportunity to boost production and exports. Services like Yelo, Tookan, Panther and Fugu are entirely local and made for a global audience. In his speech, PM Modi has made it clear that his vision for a new India would see it ramp up its manufacturing across all sectors, not just to serve the nation's demand, but to turn it into a prime global exporter as well. As such, it imperative that the products India makes should not be founded on an inward-looking perspective, but match global standards such that Indian producers are able to compete across the world.

References

https://jungleworks.com/be-vocal-for-local-support-the-indian-economy-during-the-covid-19-crisis/

https://www.commercefiber.com/benefits-of-adopting-vocal-for-local-commerce-fiber/

https://www.newindianexpress.com/opinions/2020/may/26/self-reliant-india-the-bounce-of-vocal-for-local-2147966.html

Atkinson, R., Dörfler, T., &Rothfub, E. (2018). Self-organisation and the coproduction of governance: The challenge of local responses to climate change. Politics and Governance.

Berning, C. C. (2016). Contextual perceived group threat and radical rightwing populist party preferences: Evidence from Switzerland. Research & Politics, 3(1), 2053168016635670.

Chapter - 13

Combatting Corona: The Role of Political Framework, Our Perspectives and the Prospects

Stuti Ghosh and CS Sameer Gahlot

Abstract: The dawn of the new politics has emerged at the helm of Corona pandemic wherein opportunist governments are taking action which otherwise might be difficult to implement. It has magnified the impact of the draconian measures taken by the Governments, from time to time, on social and economic health across global frontiers. The economies are witnessing a recessionary condition much severe than the Great Depression of 1930.The Politics all over the globe is fragile considering both the loss of lives and economic blowout due to complete lockdown implemented by the Government. Through this paper we strive to analyze if a certain political framework has a crucial role in alleviating or aggravating the challenges faced by the different countries under different government structures. Also, a brief study into the steps taken by the Indian Government to make India "Atmanirbhar Bharat" has been undertaken. The data relied upon for this research is of secondary nature. It has been sourced from various Governmental websites, national and international reports and newspapers. Through the analysis of the data collected it was observed that an ideal political or government structure could have saved the economy of a country is a myth. What the world needed was pro-active behavior and careful listening instead of outright inflexible decisions. The corrective measures for combating the corona aren't a secret, but their implementation demands commitment and resilience. Remaining politically unchallenged takes a country farther away from the greater goal of mass good. Every government has a journey filled with highways, potholes and rugged roads. However, the difference lies in the attitude of both- the leader and the public.

Keywords: COVID 19, Combating Corona, Pandemic, Politics, India, Atmanirbhar Bharat

Introduction

The dawn of the new politics has emerged at the helm of Corona pandemic wherein opportunist governments are taking action which otherwise might be difficult to implement. It has magnified the impact of the draconian measures taken by the Governments, from time to time, on social and economic health across global frontiers. While global economy is in the shackles of the Corona virus, in a matter of weeks, the world had no option but to surrender itself to this highly contagious and deadly disease. So much so that the economies are witnessing a recessionary condition much severe than the Great Depression of 1930. Several factors, including the virus itself, the economic interventions and the public health responses play a crucial role in determining the depth and duration of this wrath on the world economy. This unannounced pandemic-induced crisis has left the policy makers and the leaders working without a playbook.

According to JonghyunChoe (Secretary General, Association of World Elections Bodies), "the best disinfection measure is the best election management" (Association of World Election Bodies, 2020). Due to the Corona pandemic, election in various countries are either deferred or postponed. The postponed elections are either conducted through postal ballot or after adopting appropriate safety measures for the citizens. In the coming days, it is inappropriate to mention that the Election Day shall become the election month in addition to that electronic voting shall be in mainstream and voting by mail be the new normal. The Politics all over the globe is fragile considering both the loss of lives and economic blowout due to complete lockdown implemented by the Government.

According to the Johns Hopkins University of Medicine (Corona virus Resource Centre), the three worst affected countries (with respect to the number of deaths) as on March 31, 2021, were United States followed with Brazil and Mexico and least affected countries were Samoa followed with Saint Kitts & Nevis and Micronesia, whereas the three worst affected countries (with respect to the number of cases) were United States followed with India and Brazil while three least affected countries were Micronesia followed with Vanuatu and Samoa. (Johns Hopkins University & Medicine, 2020).

In order to fight against the Corona pandemic, there has been a paradigm shift in the role erstwhile played by the three organs of the government i.e. executive, legislative and judiciary. With the unending destruction due to the Corona pandemic, the most common word in year 2020 could be state of emergency in order to tackle with the rising number of cases and deaths.

This paper seeks to study the preventive actions taken by the authorities round the globe and its various implications. Through this paper we strive to analyze if a certain political framework has a crucial role in alleviating or aggravating the challenges faced by the different countries under different government structures. The sectional division of the paper is such that the introduction is followed by the research methodology, then the data and its analysis with respect to various countries in comparison to Indian situation and thereafter the conclusion.

Research Methodology

The data relied upon for this research is of secondary nature. It has been sourced from various Governmental websites, national and international reports and newspapers. The limitation of this research lies in the fact that, the data is volatile and analysis is subjective in nature.

Data and its Analysis

India

Corona pandemic has challenged the Indian administrative and constitutional framework to handle the first pan India biological disaster. It must be noted that India reported its first case in the state of Kerala on January 30, 2020 (Ward, 2020) and the nationwide lockdown which was announced on March 24, 2020 was imposed under the Disaster Management Act, 2005 by the order of NDMA (National Disaster Management Authority), "to take measures for ensuring social distancing so as to prevent the spread of COVID - 19". This unexpected drastic step by the Indian Government called for mixed reactions from the citizens. It also led to multifarious implications on the country and its citizens as a whole.

In order to ameliorate the situation, the Government had no other recourse but to abide with the provisions of the following acts:

The Epidemic Disease Act, 1897

The Epidemic Disease Act, 1897 is a short legislation that was enacted to stonewall the 1896 Bubonic plague that devastated lives in Mumbai (formerly Bombay Presidency). It is the primary and the major legal weapon that the Government of India possesses today after almost 120 years. The Act was drafted, back then, with the objective to provide for better prevention from the spread of Dangerous Epidemic Diseases.

The Disaster Management Act, 2005 (DMA, 2005)

The enactment of the Disaster Management Act, 2005, by the Government of India, envisaged the creation of

National Disaster Management Authority (NDMA) chaired by the Prime Minister of India brought a paradigm shift in the disaster management in India. The NDMA is mandated to issue guidelines for preparing action plans for holistic and coordinated management of all disasters (ndmindia.nic.in, 2005).

The Essential Commodities Act, 1956

The enactment of the Essential Commodities Act, 1956, by the Government of India, in order to control the production, supply and distribution of, and trade & commerce, in certain commodities.

In 2008, when the Centre drafted the Management of Biological Disaster Guidelines, which is being followed in letter and spirit even today, it was apprehended that the Epidemic Disease Act, 1897 was deficient when it came to bio-terrorism and international spread of disease (Sharma, 2020). It further restricted the powers of the Centre to just issuing advisories and coordinating. The Centre wasn't empowered enough to intervene in case of biological emergencies. It demanded an Act which could address the prevailing and predicable public health needs and use of biological weapons by an adversary as well (ndma.gov.in, 2008).

It was argued that the Act wasn't repealed as the States thought their powers were being infringed upon. A public health emergencies bill, drafted during the first term of the UPA government also didn't see the light of the day due to similar concerns from the states. It was during the first term of the Modi Government when a similar draft was considered by the health and family welfare ministry, named Public Health (Prevention, Control and Management of Epidemics, Bio-terrorism and Disasters) Bill 2017, proposing The Epidemic Disease Act, 1897 to be repealed.

As Swami Vivekananda said, "each work has to pass through three stages- ridicule, opposition and then acceptance. Those who think ahead of their times are sure to be misunderstood". The fundamental changes, like the steps towards digitization, direct benefit transfers, gas cylinders to poor, etc., incorporated by the Modi Government has served as a boon in the times of crisis. The legal inability and inadequacy to address disease outbreaks were known for long and baby steps were being taken, but in the end, the country was caught off guard when the pandemic broke, the severest since the 1917-18 Influenza that killed millions.

As stated by Kamal Kishore, a member of NDMA, a lot of peacetime work, including drafting of the National Disaster Management Act, 2019 was undertaken in view of the possible biological disaster, in addition to the 2008 Biological disaster Guidelines. However, only knee jerks and haphazard responses are being witnessed at the ground level, despite the annual National plans, State plans and district plans to address impending disasters (including "Biological and public health emergencies") are being made under the DMA, 2005.

USA

The United States which is scheduled to face the Presidential elections in November 2020 has forced the Government to take abnegated measures which are vital for people other than its citizens. The obscurantism of the Government which has been lashed out by people of its own country is currently facing the hardest blow due to the Coronavirus pandemic and long battling fight of rights by the black people. The Elections which is part and parcel of democratic life shall pave the way for justice regardless of its consequences. The government has taken the following measures in helter skelter so as to cope up with the Corona virus pandemic:

National Emergency Act

It is an act which was enacted in order to provide for orderly implementation and termination of future national emergencies (fema.gov.in, 2020).

Stafford Act

An act which provides an orderly and continuing means of assistance by the Federal Government to State and Local governments in carrying out their responsibilities to alleviate sufferings and damage which result from disaster (like Corona pandemic). After due implementation of the provisions of this act, the federal government became more powerful and can issue directions to all the states. It is equivalent to Indian counterpart which is National Disaster Management Act, 2005 (fema.gov.in, 2020).

Defense Production Act

An act wherein the Federal Government can expedite and expand the supply of materials and services from US Industrial base needed to promote the national defense. For example, in order to ensure uninterrupted supply of ventilators and other essentials, the US Government has required General Motors and later extended to 3M to produce ventilators (https://www.brookings.edu/).

In addition to these regulations, US has enacted the Coronavirus Aid, Relief and Economic Security Act or CARES Act in order to repeal the excise tax on high cost employer-sponsored health coverage (fema.gov.in, 2020).

Hungary

As stated in the beginning that opportunist government are taking action which otherwise might be difficult to implement which was proved by Hungary. The Government in the

Hungary under its emergency provisions has taken control over all matters terming them as necessary for corona virus. The critics have said that Hungary has taken a step closer to dictatorship (Szekeres, 2020).

Algeria

Algeria which is located in the Southern Europe is currently dealing with dual blow to its system in the times of pandemic, facing with political as well as economic uncertainty. The country enacted new legislation on the pretext of curbing the fake news during the pandemic in order to repress the rights movements or what is popularly known as Hirak in Arabic. The regime's use of the pandemic to quell popular dissent is pushing Algeria deeper into crisis (Serrano, 2020).

South East Asian countries

In the ASEAN region (i.e. group of 10 countries which includes Brunei, Cambodia, Indonesia, Laos, Malaysia, Myanmar, the Philippines, Singapore, Thailand and Vietnam), the corona virus pandemic has impacted people from every walk of life, including the political, economic and social aspect as seen in the Philippines where government took illiberal actions without public scrutiny to crack down on their opponents.

Cambodia on the other hand adopted worst strategies from the People's Republic of China i.e. an unnecessary crackdown on human rights. Also it restricted the freedom of expression and peaceful assembly.

Coronavirus has revealed to us fragile conditions of human rights and civil liberties across the region that highlighted that in countries like Indonesia and Singapore how existing regulation on speech, criticism and fake news may be used to combat emergent public threats (Research, 2020).

On the other hand, Vietnam is not a democracy, and those left behind by development have only limited access to the ears of policymakers in Hanoi, but local governance has improved nevertheless, and the country's political economy has been transformed as a result. And indeed, Vietnam's enviable record of managing Coronavirus pandemic by prioritizing health over all other concerns illustrates how such transparency-enhancing reforms can have enormous social and economic benefits (Nguyen & Malesky, 2020).

The people in these countries clearly remembered SARS and other epidemic, so were quick in responding to the Covid crisis.

Lebanon

The Lebanese capital Beirut has galvanized the entire world after ramification of explosion due to ammonium nitrate that was stored in the warehouse at the port city. The country which was battling with political instability and corona pandemic has shocked the world with its management.

Notwithstanding the government structure, i.e. democracy, dictatorship or any other form, the deadly virus has taken a toll on all the countries across the globe. The intensity and the plight may differ for all, but, none remained untouched. The prevailing conditions ask for a co-operative federalism, and the administration and the leaderships, at every level, cannot and ought not to fail its citizens.

Atmanirbhar Bharat and Relevance

Atmanirbhar Bharat or Self-Reliant India is based on the premise of the culture that considers the earth to be the mother. In order to make our country self-reliant, India needs to work on its five rudimentary pillars i.e. Economy, Infrastructure, System, Vibrant Demography and Demand.

As pointed out by the Economic Survey 2019-20 that India's demographic dividend will peak around 2041 when the share of the working age population will be 59% making India the most populous country in this century. The initiatives taken by the Government in the direction of reviving demand in the economy or making structural reforms by way of introducing various schemes under the Atmanirbhar Bharat Abhiyaan or enactment of new labour codes are pivotal.

The prime objective of the Production Linked Incentive (PLI) scheme launched by the Government is to make manufacturing in India globally competitive by removing sectoral disabilities, achieving objectives of the National Manufacturing Policy 2011, creating economies of scale and ensuring efficiencies. It is designed to create an incisive ecosystem in India and make India an integral part of the global order.

The recent enactment in the Labour codes has paved the way for recognising unorganised, gig and platform workers. Thereby, concomitantly simplifying bunch of central government laws dealing with labour into four codes (i.e. the Industrial Relations Code, the Code of Social Security, the Occupational Safety, Health and Working Conditions Code and Code on Wages).

Looking at the bigger picture, the unwavering one step at a time will bring us closer to an "Atmanirbhar Bharat". Every change shall bring with it a journey full of potholes and criticism. However, a complete analysis and understanding of the plight of the citizens of India, belonging to various strata, plays a crucial role in forming a supportive team that acts as a catalyst in achieving the goal seamlessly.

Conclusion

Policies and regulation formulations for disasters and public health over a long period of years took a backseat as the world was hit by this unprecedented corona pandemic. An ideal political or government structure could have saved the economy of a country is a myth. What the world needed was pro-active behavior and careful listening instead of outright inflexible decisions.

Democracy is believed, to give major incentives to the government to work for its citizens since it is bound to respond to people's needs due to public discussions and elections. A free media and open public discussions bring to light the plight and distress of the vulnerable and socially advantaged sections of people and those in need, thus, destabilizing the government standing. Although a section of the entire population may be suffering, but the majority listening to these concerns makes a government responsive.

However, India, like US has been ignorant and woefully unprepared, thus losing out the initial few weeks. All this was not on account of anti-science attitude, but due to the virus of political hate and intolerance. When actions were taken, they were thoughtless with no alternate arrangements for those who were unemployed overnight. The national lockdown without any notice and preparedness triggered a stampede, unemployment, starvation and a situation of "reverse migration". The relief plans and packages announced within a few days could do little in such a chaos.

Even in US, the announcement of income subsidies through massive federal spending was a result of public discussion and advocacy by opposition.

China, an openly authoritarian government, with its preparedness post the SARS epidemic, could do little and fumbled as here the local officials are apprehensive in sharing bad news with the higher authorities. However, the advantage of being the world leader in manufacturing and infrastructure construction couldn't be overlooked as the other countries were on the back foot as they had outsourced it to China over all these years. This came to the rescue of China as it was quick in building hospitals, manufacturing ventilators and other medical equipment.

Reportedly, the comparatively successful New Zealand, South Korea, Taiwan and Singapore demonstrated effective state machinery with their pro-active steps and mass-testing for infection in the early stages. Of these, New Zealand is a constitutional monarchy with parliamentary government, South Korea, a centralized democracy; Taiwan is a more decentralized civic- participatory democracy and Singaporean autocracy. Though the quick reflexes and effective decisions worked in the favor of these countries, the same couldn't be compared with bigger democracies like India.

However, the early decisions to seal the borders to restrict foreign influx, contract tracing, screening at the airports and mass-testing are lessons to be taken from them. Negligence and ignorance are the crucial factors in the failure of major countries in this biological war.

The corrective measures for combating the corona aren't a secret, but their implementation demands commitment and resilience. Remaining politically unchallenged by restraining the media, threatening the dissenters with punitive measures and discouraging open public discussions takes a country farther away from the greater goal of mass good. Listening to public discussions and proper consultations catalyze the process of effective and informed decisions. Well-informed and motivated citizens are the support system for a smooth running government. Small gestures and symbolic exercises encouraged by our honorable Prime Minister Narendra Modi were attempts at making the people believe that we all are together in this fight against the pandemic, following the Rig Vedic dictum, "Sangachadwam", which means 'May we walk together', "Vasudhaiva Kutumbkam" which means 'the world is our family' and "Sarva Loka Hitam" which means 'well-being of all stakeholders'. Every government has a journey filled with highways, potholes and rugged roads. However, the difference lies in the attitude of both- the leader and the public.

References

Association of World Election Bodies. (2020, September). News from Member Organiztions- contributed by EMBs. *A-WEB Newsletter.*

cdc.gov.

fema.gov.in. (2020).

http://www.aweb.org/eng/main.do.

https://www.brookings.edu/.

Johns Hopkins University & Medicine. (2020). *COVID-19 Dashboard by the Center for Systems Science and Engineering (CSSE) at Johns Hopkins University (JHU).* Coronavirus Resource Center.

Mohan, M. R., & Alex, J. P. (2020, April 26). COVID-19 and the ambit of the Disaster Management Act. *The Week .*

ncbi.nlm.nih.gov.

ndma.gov.in. (2008). *Management of Biological Disasters.* National Disiaster Management Guidelines.

ndmindia.nic.in. (2005). *Section 6, Disaster Management Act, 2005).*

Nguyen, T. (., & Malesky, E. (2020, May 20). Reopening Vietnam: How the country's improving governance helped it weather the COVID-19 pandemic. *Brookings .*

Research, T. N. (2020, June 11). The Political and Economic Impact of Covid-19 in Southeast Asia. *The National Bureau of Asian Research .*

Serrano, F. (2020, August 2020). In Algeria, Protests Pause for COVID-19 as the Regime Steps Up Repression. *World Politics Review .*

Sharma, S. N. (2020, March 22). How India is fighting Coronavirus with a colonial-era law on epidemics. *The Economic Times .*

Szekeres, E. (2020, March 31). Hungary 'No longer a democracy' after coronavirus law. *Reporting Democracy .*

Ward, A. (2020, Macrh 24). India's coronavirus lockdown and its looming crisis, explained. *Vox.*

Chapter - 14

Entrepreneurship and Vocational Skills

Sheetal V Barshi and Nandini N Doddamani

Abstract: The objective of Entrepreneurship is an important objective for education and lifelong learning policies. This article reports the results of a research project on entrepreneurship competencies in Higher and vocational education. Marketing, health and nutrition, tourism, fashion and fabric are the most crush Opportunities where one can get a good platform of entrepreneurship. Food and nutrition entrepreneurship addresses significant and ongoing changes in the food industry with sound nutrition principles and business acumen that will allow them to competitively participate in a growing field. Entrepreneurial skills are of paramount importance. The aim of this paper was to understand the perspective of tourism students on the relevance of entrepreneurship education within their courses. This study proposes a vision of entrepreneurship in fashion design. Fashion design courses have evolved and moved to a more entrepreneurial concept, as a generation of fashion designers has transformed past experiences and professional vision to become entrepreneurs. Authors and reports linked to entrepreneurship observe more than ever the importance and necessity to bring entrepreneurship very early to classrooms. This pathway provides early entrepreneurs the option to explore entrepreneurship, career opportunities and demonstrate advanced skills in apparel construction, textiles and technology. This pathway provides early entrepreneurs the option to explore entrepreneurship, career opportunities and demonstrate advanced skills in interiors fabrication, textiles and technology.

Key Words: Entrepreneurship, Vocational skills, Demonstrate.

Introduction

Supporting entrepreneurship in vocational education and training is increasingly important for governments as they seek to improve pathways to the labour market for youth. Given the youth unemployment challenge that is currently faced in Tunisia, entrepreneurship can offer opportunities for youth to create jobs for themselves and for others. The vocational education and training system has an important role to play in supporting this agenda by providing entrepreneurship training and business start-up support. The OECD is undertaking a series of reviews of entrepreneurship support in vocational training and higher training in selected regions and countries as part of its activity on skills and competencies for entrepreneurship. The reviews on entrepreneurship support in vocational education and training are based on a framework that was developed from international case study work and the ongoing academic debate on the role of training in generating entrepreneurial motivations, intentions and competences.

The Context of the Study

Entrepreneurship skills are increasingly important to help the labor force adjust to the changing needs of the economy and vocational education and training (VET) systems can play a significant role in helping many youth acquire these skills. These skills refer to both entrepreneurial mind-sets as well as the set of skills that are needed to start and successfully operate a business. Entrepreneurship skills will be beneficial for all, particularly students, regardless of whether they go on to start a business or not because entrepreneurial behavior can be an asset in any workplace. Supporting the development of entrepreneurship attitudes and skills is a timely issue, as many governments are looking for methods of achieving job creation and economic growth. Entrepreneurship can be part of the answer. It is particularly important in Tunisia where there are many challenges related to labor market outcomes for youth. This study aims to review practices in promoting and supporting entrepreneurship in vocational training centers. It is part of a series of reviews on Skills and Competences for Entrepreneurship carried out by the Local Economic and Employment Development (LEED) Programme of the Organization for Economic Co-operation and Development (OECD) that assess current practices in higher education institutions in entrepreneurship training and specialized business start-up support.

Atama Nirbhar Bharat

Prime Minister Narendra Modi has said "Atmanirbhar Bharat is not about being self-contained or being closed to the world, it is about being self-sustaining and self-generating. We will pursue policies that promote efficiency, equity and resilience. Its proponents have said that this self-reliant policy does not aim to be protectionist in nature; the Finance Minister said, "self-reliant India does not mean cutting off from rest of the world. The law and IT minister, Ravi Shankar Prasad, said that self-reliance does "not mean isolating away from the world. Foreign direct investment is welcome; technology is welcome self-reliant India translates to being a bigger and more important part of the global economy. Further, in May 2020, Prime Minister Modi laid down the five pillars of 'Atmanirbhar Bharat' are stated as economy, infrastructure, technology-driven systems, vibrant demography and demand.

Vocal for Local

Not only should products be 'made in India', but the promotion of those products should take place so as to make those products competitive. During the Independence Day speech in 2020, Prime Minister Modi said that "The mindset of free India should be 'vocal for local'. We should appreciate our local products, if we don't do this then our products will not get the opportunity to do better and will not get encouraged. Amul Managing Director RS Sodhi explained that the phrase vocal–for–local meant that products be made global brands" and that it didn't mean that one must only buy products that have a logo 'made in India' on it. An extension of this slogan is 'local for global', that local products in India should have global appeal and reach.

Importance of Vocational Skills in Marketing

Marketing Education is the instructional program designed to prepare individuals for the major occupational areas within marketing and management (Gordon, 2008). Marketing, simply defined, is the selling of ideas, products and services of all kinds to identified and qualified markets.

Since Business Administration is the number one declared major of college freshmen and it accounts for 39% of all US jobs, including the largest number of career positions annually, it is imperative that students in Wisconsin's high schools have access to Marketing Education programs. These programs must evolve and create new opportunities for the success of their students, schools and communities.

Marketing includes channel management, recruiting, image building, promoting, marketing information management, market planning, product service management, selling and training, financing, and communicating. Marketing is a process that can be adapted to virtually every economic, social, or public activity and is an essential ingredient in making our free enterprise system work.

Marketing includes channel management, recruiting, image building, promoting, marketing information management, market planning, product service management, selling and training, financing, and communicating. Marketing is a process that can be adapted to virtually every economic, social, or public activity and is an essential ingredient in making our free enterprise system work.

Vocational Skills in Health and Nutrition

Nutrition is a critical part of health and development. Better nutrition is related to improved infant, child and maternal health, stronger immune systems, safer pregnancy and childbirth, lower risk of non-communicable diseases (such as diabetes and cardiovascular disease), and longevity.

Healthy children learn better. People with adequate nutrition are more productive and can create opportunities to gradually break the cycles of poverty and hunger. Malnutrition, in every form, presents significant threats to human health. Today the world faces a double burden of malnutrition that includes both under nutrition and overweight, especially in low- and middle-income countries. WHO is providing scientific advice and decision-making tools that can help countries take action to address all forms of malnutrition to support health and wellbeing for all, at all ages. This fact file explores the risks posed by all forms of malnutrition, starting from the earliest stages of development, and the responses that the health system can give directly and through its influence on other sectors, particularly the food system.

So, where do nutritionists work? The possibilities are plentiful, depending on their specific qualifications. Jobs for nutritionists can be found in:

- Hospitals, clinics, and other health care facilities
- Training gyms and fitness centers
- Food manufacturing companies
- Academic institutions
- Public health organizations

- Government agencies
- Community centers
- Health food markets
- Wellness centers

Many nutritionists also go into private practice and offer their services as consultants.

Many people mistakenly use the terms "dietician" and "nutritionist" interchangeably. Although these two professions are undoubtedly related, they maintain distinctive qualities. **Dietetics** emphasizes on **food management**, whereas **nutrition** emphasizes on **the promotion of health by way of healthy food.**

The main difference between Nutritionists and Dietitians is that Nutritionists are not held accountable by a regulatory college so that anyone can use the Nutritionist title. However, if you're looking to make a career as a Nutritionist, it's best to gain as much educational and hands-on experience as possible.

A person can be an entrepreneur in the field of nutrition in the following field.

Nutriprineurship is the practice and process that results in innovation, development, and growth of nutrition business.

Vocational Skills in Tourism

Tourism industry is growing rapidly all around the world to be the number one service industry in terms of revenue generation in comparison to the investments. Again its going to be the number one industry in terms of number of employment generation from the point of invested money for the business. Tourism is the phenomenon of the 21st century globalization where the world behaves like one small village. In India the tourism business is still its initial phase of development where opportunities are immense for the people engaged in the business of tourism. Culturally India is so rich that it can be the top most destinations in the world for the foreign tourist travelling all around the world. Naturally India's beauty is unmatched to any other part of the world comprising all the different features of the world in a single nation. Potential of India as a destination for tourism business comes right from the history as well where people are still in the form of their pristine beauty, consisting the old traditions of their ancestors & embracing the modernity in the same time. India is more like an amalgamation of past & present that should be handed to the future generations to come. Presenting the options for the foreign tourism opportunities India has its Domestic tourism potential in great abundance. Comprising the forms of tourism like Religious Tourism is the most important form of tourism prevalent in India. People from all around the country visit places of religious importance in numbers. Current business developments in the country present ample opportunities for the MICE (Meeting, Incentive, Conferences & Exhibitions) for the tourism practitioners. Other important factor suiting the development of the tourism business in India from all around the world is its geographical situation consisting the sea all to the three sides & economic conditions. Tourists travelling around the world while crossing their native country tend to stopover to the places of important in between their actual destination for tourism. India in this category get numbers of tourists around the world tourists travelling from Europe & America to South-East countries like Singapore, Malaysia, Indonesia, Thailand etc visits India in numbers in between.

Essential Soft Skills for Careers in Hospitality and Tourism

Empathy and emotional intelligence

It goes without saying that digital transformation carries the future of the hospitality and tourism industry, but this does not mean the industry will become depersonalized. On the contrary, investing in human capital is key to finding innovative solutions in an ever-changing scenario. People determine the success of an organization and, if this holds true across all fields, it is even more important for service-based industries like hospitality and tourism.

Teamwork

Among specific qualifications demanded by a wide range of host companies and organizations, the ability to integrate into the existing team is often considered essential when choosing a candidate. In order to satisfy this need, IULM's internship and placement department offers a counseling service aimed at supporting and preparing students for the interview process, and to ensure appropriate mentoring during the internship. "We help students improve their personal skills," explains Cristina Sottotetti, IULM internship and placement director, "which are necessary to achieve professional success."

Stress and time management

Hospitality managers will often work on several things at once, managing a heavy work load at a fast pace. It's easy to let your emotions run wild when you are asked to do several things at once over a short time span and forced to deal with unexpected problems... For careers in hospitality and tourism, you need to be prepared to multi-task and remain cool and collected if you are to achieve greater efficiency and customer satisfaction!

Problem-solving

Whether you're dealing with a difficult client or faced with internal issues, the ability to think on your feet and suggest feasible solutions to problems is one of the most valued soft skills for careers in hospitality and tourism, and certainly a determining factor when it comes to professional success.

Whatever your specialty, you will need to learn how to manage a crisis, from identifying the problem to evaluating how well you did and what could be improved in future.

Strategy and innovation

Hospitality and tourism HR managers tend to favor candidates who are allergic to the "if it ain't broke don't fix it" mantra and will go the extra mile to innovate. "At Starwood [Hotel and Resorts]," explains Arianna Agresti, Starwood Milan Area HR Supervisor, "we look for talents with strong team-working skills and this is yearly measured through our apposite survey." She adds, "Among strategic and innovative skills we mention the 'going beyond borders' attitude: the ability to keep looking for new opportunities and solutions even if there are established procedures."

Education and Vocational Skills in Fashion and Fabric

Why is fabric important in fashion?

A good quality of the fabric is important because it makes wearing an outfit a pleasant experience. Using of good quality of fabric makes the cloth durable and well to do. Even after washing them the fabric remains up to date and the quality of clothes remain well.

Many fashion designers have a **bachelor's degree** in a related field, such as fashion design or fashion merchandising. Employers usually seek applicants who are creative and who have technical knowledge of the production processes for clothing, accessories, or footwear.How starting to leverage these technological advancements and merge them with fashion to create extraordinary work that speaks for itself.

Whether it is for a fashion line or ready-to-wear range, designers are creating ingenious designs that are pioneering as a new frontier in the world of fashion. If you dream of being the next Coco Chanel or Ralph Lauren, it's important to break the mould and work towards refining your art and skills.

Let's first review the main responsibilities of a fashion designer, then look at how you can improve your fashion designing skills, and finally examine the top 9 fashion designing skills you will need to be a successful designer in the future.

Career as a Fashion Designer

About Fashion Designer

Fashion designers are creative, innovative and determined individuals having knowledge and awareness of the fashion market requirements. Fashion designers have to be interested in learning new things and reading journals, magazines, and books on fashion design history and new trends. The profession of fashion designing involves a set of skills that range from market research and creativity to sketching and fabric selection. It is a profession that requires designers to constantly be in tune with the market trends. To be successful, fashion designers must have a good understanding of the audience's lifestyle, customer needs and requirements.

A career in fashion is referred as fashion designing which is an art of inventing/innovating or adding beauty to clothing by using certain accessories. The job of a fashion designer includes, sketching fashion ideas, cutting out and sewing the clothing item, attending fashion shows, using tailoring skills to perfect the fit, drawing patterns to create garments, selecting fabrics and any special additions for the outfit and reading magazines to keep up with the latest fashions. Hence, a strong business sense plays an important role in a successful career of a fashion designer.

Types of Job Roles Fashion Designer

The conceptualization and development of intricate design details of a fabric are the work areas of a fashion designer.

There are various job profiles for fashion designers after pursuing a fashion designing course, however, taking a job will depend on your interests and skills. Following are some of the job profiles for fashion designers that one can opt for:

Retail Manager

A retail manager is responsible for ensuring that promotions and marketing gimmicks work smoothly, sets daily targets for the staff, and ensures customer satisfaction etc. He/she also heads the human resources and finance department in smaller enterprises.

Fashion Coordinators

Fashion coordinators look after the advertising and promotions of the brand. They work closely with fabric dealers to bring out the best of products.

Fashion Stylist

A stylist is responsible for choosing the entire wardrobe of a fashion show. His/her job is to pick the right pieces from anyone's wardrobe or from a designer's collection, which would suit the client's character, body type, the kind of occasion the dress is getting selected for.

Fashion Consultant

As a fashion consultant, one has to keep a close eye on the latest trends of the market. The role of a fashion consultant also requires individuals to be keen observers of the changing fashion trends.

Textile Designer

Textile designers work both independently or as part of a design team in both indusrial and non industrial settings. They are responsible for designing 2D patterns, both repititive and unique for knit patterns, weave and printed fabrics etc.

Make Up Artist

Make up artists are hired for fashion events, weddings, pre-wedding photoshoots, bridal makeup, for models and celebrities. These artists are different than beauticians, as they do not take up normal beauty treatment jobs.

Sketching Assistant

He/she is responsible for making technical sketches of garments for various presentations. These sketches are used as specifications on the designing and fabrication of the garments.

Fashion Journalist

The fashion journalist has a job to write or report about latest fashion trends for a magazine. To be a fashion journalist one should to know the latest fashion trends and be in touch with the news of the fashion world.

Pros of becoming a Fashion Designer

The work of fashion designer is very creative and fun provided you have an eye for fashion. It all about coming up with new innovations which are trending or could trend in the future among people.

The profession of fashion designing involves self satisfaction. A fashion designer comes up with new and improved trends to influence people to start using that particular clothing or accessory. So, if the product is used by large number of people, then the fashion designer will have the utmost satisfaction knowing that people are using something that has been his/her innovation.

A career in fashion designing can prove very promising for those who love to travel. A career in fashion designing offers a lot of opportunities of traveling abroad if the clients are residing over there.

You're surrounded by creativity : Even if you're not interested in a creative role within the fashion industry, you'll still be around a lot of people who enjoy expressing themselves in artistic and creative ways. The fashion industry is colorful and full of flavor, as it is centered around clothing design and style.

Working in the fashion industry *can* be very glamorous. You never know when famous designers, celebrities, models and actors will make an appearance. However, meeting famous people and attending fashion shows and fancy industry events are a small part of a career in fashion. The career is so much more than the glossy photos that you see in magazines.

The fashion industry is moving away from rigid job roles and moving towards employing people with many different skills who can take on a variety of tasks. These jobs are far more dynamic and multifaceted than they used to be, making the positions more interesting than before.

The fashion industry moves fast and is always shifting and evolving – just like fashion trends. Every year thousands of designers are showing new collections and designs that then set the trends for the following year. Fashion industry professionals are constantly working on what's new

Conclusion

The developments in education over the last few decades have had strong links with the demands in the society, as society has changed so as the purpose of education and as a result a number of initiatives have been developed to address these needs. However there use a method of improving the qualifications of people that have traditionally left the educational system with limited qualifications have reduced the status of these qualifications when compared. Its an attempt to improve the status of vocational qualifications thus allowing to have a wider choice. Ultimately there is a need of education as well as vocational education to meet the needs of an ever changing society.

References

Vocational Education by Mark S Tucker

https://medium.com/@siddharthscholar/vocational-tourism-education-an-answer-to-contemporary-education-system-cfd752b5af34

https://www.google.com/search?q=educational+and+vocational+skills+in+fashion+an+fabric&source=lnms&tbm= isch&sa=X&ved=2ahUKEwikq8XsgP3uAhW9yjgGHUxZA8YQ_AUoAXoECBA QAw&biw=1600&bih=789#imgrc=SYCn3K9dca0xrM

Chapter - 15

The Contribution of Women Entrepreneurs in Creating an Atmanirbhar Bharat- A Step towards Women Self-reliance

SHEPHALI MATHUR AND PRASHANT KUMAR

Abstract: Entrepreneurship refers to the concept of developing and managing a business venture in order to gain profit by taking several risks in the corporate world and is considered as one of the most important factors contributing to the economic development of the society. In India, concept of women entrepreneurship is of recent origin. Women have become aware about their rights and situations and entered in different fields of business. They have established their own successful business empires and are contributing towards the growth of economy to build an Atmanirbhar Bharat.

Purpose of the Study: The primary objective of this study is to examine the different financial assistance provided by government for development of women entrepreneur and the contribution of women entrepreneurs in making an Atmanirbhar Bharat.

Methodology: The secondary data were taken for purpose of present study. The researchers reviewed different areas of women entrepreneurship and various financial assistance provided by government for development of women entrepreneur and making women self- reliance and based on the content available tried to give answer to the research questions taken in the present study.

Findings: The idea of business for the women was like a dream as they were busy doing the house work but now the time has changed, there is no shortage of women who have grown up beyond many such forms of domination. For example, Indira Nooyi, Chanda Kochhar, Ekta Kapoor and our current finance minister, Mrs. Nirmala Sitharaman, are also a witness to women empowerment. Various schemes were introduced by financial institutions in India including nationalised banks for the upliftment of Women entrepreneurship like Annapurna Scheme, Stree Shakti Package for Women Entrepreneurs, etc. and would be able to contribute towards Atmanirbhar Bharat and will become self-reliance.

Keywords: Entrepreneurship, system of patriarchy, Annapurna Scheme, Stree Shakti Package for Women Entrepreneurs, Cent Kalyani Scheme, Mudra Yojna Scheme, Bharatiya Mahila Bank (BMB) business loan, Udyogini Scheme, TREAD Scheme

Introduction

Atmanirbhar Bharat, which translates to 'self-reliant India' or 'self-sufficient India', is a term used by the Prime Minister of India Narendra Modi in relation to economic development in country. The term has been used in relation to making India "a bigger and more important part of the global economy", pursuing policies that are efficient, competitive and resilient, and being self-sustaining and self-generating. Atmanirbhar Bharat does not mean "self-containment", "isolating away from the world" or being "protectionist".

Women-led development will pave the way for self-reliant Bharat in a real sense. We should not forget that 50% population belongs to our women. The resilience, passion and commitment for family, society and country are shown at different periods of time for different sections, like to save the dignity of women, freedom struggle, uplifting education, economic empowerment, art, literature and culture, sports, medicine, science and technology, research and development, rural and urban area development, environment management, the spiritual progression of individual and society, administration and civil services, leadership, political movement, social media ad journalism and fighting against evils in society.

Women entrepreneurs may be defined as a woman or a group of women who initiate, organise and run a business concern. According to Schumpeter- "Women entrepreneurs are those women who innovate, initiate or adopt a business activity".

According to Government of India – "A woman entrepreneur is defined as an enterprise owned and controlled by a woman having a minimum financial interest of 51 percent of the capital and giving at least 51 percent of the employment generated in the enterprise to women."

Women entrepreneurs are those women who think of a business enterprise, initiate it, organise and combine factors of production, operate the enterprise and undertake risks and handle economic uncertainty involved in running it.

The features of women entrepreneurs found in India are

1. Most women with small income and small facilities are likely to become entrepreneurs.
2. A majority of women entrepreneurs are married. With the support of their husband, they accepted entrepreneurship.
3. Most spinsters face difficulties in obtaining financial support to start their enterprises.
4. A large number of women with little or no education and training enter into the business field.
5. Many women become entrepreneurs out of economic necessity and their sincerity and hard work is the cause for sustainability and growth.
6. Women entrepreneurs are security oriented rather than growth oriented.
7. Most women prefer stabilization of income and minimization of risk.

Business enterprises of women lack working capital; this causes low profit margin.

Why women become entrepreneurs?

Women become entrepreneurs basically to become economically independent and to establish their identity in the society and to build confidence in themselves, to develop risk assuming ability and to claim equal status in the society.

"When woman moves forward, the family moves, the village moves and the nation moves." is rightly said by Pandit Jawahar Lal Nehru. Employment gives status and economic independence to women leading to an empowered woman.

Women set up an enterprise due to economic and non-economic reasons as well.

Various reasons can be due to

1. Motivational factors, and
2. Facilitating factors.

1. Motivational Factors include Economic necessity, Independence, Self-actualisation, Government Policies and Programmes, Education and qualification, Self-Identity and social status, Employment generation.

2. Facilitating Factors include Adequate Financial Facilities, Self-satisfaction, Innovative thinking, Co-operation of family, Experienced and Skilled people at work.

Literature Review

Since independence India has adopted a planned approach to development. Five-year plans were the fundamental plans outlaying targets and mechanisms to achieve development and growth.

First Five-year plan (1951-56): Community based approach aiming for welfare of women. Establishment of Central Social Welfare Board.

Second Five-year plan (1956-61): Allocation for welfare extension projects was hiked.

Third Five-year plan (1961-66): Special aid to Mahila Mandals for welfare extension services. Providing financial support to voluntary organizations for implementing socio-economic programs for women beneficiaries. Provisions for vocational and skill development training to adult women.

Fourth Five-year plan (1969-74): Budgetary allocations hiked for family planning activities.

Fifth Five- year plan (1974-78): Focus shifted to functional literacy programs for women.

Sixth Five -year plan (1980-85): Focus shifted to addressing the issue of economic upliftment of women. Women's health, nutrition, education and employment were the prime target in this plan.

Seventh Five -year plan (1985-90): Policies and programs were focused on increasing gainful employment for women.

Eighth Five- year plan (1992-97): National commission for women was established in 1992. Rashtriya Mahila Kosh was established in 1993. Mahila Samriddhi Yojana was initiated in 1993. Indira Mahila Yojana was launched in 1995-96.

Ninth Five- year plan (1997-2002): National policy for empowerment of women was adopted. Integrated Rural Development Programme (IRDP), Training of Rural Youth for Self-Employment (TRYSEM), Nehru Rozgar Yojana (NRY), Jawahar Rozgar Yojana (JRY), Prime Minister's Rozgar Yojana (PMRY), Development of Women and Children in Rural Areas (DWCRA), Indira Mahila Yojana (IMY), Support for Training and Employment (STEP), NORAD-assisted Training-cum-Production Centres (popularly known as NORAD), Socio-Economic Programme (SEP) were implemented. Bill proposing reservation of seats in parliament and state assemblies was first proposed. Focus shifted to financial inclusion of women.

Tenth Five-year plan (2002-07): National policy for empowerment of women was further strengthened through concrete measures. Swayamsidha scheme was implemented in support to Training and Employment Program for Women (STEP), Swawlamban Scheme, Hostels for Working Women and Swadhar schemes aimed at providing shelter, food, clothing, and care to the women living in difficult circumstances were implemented.

Eleventh Five Year Plan (2007-12): Focus shifted to programs for vocational training and skill development of women. **Swayamsiddha** scheme for women empowerment was pursued. Self- help groups gained momentum. **Rashtriya Mahila Kosh** was integrated with STEP and Swayamsiddha.

Twelfth Five -year plan (2012-17): Rashtriya Mahila Kosh was allocated larger budget. Central Social Welfare Board was given target to provide vocational training and financial assistance to women. STEP, Priyadarshini and working women's hostel, *Ujjawala, Swadhar Greh Scheme* to provide institutional support for women. Gender Budgeting Cells were strengthened. All ministries and departments were directed to maintain gender disaggregated data.

Women entrepreneurship in India is still emerging. The representation of women as entrepreneurs is quite limited. In this section representation of women entrepreneurs in India is analyzed through data available in key government publications. The ranking of India on parameter of women entrepreneurship according to the Global reports is also very dismal. According to the "Female Entrepreneurship Index Report", 2015 compiled by Global Entrepreneurship Development Institute, India ranked 70 with a low score of 25.3 among 77 countries studied. India lags behind even African countries, **(Terjesen & Lloyd, 2015)**. According to the Global Entrepreneurship Monitor Report on Women's Entrepreneurship 2016-17, India needs a lot of improvement as far as women entrepreneurial activity is concerned.Total early stage entrepreneurial activity in Indian females is only 7.6 percent while percentage of women having established business activity is only 3.4 percent.

Awasthi (2011) argued that Entrepreneurship education in India is rather in a nascent stage. EntrepreneurshipDevelopment Institute (EDI) is the only Institute in the country that has a full 2-year PostGraduate Programme in Entrepreneurship which started in 1998. **Christopher and Meyer (2011)**, in their study examined that two entrepreneurship education variables, i.e. theuniversity's role to promote entrepreneurship and the entrepreneurial curriculum and content along withgender, working experience and mother's occupation are statistically significant. **Mohammad and Aparna (2011)** examined that self-efficacy play an important role inshaping (or limiting) perceived careeroptions as most of students are inclined towards corporate or government careers. **Santhi and Kumar (2011)** argued that most entrepreneurs simply got tired of working for others, had a great idea they wanted to commercialize, or woke up one day with an urgent desire to build wealth before they retired.

Digal and Bal (2010) in the study attempted to analysed the motivating factors, reasons for success for failure and the problems faced by the women entrepreneurs and found that the major problem faced by them was procuring finance and they depended mostly on the local markets to sale their products. EDP trainings programmes organized by the district authorities and Anganwadi Kendras were attended by most of the entrepreneurs. **Fitzsimmons and Douglas (2005)** explained that entrepreneurial attitudes to ownership, income, independence, risk and work effort are likely to be significant in explaining an individual's entrepreneurial intentions. **Lüthje and Franke; (2002)** stated that in recent years fostering entrepreneurship has become a topic of highest priority in public policy. This trend is due to the widespread recognition that business start-ups are a driving force of economic growth andsignificant job creation.

Reviewing the different researches in area of entrepreneurship it was found that there is good scope in entrepreneurial development and it is a commendable idea to analyze what are the financial assistance provided by government that motivate or discourage women in becoming successful entrepreneurs. It is further observed that the scores of Government schemes are not catering to the requirements of needy entrepreneurs. Hence, there is a need formulate area specific schemes and make finance available at their doorsteps.

Purpose of the Study

The primary objective of this study is to examine the different financial assistance provided by government for development of women entrepreneur and the contribution of women entrepreneurs in making an Atmanirbhar Bharat. In addition, the study attempts to answer the following research questions;

To what extent do financial assistance provide by government for development of women entrepreneur is successful.

How the government schemes are helpful in motivating women for entrepreneurial development and making women self- reliance.

Methodology

Present study is based on the different financial schemes available to women entrepreneur in India. For the purpose the secondary data were taken which comprises of the review of different schemes provided by government which are reviewed by researchers. The data were obtained from official website and those sources are mentioned in references.

The researchers reviewed different areas of women entrepreneurship and various financial assistance provided by government for development of women entrepreneur and making women self- reliance and based on the content available tried to give answer to the research questions taken in the present study.

Areas for Women Entrepreneurship

Women entrepreneur in earlier years after independence were confined to entrepreneurship in traditional areas like food, fruits, vegetables, pickles, papads, tailoring, hosiery etc. Women entrepreneurs have branched out to several new areas like engineering, beauty parlours, jewellery, handicraft, electrical, electronics, chemical and other manufacturing. This shows that entrepreneurial base of women expanded from traditional line of business to modern. Now today the women are making their career even in Direct Selling Industry.

There are vast numbers of industries under small business sector where women are playing a major role like:

1. Agriculture and Allied industries – such as sericulture, horticulture, dairying and animal husbandry etc.
2. Home based industries-such as handicrafts, Agarbati, Candle making, bidi industry, hosiery, and textile, doll making, jewellery pottery, designing etc.
3. Outside home industries – such as electrical and electronics, food processing etc.

Apart from the above, most Indian Women have performed well in both organized and unorganized sector. For example, **Kiran Mazumdar shaw, Shahnaz Hussain, Ekta Kapoor, Kathi Ben** who started their enterprises in small scale and achieved wonders and created history.

There are few women's which proves the mettle of a woman and their contribution in Aatmanirbhar Bharat like

Bachendri Pal (Sports): A hugely famous name when it comes to mountaineering. Bachendri Pal had become the first Indian woman to scale the Mt. Everest way back in 1984. She has been conferred with Padma Bhushan award. **Godavari Dutta (Art-Painting)**: This great mother is a national award winner is known for her contribution to the beautiful art of Madhubani painting not just in India but also across the globe.

Rohini Godbole (Science and Engineering -Nuclear): Indian Physicist, professor at the Centre for high energy Physics, Indian Institute of Science, Bangalore. She has authored over 150 research papers. She is known for her work in new particle production at current and future collides, physics at large Hadron collider and next linear collider, QCD Phenomenology, structure functions of the proton, photon and nucleus plus supersymmetry and electroweak physics. She is a Padma awardee in2019.

Rajkumari Devi (Agriculture): Fondly known as Kisan Chachi. She hails from Muzaffarpur has been doling out tips on farming that ensures successful harvests. She has mobilised over 300 women to form self-help groups. She is a Padma awardee in 2019.

Financial Assistance Provided by the Government for the Upliftment of Women Entrepreneurship

The various schemes introduced by financial institutions in India, including nationalised banks for the upliftment of Women entrepreneurship are:

1. Annapurna Scheme: Under this scheme, the Government of India offers women entrepreneurs in food catering business, loans upto Rs. 50,000. The loaned amount could be used for working capital requirements such as buying utensils, cutlery, gas connection, refrigerator, mixer cum grinder, hot case, utensil stand, tiffin boxes, working table, water filter etc.

A guarantor is required to avail the loan and the assets of the business have to be pledged as collateral. Once sanctioned, it has to be repaid in 36 monthly instalments (which equals to a period of three years). After the loan is sanctioned, the lender doesn't have to pay the EMI for the first month. The interest rate is determined depending upon the market rate and the bank concerned. The State Bank of Mysore and Bhartiya Mahila Bank currently offers this scheme.

2. Stree Shakti Package for Women Entrepreneurs: The Stree Shakti Package is a unique SBI-run scheme to support entrepreneurship among women by providing certain concessions. This scheme is eligible for women who have majority ownership (over 50 percent) in a small business. Another requirement is that these entrepreneurs have to be enrolled in the Entrepreneurship Development Programmes (EDP) organised by their respective state agency. This scheme allows women to avail an interest concession of 0.05 percent on loans exceeding Rs. 2 lakh. No security is required for loans up to Rs. 5 lakh in case of tiny sector units.

3. Cent Kalyani Scheme: This scheme under the Central Bank of India can be availed by both existing and new entrepreneurs and self-employed women for micro/small enterprises like farming, handicrafts, circulating libraries, day creches, STD/Xerox booths, tailoring etc. (in other words, agriculture, cottage industries, small and medium enterprises, government sponsored programs and retail trade.) Under this scheme, loans up to Rs. 1 crore are sanctioned with a margin rate of 20 per cent. You do not require any collateral security or guarantors for this loan. Interest on loans depends on market rates. The loan tenure will be a maximum of seven years including a moratorium period of 6 months to 1 year.

4. Mudra Yojana Scheme: This is a general scheme for small units that women entrepreneurs can avail of too. Offered by nationalised banks under the Pradhan Mantri Mudra Yojana, this can be used to set up beauty parlour, tuition center, tailoring unit, etc. Loans between Rs.50, 000 to Rs. 50 lakh are sanctioned under this scheme. No collateral and guarantors are required for loans below Rs. 10 lakh. The scheme has three plans:

Shishu– Grants you loans up to a maximum limit of Rs.50,000 for a new business with rate of interest being 1 per cent per month or 12 per annum. The repayment period up to 5 years.

Kishore – Grants loans from Rs 50,000 up to Rs 5 lakh for well-established businesses. The rate of interest varies with banks as it depends on the scheme guidelines and credit history of the applicant. Repayment period also depends on the discretion of the bank.

Tarun – Grants loans from Rs 5 lakh up to Rs 10 lakh for business expansion. The rate of interest is dependent on the bank as per the scheme guidelines and credit history of the applicant. Repayment period depends on the discretion of the bank.

5. Mahila Udyam Nidhi Scheme: Offered by Punjab National Bank and Small Industries Development Bank of India (SIDBI), this scheme supports women entrepreneurs to set up a new small-scale venture by extending loans uptoRs10 lakh to be repaid in 10 years. SIDBI also includes a five-year moratorium period. The interest depends upon the market rates.

Some of the other Government schemes for women entrepreneurs are:

1) Bhartiya Mahila Bank (BMB) business loan: BMB Inaugurated on 19th November 2019 and was merged with State Bank of India on 1st April 2017. This loan is for women who wanted to start their own business. It offered women entrepreneurs business loans up to 20 Crores for manufacturing enterprises with an interest of 10.15% and more. It also offers collateral-free loans up to 1 crore under Credit Guarantee Fund Trust for Micro and Small Enterprises (CGTMSE) cover. The loans under this bank loan scheme are to be repaid in seven years.

2) Orient Mahilavikas yojana scheme: This scheme is launched by Oriental Bank of Commerce. It provides capital for women for starting small businesses. Womenwith 51% share in the business are eligible for the loan. Collateral is not needed if loans are between Rs.10 lakhs to Rs.25 lakhs for small-scale industries.Repayment is for 7 years period. And it offers concession of 2% on the rate of interest.

3) Dena shakti scheme: This scheme is provided by Dena bank to those women entrepreneurs in the fields of Agriculture & allied activities, Retail Trade, Micro Credit, Education, Housing and retail & small business enterprises. There is a concession of 0.25 % on rate of interest. Scheme offers loans up to Rs 20.00 lakhs under retail trade, Rs 20 lakhs under education and housing and Rs 50,000/- under micro credit.

4) Udyogini scheme: Women entrepreneur aged 18 to 45, who are involved in agriculture, retail and similar small businesses are eligible for loans upto Rs. 1lac under this scheme. And her family annual income should be 45,000 or less to avail this loan. There is exception for widowed, destitute or disabled women. For widowed, destitute or disabled women from SC/ST categories, a subsidy of 30 percent of the loan, up to Rs 10,000, is provided and for women with general category a subsidy of 20% of the loan or Rs.7,500 whichever lower is provided. Panjab and Sind bank and KSWDC are offering this loan.

5) TREAD (Trade Related Entrepreneurship Assistance and Development) scheme: This scheme aims to economic empowerment of women by providing credit (through NGOs), training, development and counselling extension activities related to trades, products, services etc. Government grants up to 30% of the total project cost as appraised by lending institutions which would finance the remaining 70% as loan assistance to applicant women.

Impact of Study

Study focus on the various scheme and its success in development of women entrepreneurs and making the women atmnirbhar and making them more independent and help them in contributing in upliftment of Indian Economy. Entrepreneurial base of women expanded from traditional line of business like food, fruits, vegetables, pickles, papads, tailoring, hosiery etc. to modern line like engineering, beauty parlours, jewellery, handicraft, electrical, electronics, chemical and other manufacturing even in Direct Selling Industry. Today the womens are playing a major role in different industries like Agriculture, sericulture, horticulture, dairying and animal husbandry , handicrafts, , hosiery, and textile, doll making, jewellery pottery, designing, electrical and electronics, food processing etc.

The financial assistance provided by government paid a vital role in successful development of women entrepreneur in India. Annapurna Scheme India offers women entrepreneurs in food catering business, loans upto Rs. 50,000. Stree Shakti Package for Women Entrepreneurs allows women to avail an interest concession of 0.05 percent on loans exceeding Rs. 2 lakh. No security is required for loans up to Rs. 5 lakh in case of tiny sector units and it is helpful for women to start their own venture who don't have any security to keep against loan. Cent Kalyani Scheme can be availed by both existing and new entrepreneurs and self-employed women for micro/small enterprises like farming, handicrafts, etc. Under this scheme, loans up to Rs. 1 crore are sanctioned with a margin rate of 20 per cent. Mudra Yojana Scheme is a general scheme for small units that women entrepreneurs in which Loans between Rs.50, 000 to Rs. 50 lakh are sanctioned without any collateral and guarantors for loans below Rs. 10 lakh. Mahila Udyam Nidhi Scheme supports women entrepreneurs to set up a new small-scale venture by extending loans uptoRs10 lakh to be repaid in 10 years. Beside these the various Government schemes for women entrepreneurs boostup the motivation of womens to become atmnirbhar like Bhartiya Mahila Bank (BMB) business loan, Orient Mahilavikas yojana scheme, Dena shakti scheme, Udyogini scheme and TREAD (Trade Related Entrepreneurship Assistance and Development) scheme.

Conclusion

Women entrepreneurs play a significant part in making Atmanirbhar Bharat and the global expedition for sustained economic development and social progress. Due to the growing industrialization, urbanization, social legislation and along with the spread of higher education and awareness, the emergence of Women owned businesses are highly increasing in the economies of almost all countries.

Indian women had undergone a long way and are becoming increasingly visible and successful in all spheres and have shifted from kitchen to higher level of professional activities.

Women entrepreneurs are fast becoming a force to reckon with in the business world and are not only involved in business for survival but to satisfy their inner urge of creativity and to prove their capabilities. Educated Women is contributing to a great extent to the social transformation and in the future, will be seen that more women venturing into areas traditionally dominated by men.

Today's women are taking more and more professional and technical degrees to cope up with market need and are flourishing as de signers, interior decorators, exporters, publishers, garment manufacturers and still exploring new avenues of economic participation. It is perhaps for these reasons that Government Bodies, NGO's, Social Scientists, Researchers and International Agencies have started showing interest in the issues related to entrepreneurship among women in India and government is providing so many financial schemes for the upliftment of women and to make them self-reliance.India is one of the fastest emerging economies and the importance of women entrepreneurship is realized across the globe.

Contribution of women in the growth history is quite visible, however, as a society, we have failed to maintain the dignity of a woman. We need to change our mindset and vision not to see the woman as a mere housekeeper but to encourage them more for becoming self-reliance.

References

Awasthi, D. (2011); "Approaches to entrepreneurship development: The Indian Experience", *Journal of Global Entrepreneurship Research Winter & Spring*, vol 1, 107-124

Chowdhary, N., and Monika Prakash(2010); "Entrepreneurship Development: Program or Process", *IIMS Journal of Management Science,* Vol.1, No.1, Jan-June 2010, pp.46-59

Digal, S. K., & Bal, R. K. (2010). Motivating Women Entrepreneurs in Orissa: An Enquiry into its Dynamics in a Comparative Setting. *Vilakshan: The XIMB Journal of Management*, *7*(1). retrieved from *https://web.a.ebscohost.com/abstract?direct* on 16-01-2021

Dr. N. Santhi and Rajesh Kumar (2011); "Entrepreneurship Challenges and Opportunities in India", Bonfring International Journal of Industrial Engineering and Management Science, Vol.1, 14-16

Entrepreneurship in India; A Study by National Knowledge Commission government of India 2008

Fitzsimmons, J., and Evan J. Douglas "Entrepreneurial Attitudes and Entrepreneurial Intentions: A Cross-Cultural Study of Potential Entrepreneurs in India, China, Thailand and Australia", Babson-Kauffman Entrepreneurial Research Conference, Wellesley, MA. June 2005

https://amity.edu/UserFiles/admaa/db0c0Paper%204.pdf

https://en.wikipedia.org/wiki/Atmanirbhar_Bharat

https://journal-jger.springeropen.com/articles/10.1186/s40497-016-0055-x

https://savvywomen.tomorrowmakers.com/wise/government-schemes-can-help-women-entrepreneurs-india-grow-their-small-businesses-article

https://smefutures.com/atmanirbhar-bharat-chronicles-of-women-entrepreneurs-powering-self-reliant-india-through-innovation-and-entrepreneurship/

https://timesofindia.indiatimes.com/readersblog/youth2020/atmanirbhar-bharat-and-women-empowerment-26777/

https://www.mudrahome.com/blog/7-government-schemes-for-women-entrepreneurs/

https://www.yourarticlelibrary.com/women/women-entrepreneurship/women-entrepreneurship/99813

Keat, O.Y; Christopher Selvarajah and Denny Meyer (2011), "Inclination towards entrepreneurship among university students: An empirical study of Malaysian university students", International Journal of Business and Social Science, Vol 2, issue 4, 206-220.

Luthje, C. and Nicolaus Franke (2002); "Fostering entrepreneurship through university education and training: Lessons from Massachusetts institute of Technology", 2nd annual conference on Innovative Research in Management May 9-11, 2002, 1-13.

Luthje, C. and Nikolaus Franke; (2002)"Fostering entrepreneurship through university education and training: Lessons from Massachusetts Institute of Technology", European academy of management 2nd Annual Conference on: Innovative Research in Management May 9 – 11, 2002, Stockholm, Sweden. Session: Management Education in a Technology Driven Economy

Mohammad, M. and M.P. Aparna (2011); "Entrepreneurial Intentions of MBA Students – A study in Hyderabad", Entrepreneurial practice review, vol 1 issue 4, 20-37.

Chapter - 16

Atmanirbhar Bharat from the Perspective of Young Entrepreneurial Skills

Y. H. Bilagi

Abstract: Atmanirbhar Bharat Abhiyan, which translates to self – reliant India or self -sufficient India, is the vision of the prime minister of India Narendra Modi of Making India "a bigger & more important part of the global economy". Pursuing policies that are efficient, competitive and resilient and being self-sustaining and self generating. Aatmnirbhar Bharat does not mean "self- containment". Isolating away from the world or being "protectionist". the first mention of this came in the form of the 'Atmanirbhar Bharat abhiyan are or self-reliant India mission during the announcement Indians covid-19 pandemic related economic package on 12th may 2020. The five pillars of 'atmanirbhar Bharat'are started as economy, infrastructure, technology -driven systems,vibrant demography and demand.

On 15th August 2020 PM address the nation from the red fort on the occasion of 74th Independence Day of India. In a 90 minutes of speech. He forced on Atmanirbhar Bharat (self Reliant India), vocal local, make in India to make for world. However the term was already coined by the the PM of of India on 12th may 2020.there are two different opinions coming for the same, first is to stop importing goods from foreign Nations and boycotting all foreign products,the other is to promote and give reference to Indo genius products by ensuring good quality and competitive price with imported goods.

This paper aims to study the requirements to develop the creative and innovative society

Key words: self -reliant, boycotting, protection

Introduction

Atmanirbhar Bharat Abhiyan (Self-reliant India Mission) a Post pandemic financial package to Help Restore Economic Growth and Make India Self -Reliant. The vision of the prime Minister of India Nerendra Modi of making India a self – reliant nation. The first mention of this came in the form of the 'Atma Nirbhar Bharat Abhiyan' or self – Reliant India Mission during the announcement of the coronavirus pandemic related economic decisions have taken place such as changing the definition of MSMEs. Boosting scope are of private participation in numerous factors increasing FDI in the defence sector, and the vision has found support in many factors such as the solar manufacturers sector. The special economic package would be the main component of Atma-Nirbhar Bharat (Self – reliant) Modi side in his fifth address to the nation "Corona will be with us for a long time but our lives cannot revolve around Corona". the prime minister said emphasizing on migrant workers several of whom lost their lives while the trying to reach their native places during the lockdown some even staged protests demanding transport facility to their homes.

RBI announced an Rs.3.4 lakh core monetary stimulus. Modi's Rs 20 lakh a marathon six – hour meeting with chief ministers, with almost all of them asking for a large financial package. He said self – reliant India will stand on five pillars – Economy, infrastructure, tech – driven system vibrant demography and demand. Prime minister Modi, in his fifth address to the nation scenes the great lockdown announced Atma Nirbharta Bharat Abhiyan package of rupees 20 lakh crore to review the Indian economy, to help farmersMigrant workers,etc. And to review the industrial sector. This package is a 10% of Indians total GDP.the details about the package were announced by the finance minister Nirmala sitharaman in

5 tranches. These tranches announced by the finance minister via press conference from May 13,2020to May 17, 2020.. The package including rupees 8 lakh crore in liquid ATI measures announced by the RBI. the government will also provide a 100% guarantee to rupees 3 lakh crore in small business loans self reliance are self sufficiency. Has made tremendous progress in improving easy of doing business in India through various measures to simplify the company registration process. On the eve of 74 th India Independent, India's largest cloud – based business registration and compliance services platform India feelings.com has taken a pledge to help over 10000 startups registered their business under the Aatmnirbhar Bharat mission. From 142 to 77 th place on Ease of doing Business ranking in merely four years, India has made tremendous progress to make it simpler for Entrepreneurs to register a company. The government has streamlined various services and simplified the forms to make same day incorporation of the company possible in India.

Objectives of Atama Nirbhar Bharat

1. The aim is to make the country and its citizens independent and self-reliant in all senses. He further outlined five pillars of Aatma Nirbhar Bharat – Economy, Infrastructure, System, Vibrant Demography and Demand.
2. Finance Minister further announces Government Reforms and Enablers across Seven Sectors under Aatmanirbhar Bharat Abhiyaan.

Atmanirbhar Bharat various business start up services

Under the ' Atmanirbhar Bharat' mission, India feelings fillings offer various business startup services at a very nominal cost. Also, those signing up under this initiative will be provided access to other software for Accounting and HR at no additional cost for one year. Swadeshi does not necessarily mean boycotting every foreign products RSS chief Mohan bhagwat sale on and asserted that that only those technologies are materials may be important which the country lacks traditional or are not available locally. Talking about the relevance of being self reliant and Swadeshi in the wake of covid-19 he suggested that the gandamak has made it clear that globalisation did not yield desired results and one economic model cannot be applicable everywhere. Mutual cooperation among self reliant countries while countries while considering the world as one family and not one market, seems to be the economic model required for post – COVID world, Bhagwat said while speaking at a virtual book lunch event.

Backing the BJP - led NDA government's pitch for a self -reliant India, the RSS chief said Swadeshi means to promote and give preference to indigenous products or technologies and not necessarily boycott all foreign items. He made it clear that only those materials or technologies should be imported which are not available locally or India lacks traditionally and these should be modified in an India manner. Citing a few examples when traditionally available products and technologies were overlooked for imported ones, Bhagwat emphasized on the need for change in mind set and not considering domestic times as inferior. Nothing that even after independence policy making in India was lovely answer the bible rest and a therefore and countries Bhagwat said as a the many locally available products and technologies way overlooked in favour of foreign items. the concept of Swadeshi she which talk about promoting local products and restricting inflow foreign investment and items, features prominently in RSS ideology .it's affiliate Swadeshi jagran Manch has been at the forefront of a campaign to boycotting Chinese products.

In the recent items political conditions coupled with India's economic situation has given rise to widespread sentiments around boycotting Chinese products. read Indians Smartphone market being one of the most back to in the world manufacturers naturally heeded to Prime Minister Narendra Modi's. Make in India 'call in September 2014, to unveil local manufacturing plans. Howere, as India stands at our critical economic and political juncture, completely removing China's influence in the heavily valued segment still seems like a tall task, even through numerous brands have claimed otherwise. The critical roadblocks India has graduated from a SKD (semi Knocked – Down) – type manufacturing, to CKD (Completely Knocked – Down).However, all the major components (manufacturing a Smartphone) are sourced from chain, and are only assembly in India.

Atmanirbhar Bharat, which translates to' self-reliant India' or 'self-sufficient India' Indian,is a term used by the prime minister of India Narendra Modi in relation to economic development in country.the term has been used in relation to making India" a bigger and more important part of the global economy", pursuing policies that are efficient, competitive and resilient,and being self sustaining and self- generating . Atmanirbhar Bharat does not mean self – containment ,isolating always from the world or being protectionist. the first mention of this came in the form of the Atmanirbhar Bharat packing or self Reliant India Mission during the announcement of India's COVID -19 pandemic related economic package on 22 May 2020. Subsequently, two more Atmanirbhar Bharat package where announced on 12 October 12 November 2020, bringing the total economic stimulus to 39.87 lakh crore.

Vocal for Local

The Indian Prime Minister's televised address to the nation on 12 May 2020 included a financial package of Rs 20 lakh crore to revive India's stalled economy on account of COVID-19. Simultaneously, the package intended to kick start a process towards making India self-reliant. Besides the financial stimulus, the PM spoke about the importance of India as a huge local market and how India has the potential to take its local products global.

As a part of the speech the PM emphasized the need for India to recognize the importance of local manufacturing, local markets and local supply chains. He said that COVID-19 taught India the importance of being local. He said, "All our demands during the crisis were met locally. Now, it is time to be 'vocal about local' products and help them become global."

The PM felt that leading brands of the world were once local brands and they became global brands when local people started buying and using them. They branded them and then felt proud of them and started promoting them. They were the catalysts to make them global brands from local brands.

The call for "vocal for local", made by our Prime Minister Shri. Narendra Modi has come as a strong support for many industries in India as this allows the Indian industries to emerge and expand after the havoc caused by the Coronavirus pandemic. Though being vocal for local is indeed a positive step for India but to understand how beneficial it will be for India, we need to first understand what actually "vocal for local" means.

The narrative of "vocal for local" has emerged with many interpretations, as some have given it the colours of "Swadeshi movement" led by Mahatma Gandhi in 1905, which means to completely disassociate from the foreign brands and the global market but here the question arises how feasible would it be for India to completely close its door to the foreign market especially in this global and technologically connected world?

Vocal for Local = Swadeshi Movement 2.0?

Rationally speaking India cannot close its doors to the foreign market because today Indian has made a prominent presence in the global market where it is not only a consumer but also a seller of its products such as dry-fruits, cooking oil, spices etc therefore, closing doors to the foreign market would also mean closing its selling business with its foreign clients which in every aspect would be a bad deal.

Therefore, one has to understand that being vocal for local doesn't mean completely closing down or stepping out of the foreign market but it means to believe, promote, consume and grow the Indian brands within the homeland to such an extent that they can easily be a strong competition to the foreign brands in the global market revamping the "Swadeshi movement" and making it "Swadeshi movement 2.0".

In this light, we need to understand that India has to buckle up and embrace the call for vocal for local in high spirits especially in the field of FMCG industry as post coronavirus a lot of changes are under way and to reap the benefits of these changes one must understand these following 7 reasons that prove how vocal for local for Indian FMCG products is going to be beneficial for everyone-

Indian Infrastructure

The most important reason for being part of this "vocal for local" wagon is that this is purely for Indians and by the Indians. The Indian Government is encouraging the nation to start using products that are made by Indian raw materials, in Indian certified facilities and by Indian skilled labour. The ideology behind this is simple- the quality of Indian raw materials is going to be fresher and rich in quality as compared to the stale and cheap quality imports.

The seriousness for consuming only Indian FMCG products can be seen by the steps taken by the Indian Government who has asked companies like Nestle India, a subsidiary of a Swiss company Nestle, whether the products are being manufactured in India? Whether the raw materials are being taken from India or not?

The main objective behind the government to take strict initiatives for "vocal for local" is that it wants all FMCG companies whether domestic or International to work according to the Indian frame structure which shall involve workforce of lakhs of Indian labourers and farmers who will only use Indian raw materials like milk, wheat, spices and coffee that shall intrinsically enhance the Indian FMCG industry, employment and economy.

Healthy Indian Grocery

Since the advent of coronavirus, the attitude towards hygiene lifestyle has heightened as now people have understood that even the slightest compromise on their hygiene routine can bring grave consequences because of which FMCG industry is seeing a drastic change in the behaviour of consumers, as now there is an increase in demand for only healthy products, whether it is for food consumption, house cleaning, personal hygiene etc, consumers now only want healthy products around them.

Market experts believe that consumers shall no more compromise when it comes to hygienic products as a visible rise of 37.9% of Indian FMCG products have already been witnessed during the coronavirus because even the consumers have understood that the products made in the homeland would naturally be purer and fresher than those which are imported from other countries.

To cater to the changed behaviour during the pandemic, Pansari Group made it a point that the public is able to consume products such as cooking oil, rice, flour that are of the highest quality and made by the safest techniques; it has seen a massive hike of 35% as consumers have chosen their products for its nutritional value, hygienic and safe production, efficient supply chain and most importantly because of being a premium quality Indian FMCG product.

Furthermore, it was also observed that the sales of Indian FMCG products was not only limited to the domestic boundaries but also in the international market. For example, there was a massive increase in the export of Pansari products to South America, Canada, Australia, New Zealand, HongKong, Singapore, Malaysia, Middle East, Gulf Countries & West Africa, and to meet this high demand Pansari group efficiently increased its production from 700 metric tons per day to 1300 metric tons per day with an expanded supplying chain mechanisms.

As a believer of "customer being the boss" Pansari Group has geared up to pull up India as a whole by boosting the health with local but finest quality products along with being a unified society and a strong economy on the lines of the "vocal for local".

Kiranas Durability

Kirana's are traditional businesses of essential goods which have been persisting in India for centuries but since the advent of Modern Trade Landscape in both rural and urban India, a noticeable decline of kiranas was witnessed. But, the pandemic has also brought back these traditional Kirana businesses, as they have proved it again that they truly know the pulse and pain of the customers. This was realised when the e-commerce deliveries were delayed during the pandemic or barred in many containment zones and it was only because of the kiranas that people could get their essential products.

Though it is undeniable that e-commerce platforms for the supply of FMCG products cannot be disregarded as 79.7%

of the households now depend on it but at the same time, it has to be considered that Kiranas too have digitised themselves and because as they have easier accessibility in the vicinity, they shall always be a crucial part of the Indian FMCG Industry.

Revamp of Traditional Products

There is no doubt that India has ocean of natural resources especially when it comes to fruits and dry fruits but in the past, it has been observed that fruits being exported from foreign countries like kiwi, strawberries and plums have overshadowed homegrown traditional items such as apples, pears, walnuts, almonds and other dry fruits. Therefore, experts believe that the call for vocal for local will allow these traditional products to make a comeback into the market, if the Indian FMCG companies can develop organic and healthy products from these products along with business models that are self-reliant through a strong value chain via brand, package, price and channels.

SKD (Semi Knock Down)

This service consists of dismantling and packaging up certain parts of a vehicle for shipment to other assembly plants where the parts will then be re-assembled. We design custom packaging and selecting the right material for the needs of your product, also can put them inside for optimal fastening and protection of parts, cardboard, foam, plastic... Whatever part of the car to be packaged, we know the package that suits you best.

CKD (Complete Knock Down)

Shipment of automobile parts for certain vehicles from the manufacturing plant for these vehicles to plants in different countries where they are assembled. We design custom packaging and selecting the right material for the needs of your product, also can put them inside for optimal fastening and protection of parts, cardboard, foam, plastic... Whatever part of the car to be packaged, we know the package that suits you best.

Atmanirbhar Bharat Abhiyaan: A Campaign for Self-Reliant India

Amid coronavirus outbreak, the Prime Minister, Mr. Narendra Modi, announced a special economic package of Rs 20 lakh crore under Atmanirbhar Bharat Abhiyaan. The primary aim of this package is to make the country independent and combating the competition in the global market. It is also helpful in filling the gap between demand and supply of essential goods and services in the present debilitating situation. It gives the upliftment to weaker sections and empowering migrated laborers, who are drastically affected by COVID-19. Below is the note summarises the important measures proposed under the Abhiyaan.

It has divided into below mentioned tranches that have their separate focus areas. Take a look at its break-up:

- Relief measures for MSMEs, NBFCs, HFCs, contractors, real estate, and salaried workers.
- Fund for migrant workers, small farmers, street vendors, and poor people.
- Relief fund for agriculture and allied sectors such as dairy, animal husbandry, and fisheries.
- Package for eight critical industries includes coal, minerals, defense production, airspace management, social infrastructure projects, power distribution companies, atomic energy, and space sector.

Atmanirbhar Bharat Abhiyaan Highlights

India has demonstrated that it can cope up with any problematic situation and uncovers opportunities. The focal point of the

Abhiyan is to make the country self-reliant. Let's understand its highlights:

- Rise in borrowing limits: With the relief package, state governments now have a rise in their borrowing limits. The increase is from 3% to 5% of the gross state domestic product for the annual year 2020-21. In this way, states have extra resources to spend on health care, employment, and infrastructure.
- One Nation One Ration card: This universalization of ration card will enable migrant workers and their families to access public distribution benefits from any Fair Price Shop in the country. They can get the food grains at subsidized rates.
- Privatization of Public Sector Enterprise (PSEs): Under this new PSE policy, the government may likely privatize its public sector enterprises. The purpose of such an initiative is to improve the efficiency and profitability of PSEs.
- Collateral Free Business loan: All businesses such as MSMEs, agriculture, and allied sectors can get collateral-free automatic loans. It gives a financial cushion to several businesses and encourages entrepreneurs to produce maximum goods and services within the country.

Benefits of Atmanirbhar Bharat Abhiyaan

In order to regain the strength of the economy in the global market with self-reliance, the Indian government launched the Atmanirbhar Bharat Abhiyaan. Below are its benefits:

- Liquidity infusion and direct cash transfers into the accounts of laborers and daily-wage earners are helpful for their survival during the lockdown

- Long-term modifications in critical sectors keep them globally competitive and attractive
- Substantial growth in the e-Commerce industry
- Boost in the supply chain logistics industry
- Lots of employment opportunities soon in the country
- Reduction in scarcity for medical supplies and food grains

Conclusion

Atmanirbhar Bharat Abhiyaan or **Self-reliant India** campaign is the vision of new India envisaged by the Hon'ble Prime Minister Shri Narendra Modi. On 12 May 2020, our PM raised a clarion call to the nation giving a kick start to the Atmanirbhar Bharat Abhiyaan (Self-reliant India campaign) and announced the Special economic and comprehensive package of INR 20 lakh crores - equivalent to 10% of India's GDP – to fight COVID-19 pandemic in India. The aim is to make the country and its citizens independent and self-reliant in all senses. He further outlined five pillars of Aatma Nirbhar Bharat – Economy, Infrastructure, System, Vibrant Demography and Demand. Finance Minister further announces Government Reforms and Enablers across Seven Sectors under Aatmanirbhar Bharat Abhiyaan.The government took several bold reforms such as Supply Chain Reforms for Agriculture, Rational Tax Systems, Simple & Clear Laws, Capable Human Resource and Strong Financial System.

References

https://www.tatacapital.com/blog/government-updates/pm-modi-urges-you-to-be-vocal-for-local-products/

https://pansari.co.in/why-india-should-be-vocal-for-local-in-its-fmcg-industry/

https://www.nationalskillsnetwork.in/vocal-for-local-an-opportunity-to-boost-local-skills-and-products-in-india/

Chapter – 17

पंडित दीनदयाल उपाध्याय और राष्ट्र दर्शन

ऋतु राज सिन्हा

आलेख का प्रारंभ इस कविता से किया जा सकता है।

राष्ट्रगाण बन गुंजित धरा–गगन,
देश प्रेम की मधुर भावना व अमन।
बनु जागरण–गीत, हे राष्ट्र ऐसा वर देना
शत–शत दीप जले–आर्यावर्त के चरणों पर
मै बिरल दीप बन जलुं, बस इतना वर देना।।

राष्ट्रवाद तत्वतः एक मानसिक और आध्यात्मिक प्रत्यय है। यह उस पुरानी गणभक्ति (कबिला परस्ती) की गंभीर भावनाओं का आधुनिक संस्करण है जो हम प्रागैतिहासिक और प्राचीन युगों से देखते आये हैं। लोगों में प्रेम और अनुराग की जो भावना अपने कबीले अर्थात् गण, पोलित, सिविटास और देश के प्रति थी, उसी ने वर्तमान युग में विकसित होकर राश्ट्रभक्ति का रूप ले लिया है। यह सत्य है कि राश्ट्रवाद तभी पनपता है जब एकता की भावना को उत्पन्न करने वाले वस्तुगत तत्व विद्यमान होते है। सर्वमान्य द्वारा बोली जाने वाली एक भाषा, किसी एक ही वास्तविक अथवा काल्पनिक जाति से सब की उत्पत्ति का विश्वास, एक ही भूमि पर निवास और एक सामान्य धर्म – ये कुछ बहुत ही महत्त्वपूर्ण वस्तुगत तत्व हैं जिनसे राष्ट्रवाद की भावना उत्पन्न होती है। किन्तु मनोगत मनोवैज्ञानिक तत्व प्रधान हुआ करता है। भारत में जातिगत और भाशागत विभिन्नताओं की विरासत पर आधारित मानसिक एकता

की भावना विद्यमान हो। भारत में जातिगत और भाषागत विभिन्नताओं के बावजूद राष्ट्रवाद का यह मानसिक आधार महत्त्वपूर्ण रहा है। भारतीय संस्कृति की सरिता के सतत् और अविच्छित प्रवाह ने देश में इस आधारभूत मानसिक एकता को उत्पन्न करने में महान योग दिया है। औसवाल्ड स्पेंगलर ने राश्ट्रवाद को आध्यात्मिक तत्व माना है। राष्ट्रवाद विदेशी साम्राज्यवाद के विरूद्ध आर्थिक संघर्श और स्वायत्त आत्मनिर्धारित जीवन की राजनीतिक आकांक्षा का ही द्योतक नहीं है, बल्कि उससे संस्कृति की आत्मा के विकास का भी विषेश रूप से परिचय मिलता है। भारत में बंकिमचन्द्र, विवेकानन्द, तिलक, अरविन्द, विपिनचन्द्र पाल और गांधी ने राश्ट्रवाद के इस आध्यात्मिक तत्व को महत्त्व दिया है। इसके विपरीत दादाभाई नौरोजी, फिरोजशाह मेहता और गोखले ने राष्ट्रवाद की धर्मनिरपेक्ष धारणा का पोषण किया है। यद्यपि राश्ट्रवाद तत्वतः एकता के मानसिक और आध्यात्मिक बंधनों की मनोगत अनुभूति पर आधारित होता है, किन्तु उसके लिए वस्तुगत तत्वों की भी आव यकता होती है। उत्सव और समारोह राष्ट्रवाद के प्रतीकात्मक तत्व हैं। एक ओर वे उनमें सम्मिलित होने वालों में व्याप्त एकता के बंधनों को व्यक्त करते हैं, और दूसरी ओर उनसे उन एकता की भावनाओं को बल और उत्तेजना मिलती है। बुद्धिमान नेता इन भावनाओं को सृजनात्मक भात्तियों के रूप में वांछित कार्यों में नियोजित कर सकते हैं। ध्वज, राष्ट्रचिह्न, स्वतंत्रता दिवस समारोह, तथा उत्सव गंभीर भावनाओं को प्रतीकात्मक रूप देते हैं। इस प्रकार का प्रतीक प्रयोग पाशविक जीवन की मांगों और आव यकताओं की पूर्ति में डूबे रहने से कहीं अधिक प्रगतिशील है। प्रतीक प्रयोग सांस्कृतिक विकास का द्योतक है, क्योंकि उससे प्रकट होता है कि मनुष्य कोरे भौतिक जीवन से ऊपर उठ रहा है और राष्ट्र जैसी किसी अति–वैयक्तिक सत्ता के आनन्द और आह्लाद का अनुभव कर सकता है। प्रतीक की प्रकृति और उसकी भौतिक आकृति का महत्त्व नहीं है। कुछ प्रतीक सुसंस्कृत और सौन्दर्यप्रिय लोगों को भद्दे–भौंड़े लग सकते है, किन्तु सर्वाधिक महत्व इस बात का है कि सर्वमान्य को प्रभावित करने की कितनी शक्ति है।

जिन विचाराधाराओं ने यूरोपीय राजनीति एवं जीवन को विशेषतः प्रभावित किया है उनमें राष्ट्रवाद, प्रजातंत्र तथा समाजवाद की प्रमुख रूप

से गणना की जा सकती है। इनके साथ ही विश्व–एकता तथा भ्रांति का स्वप्न देखने वाले भी वहाँ हुए हैं और उस दिशा में कुछ प्रयत्न किये जा रहे हैं।

इनके विचारों में राष्ट्रवाद सबसे पुराना तथा बलशाली है। रोम के साम्राज्य के पतन के बाद तथा रोमन कैथोलिक चर्च के प्रति विद्रोह अथवा उनके प्रभाव में कमी के कारण यूरोप में राश्ट्रों का उदय हुआ। यूरोप का पिछले एक हजार वर्श का इतिहास इन राश्ट्रों के आविर्भाव तथा पारस्परिक संघर्ष का ही इतिहास है। इन राश्ट्रों ने यूरोप महाद्वीप से बाहर जाकर अपने उपनिवेश बनाये तथा दूसरे स्वतंत्र देशों को गुलाम बनाया। राष्ट्रवाद के उदय के कारण राष्ट्र और राज्य की एकता की प्रवृत्ति भी बढ़ी तथा राश्ट्रीय राज्य का यूरोप में उदय हुआ। साथ ही रोमन कैथोलिक चर्च के केन्द्रीय प्रभाव में कमी होकर या तो राश्ट्रीय चर्च का निर्माण हुआ या मजहब का। मजहबी गुरूओं की राजनीति में कोई विशेष स्थान नहीं रहा। सेक्यूलर स्टेट की कल्पना का इस प्रकार जन्म हुआ।

अपने राष्ट्र का विचार करते समय आधुनिक मानी जाने वाली विदेशी विचारधाराओं का बोध रखना पड़ता है, उनके गुणदोषों को समझ लेना पड़ता है। राष्ट्रीय स्थिति के परिप्रेक्ष्य मे उनका विचार करना होता है। कारण, राष्ट्र की सीमाओं को मिटाकर श्रमिकों का अधिराज्य निर्मित करने की बात कहने वाले मार्क्सवद के लिए मनुष्य के स्वाभाविक राष्ट्रप्रेम को मिटा देना संभव नहीं हो पाया है। ससाम्यवादी जगत् में भी रूस, चीन, यूगोस्लाविया, पोलैण्ड, हंगरी, वियतनाम आदि देशों ने अपनी पृथक राष्ट्रीय पहचान, अपनी परंपरा ऐतिहासिक राष्ट्रपुरूषों, अपनी जय–पराजय की स्मृतियों आदि को तिलांजलि नहीं दी है। कोई भी राष्ट्र अपने इतिहास को भुला नहीं सकता, क्योंकि इतिहास और उससे बनने वाली अस्मिता पर पर्दा डाल दिया तो संकटों से जूझने की प्रेरणा देने वाली शक्ति ही लुप्त हो जाती है। हिटलर के आक्रमण का सामना करने तथा जीवन–मरण का संघर्ष करने की नौबत आते ही स्टालिन ने अंततः राष्ट्रवाद और परंपरा का ही सहारा लिया । कम्युनिज्म को बचाने के लिए शत्रु का डटकर सामना करो, ऐसे आह्वान का रूस की प्रतिकार–शक्ति, समर्पण की भावना और विजय की आकाँक्षा को उदीप्त करने के लिए

स्टालिन ने 'फादरलैण्ड के नाम पर ही अंतिम आह्वान किया और राष्ट्र को उसके पूर्व–पराक्रमों का स्मरण दिलाया। यह आह्वान रूसी जनता के मन–मस्तिष्क को छू गया।

पंडित दिनदयाल उपाध्याय जी ने जिस चिंतन एवं विशुद्ध प्रेरणाओ की आवश्यकता को अनुभव किया, उन्हें बिलकुल स्पष्ट शब्दों में देश के सम्मुख रख। उनकी मृतयु के बाद इन 18 वर्षो में विश्व तथा हमारे देश में चले घटनाचक्र को देखते हुए उन तत्वों को महत्व देने की आवश्यकता आज और भी अधिक तीव्रता से प्रतीत होती है। आज राष्ट्रजीवन के प्रत्येक क्षेत्र में विचारकों को स्वदेशी विचारों एवं नीतियों की आवश्यकता प्रतीत होने लगी है। हम कहाँ पर भूल कर गये हैं, देश मे आज ऐसी भयावह स्थिति क्यों दिखाई देती है, समस्याएँ सुलझने के स्थान पर नयी जटिल समस्याएँ क्यों खड़ी हो रही हैं और जीवन इस प्रकार अधोमुखी क्यों बनता जा रहा है, इसका पुनर्विचार होने लगा है। यह पुनर्विचार केवल राजनीति तक ही सीमित नहीं रहा है, न ही वह केवल भारत में ही सिमट गया है। एक प्रकार से समूचना मानव जीवन, उसके लक्ष्य, विज्ञान तथा यंत्र–युग के भले बुरे परिणाम, आधुनिक समय का सामाजिक चिंतन, हिंदुस्तान के राष्ट्रजीवन में पाया जाने वाला विस्मयकारी सातत्य और उतरोतर विनाश की खाई की ओर फिसलते जा रहे मानव–समूल को उन्नति की दिशा दे सकने वाला जीवन–दर्शन आदि सभी जीवन–स्पर्शी प्रश्नों का आज चिंतन हो रहा है। समाजवाद,साम्यवाद, पूँजीवाद, व्यक्ति–स्वतंत्ररूवाद आदि विचारधाराओ की एकांगिता एवं मर्यादाओं का प्रत्यक्ष अनुभव करने के कारण यह चिंतन अधिक मूलगामी होता जा रहा है। इन प्रश्नों पर प्रचीन भारत में जो विचार किया जा चुका है और भारत ने उनके जो उतर खोज लिये हैं, अध्यनकर्ताओं के आकर्षण का केन्द्र बनते जा रहे हैं । इस संदर्भ में भी पं. दीनदयाल उपाध्याय जी द्वारा किये गये विचारमंथन का महत्व विशेष रूप में अनुभव किया जा रहा हे। उनके चिंतन की उड़ान समूची मानवता को अपने पंखों में समेटने वाली थी। उनका राष्ट्रविषयक विचार मानवकल्याणकारी चितन का ही क चरण था। इसीलिए आज की स्थिति मे उसे ठीक से समझ लेना चाहिए। इस विचार की विशेषता यह है कि वह किसी संप्रदायवादी संकीर्ण भूमिका या विरोधात्मक भावना

के साथ सम्मिलिति नहीं है। अपितु पूर्णतः भवात्मक एवं रचनात्मक है। किसी भी समस्या की उसमें टालमटोल नहीं हैं प्रत्येक प्रश्न का समाधान कैसे किया जाय, इसका दिशाबोध उसमें है। मुख्य बात यह है कि अपने प्राचीन राष्ट्र के जीवन लक्ष्य का सूत्र उसमें अक्षुझण भविष्य के निर्माण की आकॉक्षा को जगाकर पंडित जी ने अपने विचारों की रचना की है।

इन तथ्यों के उपस्थित रहते हुए भी पंडित दिनदयाल उपाध्याय के दर्शन में राज्य और राष्ट्र विशद व विस्तृत वर्णन है जो काफी प्रगतिशील व समकालीक है। आज राष्ट्र और राज्य दोनों शब्दों को लगभग सामानार्थी के भॉति प्रयुक्त किया जाता है तो क्या वास्तव में ये दोनों संज्ञाएँ एक ही वस्तु की परिचाक है। पंडित दिनदयाल जी ने असंदिग्ध शब्दों में कहा है कि राष्ट्र और राज्य दो भिन्न तत्व है। उन्होनें राष्ट्र और राज्य के आपसी संबंधों पर भी प्रकाश डाला है और बताया है कि वे कैसे होने चाहिए। वैसे राष्ट्र और राजय की परिकल्पनाओं के अन्तर को समझना कोई कठिन बात नहीं है। हमारे देश के इतिहास से पता चलता है कि विभिनन कालों में यहाँ न्यूनाधिक संख्या में अनेक राज्य थे, किन्तु विभिन्न राज्यों के अस्तित्व के कारण भारत के राष्ट्रस्वरूप को कोई बाधा नहीं पहुँची।

यह राष्ट्रकल्पना स्पष्ट थी। मातृभूमि और उस भूमि पर रहने वाला राज्य का तात्पर्य राष्ट्र नहीं।

एक संस्कृतिधारा मे पला पुत्ररूप समाज। यह है हमारा राष्ट्र। रामायण, महाभारत आदि महान् राष्ट्रीय ग्रंथ, सबकी श्रद्धा के केंद्र बने। तीर्थक्षेत्र, नदी, पर्वत, देवी देवता, ऋषि–मुनि, संत सत्यपुरूष आदि के साथ हमारा राष्ट्र एकात्मकता की भावना से अनेक राज्यों के समवाय में खड़ा था। आगे चलकर विदेशियों की सत्ता यहाँ आयी अर्थात राज्य विदेशियों का हो गया, किन्तु राष्ट्र जीवमान था। जीवन की रचना ही कुछ ऐसी बनायी गयी थी कि सदैव संपूर्ण भारतवर्ष का स्मरण हो। स्नान करते समय–'गंगे च यमूने चैव, गोदावरी, सरस्वती। नर्मर्दे, सिंधु कावेरी जलेस्मिन् सन्निधिंकुरु।' यह श्लोक सहज ही में कहा जाता था। राज्यभिन्नता के कारण इसमें कोई अंतर कभी नहीं आता। यह बात इतनी सुस्पष्ट होने के उपरांत राष्ट्र और राज्य की परिकल्पनाओं के बारे में संभ्रम क्यों होना चाहिए? इसका एक कारण शायद यह है कि अन्तराष्ट्रीय

संस्थाओं, सम्मेलनों, विवादों वर्तालापों आदि में प्रतिनिधित्व राज्य (स्टेट) का होता है। संयुक्त राष्ट्र संघ नामक संस्था से सभी परिचित है। दूसरे विश्वयुद्ध के बाद निर्मित इस संस्था में प्रतिनिधित्व किसे दिया जाता है, राष्ट्र को या राज्य को? उतर है, राज्य को किन्तु उसका नाम है राष्ट्रसंघ। किसी प्रदेश को राजनीतिक स्वतंत्रता मिलते ही उसे इस संयुक्त राष्ट्रसंघ की सदस्यता मिलने का मार्ग खुल जाता है। किन्तु प्रतिनिधित्व मिलता है उस देश के शासन को। राष्ट्रीयता के आधार पर प्रतिनिधित्व का चयन नहीं होता, न ही वह राष्ट्रीयता पर निर्भर होता है। राष्ट्रकुल को देखें अथवा निर्गुट राष्ट्र सम्मेलन को लें, एक–एक सरकार को ही वहॉ इकाई माना जाता है। यही कारण है कि 'नेशन' तथा 'स्टेट' की परिकल्पनाएँ समव्याप्त होने का आभास निर्मित हुआ है। राष्ट्रकुल सम्मेलन में भारत, पाकिस्तान, बर्मा और श्रीलका आदि सबको अलग–अलग राष्ट्र माना जाता है। अर्थात् राज्यों और राष्ट्रों की सीमाएँ क ही होती है। प्रत्येक राज्य 'नेशन स्टेट' होता है। ऐसा अन्तराष्ट्रीय व्यवहार की सुविधा के लिए माना जाता है।

आज हम देखते है कि राज्यों की सीमाएँ बदली जा सकती है।, राज्यकर्ता भी बदल जाते है। जहाँ एक राज से दो राज्य झारखण्ड और बिहार राज्य बनाये जा सकते हैं, वहाँ दो राज्यों को मिलाकर एक राज्य भी बन सकता है। आज उतर और दक्षिण वियतनाम के दो स्वतंत्र राज्य रहे ही कहॉ है। क्या हम उस संदर्भ में कह सकते हैं कि वहॉ दो राष्ट्रों को मिलाकर एक राष्ट्र बन गया? ऐसा कहना तो हास्यास्पद होगा। चीन ने तिब्बत पर अधिकार कर लिया है इसका अर्थ यह कदापि नहीं होता कि तिब्बत चीनी राष्ट्र हिंदू ही था। राष्ट्र एक स्थायी अवधारणा है। विशिष्ट स्वभाव वाले लोकसमूह को प्रदीर्घ ऐतिहासिक प्रक्रिया से विशिष्ट भूप्रदेश पर राष्ट्रतत्व प्राप्त होता है। राष्ट्र एक जीवमान वस्तु है, तो राज्य सुविधा के लिए निर्मित एक व्यवस्था (मशीनरी)। जैसे शरीर होता है। और उस पर वस्त्र परिधान किया जाता है, तो शरीर के लिए वस्त्र होता है या वस्त्र के लिए शरीर? हम देखते है कि शरीर के लिए वस्त्र होता है या वस्त्र के लिए शरीर? हम देखते हे कि शरीर का आकार, उसका डीलडौल, वर्ग जलवायु, ऋतु और शरीर से अपेक्षित र्का के स्वरूप के अनुसार हम

वस्त्र–परिधान करते है। बचपन के वस्त्र बड़े होने पर काम नहीं आते। शीतकाल के लिए बने वस्त्रों को गरमी के दिनों में कोई उपयोग नहीं होता। राज्य और राष्ट्र के संबंध में भी कुछ ऐसे ही होते हे। शरीर पर कोई वस्त्र न हो, तब भी शरीर तो होता ही है। वस्त्रों का उद्देश्य तन का संरक्षण करना, उसे शोभा प्राप्त करा देना और शरीर के सामाजिक व्यवहारों को सुविधापुर्ण बनाना भी होता है। राज्य भी राष्ट्र की सेवा के लिए होता है। जो राज्य राष्ट्र की उचित ढंग से सेवा न करता हो, उसे बदला जा सकता है। राष्ट्र में सतांतरण हुआ, इतना ही उसका अर्थ होता है । विदेशी सता क्यों राष्ट्र के लिए असहनीय हो जाती है। इसीलिए कि राष्ट्र के स्वतव को विदेशी प्रभुता मे घुटन अनुभव होती है। विदेशी सत्ता भले ही अच्छी क्यों न हो, विदेशी राज्य एक सुराजय भले ही क्यों न हो, स्वराज की प्यास उसे नहीं बुझ पाती। केवल स्वराज्य के आने से भी संतोष नहीं मिलता।

राष्ट्र की स्वराज्य से अर्थात् राष्ट्र के अंगभूत शासकों से कुछ अपेक्षाएँ होती हैं। मुख्यतः यह कि उसका काम काज राष्ट्र के कल्याण के लिए होना चाहिए। उससे राष्ट्र का गौरव बढ़ना चाहिए। राष्ट्रहितों की रक्षा एवं गौरव के लिए काम न करते हुए जो स्वकीय शासक एवं उनका शासन अपना कामगाज संकीर्ण स्वाथ्रे के लिए चलाते हें और उनकी रीति नीतियों का निर्धारण किसी विदेशी शक्ति को प्रसन्न करने के लिए होता है तब राष्ट्र में असंतोष फैलता है और भी एक बात यह है कि स्वराजय को स्वावलंबी होना चाहिए। लगातार विदेशों की ताल पर नाचने की स्थिति नहीं आनी चाहिए। यही राष्ट्र की इच्छा होती है। स्वराज्य को स्वालम्बी होना चाहिए। लगातार विदेशों की ताल पर नाचने की स्थिति नही आनी चाहिए। यही राष्ट्र की इच्छा होती है। स्वराज्य को स्वावलंबी बनाने में राज्य या सरकार यदि असफल होती है और राष्ट्र की भौतिक एवं आत्मिक प्रगति में बाधा पहुँचाती है, तो राष्ट्र में शासनकर्ताओं के प्रति अप्रीति अवश्य उत्पन्न होगी। स्वराज्य के सथ ही प्रभुसता का होना भी नितांत आवश्यक है। शासन–व्यवस्था और प्रभुसत्ता के बिना स्वराजय का कोई अस्तित्व नहीं हो सकता। संयुक्त राष्ट्रसंघ में सदस्यता पाने वाले राज्य सर्वभौम राज्य होते है। राष्ट्र की प्रकृति, स्वभाव, स्वाभिमान

एवं स्वत्व से विसंगत व्यवहार करने वाले राजय को स्थिरिता कभी प्राप्त नहीं होती है। उसे शांति नहीं मिलती। हमारे देश में व्याप्त अशांति एवं असंतोष की मूलगामी मीमांसा करनी हो तो इसी प्रकार करनी पड़ेगी। राज्य को ही सर्वस्व या राज्य को ही राष्ट्र मानना एक वैचारिक भूल है।

ऐसी असत्य धारणा का पोषण राष्ट्री शरीर में न हो, इस बात की चिंता करनी होती है। अन्यथा, राष्ट्र की सेवा करने के लिए राज होता है, उस राष्ट्र को ही गौण बनाकर राज्य की सर्वेसर्वा हो जाता है। फिर वह किसी न किसी की तानाशाही का शिकार बन जाता है। किसी भी परिस्थिति में परराजय तो होना ही नहीं चाहिए, किन्तु वह भी उतना ही महत्वपूर्ण है कि स्वराज्य में राष्ट्र के मानस में इस भावना का निर्माण हो कि यह हमारा अपना राज्य है। विकृति से बचने के लिए राष्ट्रशरीर का सुदुढ़ होना आवश्यक होता है। उसकी रोगप्रतिकारक शक्ति प्रखर होनी चाहिए, क्योंकि राज्य को राष्ट्र से ही बल प्राप्त होता है। राज्य का आधार राष्ट्र ही होता है। भारत के परिप्रेक्ष्य में कहना पड़ेगा कि यहॉ राष्ट्र क्षीण है, उपेक्षित है। स्वराज्य है तो सही, किन्तु वह राष्ट्रसेवा का साधन बनकर काम नहीं करता। दुर्भाग्य से आज राष्ट्र में इतनी जागृति एवं जीवमानता नहीं है कि वह अपनी शारीरिक, मानिसक, बौद्धिक एवं आत्मिक आवश्यकताओं की पूर्ति करने वाली शानव्यवस्था यहॉ ला सके। उसके बिना हम राष्ट्र का प्रतिनिधित्व अवश्य करता है, किन्तु प्रतिनिधि योग्य ढंग से काम न करता हो तो बदलने का साहस राष्ट्र में होना आवश्यक है, तभी संबंध ठीक रहते है।

इसका भी विचार करना चाहिए कि एक व्यवस्था या सेवासंस्था के नाते राज्य का वस्तुतः कार्य होता क्या है, हिंदु अवधारणा के अनुसार ये कार्य दो प्रकार के होते हैः प्रथम यह कि राज्य की प्रजा का जीवन निरापद तथा विकासोन्मुख होने के लिए आवश्यक शांति और सुरक्षा का वातावरण तथा विकासोन्मुख होने के लिए आवश्यक शांति और सुरक्षा का वातावरण बनाये रखना। दानवी या समाजविरोधी शतिक्याँ उसमें कोई विक्षेप लाती हों, तो उनका नियमन करना। इसके लिए पं0 दीनदयाल जी ने पुलिस व्यवसथा का उदाहरण दिया है। किसी बस्ती में शांति हो, कहीं कोई भी गड़बड़ या उपद्रव नह हो, चोरी डकैती की कोई संभवना

न हो, तो वहॉ हमें पुलिस के अस्तित्व का भी आभास नहीं होता। किन्तु शांति भंग, झगड़ा, संघर्ष आदि के प्रसंग आते ही हमें तुरंत पुलिस का स्मरण आता है। उसे बुलाया जाता है या वह सवयं ही घटनास्थल पर आ पहुँचती है। शांति और सुव्यववस्था को बनाये रखना शासन क प्रमुख कार्य माना जाताहै। राष्ट्र द्वारा निर्मित राज्यव्यसथा इस न्यूनतम कर्तव्यों को निभा नहीं पाती हो, शांति एवं सुवयवस्था नष्ट होकर समाजविरोधी शक्तियाँ लोकजीवन को दूभर कर रही हों, तो किसी न किसी परिवर्तन की आवश्यकता को राष्ट्र अनुभव करने लगता है। ऐसे समय वांछित परिवर्तन करने की क्षमता राष्ट्र के अंदर होना आवश्यक होता है।

राज्य का दूसरा कार्य है नागरिकों की जीवनविषयक समस्याओं का दक्षतापूर्वक निराकरण करना। उसे यह सवधानी बरतनी होती कि समाज के दुर्बल, असहाय एवं विपन्न वर्ग का शोषण सबल एवं साधनसंपन्न वर्ग द्वारा न हो सकै।

इन दो कार्यो के अतिरिक्त राज्य का एक तीसरा कार्य भी होता है। वह है राष्ट्र की ओर से विश्व के अन्य राज्यों के साथ उचित संबंधों का निर्माण करना तथा विदेशी आक्रमण की संभावना को टालते रहना। विदेशी आक्रमण होने पर राष्ट्र की संगठित शक्ति द्वारा उसका प्रतिकार प्रमुखता से राज्यव्यवस्था को ही करना होता है। राष्ट्र का अपना राजय न होने की स्थिति में राष्ट्र ही विदेशी शक्ति के विरूद्ध प्राणप्रण से लड़ता है। इसके भी उदाहरण हमारे इतिहास में मिलते हैं। यहॉ अंग्रेजों की सत्ता थी, तब हमारा अपना राजय कहॉ था? फिर ब्रिटिश सत्ता से किसने संघर्ष किया? उससे पूर्व मुगलों की बहुत शक्तिशाली सत्ता यहाँ थी। उस सत्ता के विरूद्ध स्वतंत्रता के लिए प्रदीर्घ संग्राम किसने किया? हम बड़े गर्व के साथ कहते है कि हम स्वतंत्रता के लिए लड़े थे। इसमें जो 'हम' है वही हमारे राष्ट्रस्वरूप का बोध कराता है। संभाजी की मृत्यु के साथ ही हमारी राज्यसता तो प्रायः नष्ट सी हो गयी थी। इसके उपरांत लगातार 18 वर्ष तक लड़ते रहकर मुगल सम्राट औरंगजेब को पराजीत एवं हताश अवस्था में अंतिम सॉस लेने को बाध्य करने वाली तेजस्विनी शक्ति राष्ट्री की ही थी। विदेशों का उदाहरण लेना हो, तो कहना होगा कि हिटलर के विरूद्ध रूसी साम्यवाद ने नहीं, अपितु रूसी राष्ट्रभावना

ने ही युद्ध किया था। इसी राष्ट्रभावना ने हिटलर के सारे सपने धूल में मिला दिये। मार्क्स ने तो कहा था कि राष्ट्र एक पूँजीवादी परिकल्पना हैं। किन्तु फिर भी कम्युनिस्ट क्रांति के बाद भी रूसी राष्ट्र का लोप नही हुआ। वहॉ की कम्युनिस्ट सरकार को भी राष्ट्रीय चेतनाशक्ति को केन्द्र बनाकर ही शत्रु का सामना करना पड़ा है। प्राचीन काल में समाट चंद्रगुप्त ने ग्रीक आक्रान्ताओं को धूल चटायी था। उसे तो राज्य द्वारा राष्ट्ररक्षा का अपना दायित्व दक्षतापूर्वक निभाने का ही परिचायक मानना पड़ता है। इसीलिए पं0 दीनदयाल जी इस निष्कर्ष पर पहुचे थे कि राजय राष्ट्र के लिए होता है। राष्ट्रीयता राजनीति के लिए नहीं हुआ करती राजनीति को ही राष्ट्रीयता का पोषण करेन वाली होना होता है। राष्ट्र को क्षीण करने वाली राजनीति को त्याज्य ही मानना चाहिए। यह निष्कर्ष आज की राजनीति के परिप्रेक्ष्य में इतना महत्वपूर्ण है कि उसका और स्पष्टीकरण अनावश्यक है। ब्रिटिशों ने यहॉ के राष्ट्र को क्षीण करने के उद्देश्य से ही फूट डालो और राज्य करो' वाली नीति अपनायी थी। यहॉ के प्राचीन हिंदू राष्ट्र को दुर्बल करने के लिए उन्होनें मुसिलमों को बढ़ावा दिया। ईसाई मत का प्रचार कर उसके द्वारा यहॉ के लोगों को अराष्ट्रीयकरण कराने का षडयंत्र उन्होनें रचा। राष्ट्र के बारे में भ्रांतिपूर्ण अवधराणाएँ प्रस्तुत कीं। हिंदू समाज में भीतरी कलह सुलगाने की कुटिल चाल चली। नाना प्रकार के आंतरिक झगड़े उन्होनें प्रारंभ करवा दिये। उनका हर पग इसी चाल के अनुसार उठता था कि एक राष्ट्र में अनेक परस्परविरोधी राज्य बन जायें। राष्ट्र को हतप्रभ बनाने का ही यह सारा प्रयास था और वह जानबूझकर किया गया।

इस सारी चाल को समझते हुए भी 1947 के बाद की राजनीति ने राष्ट्रीयता का पोषण करने के कर्तव्य को नही अपनाया। राज्य नामक संस्था राष्ट्र की सेवा करने के अपने मूल उद्देश्य को भुला बैठी । राष्ट्र विगठित और अपनी पहचान के बारे में भ्रांतियों में रहता हो तो राज्य पर अंकुश रखने वाली राष्ट्रीय शक्ति प्रकट नहीं हो पाती। स्वदेशी राजय भी राष्ट्र के लिए पोषक बनने के स्थान पर मारक होने लगे तो उस स्वराज्य का विरोध करना राष्ट्र के लिए अपरिहार्य बन जाता है। किन्तु स्वतंत्रता की परिकल्पना इससे कहीं अधिक व्यापक है ।सामाजिक, सांस्कृतिक एवं

आर्थिक स्वतंत्राओं का भी स्वतंत्रता में ही समावेश होता है। स्वतंत्रता का विचार टुकड़ों में नही किया जा सकता। पंडित जी का यह प्रतिपादन इसी बात का साक्षी है कि राष्ट्रविचार प्रस्तुत करते समय वे कितनी सावाानी एवं सतर्कता के साथ सारी सूक्ष्मताओं का विश्लेषण किया करते थे, उनके तर्क कितने ठोस होते थे और वैचारिक सीमा को छोड़कर उचित कर्तव्यबोध जगाने में वे कितने दक्ष हुआ करते थे। स्वराजय और स्वतंत्रता का आशय इस प्रकार लोगों को स्पष्ट समझाने और राष्ट्रहित की एकमात्र कसौटी पर प्रत्येक परिकल्पना को परखने का प्रयोग कितने राजनेअताओं ने कियाहोगा? विपक्ष की भूमिका केवल यही नहीं होती कि सतारूढ़ दल का विरोध ही करता रहे, अपितु राष्ट्रहितों का भावात्मक आग्रह भी उसे रखना चाहिए। इसी अर्थ में विरोधी दलनेता की भूमिका को पं0 दीनदयाल जी ने कुशलता से निभाया।

इस सारे प्रतिपादन द्वारा पं. दीनदयाल जी ने इस आवश्यकता को ही प्रस्तुत किया है कि क्षेत्र कोई भी हो, देश के सभी कार्यो एवं योजनाओं की प्रधान कसौटी राष्ट्रहित ही होना चाहिए। उन्होनें धर्म की सावीोमिकता, राष्ट्र की स्वयंभु, स्थायी एवं जीवमान सत्ता, राज्य के कर्तव्य, स्वराज सुराज्य और स्वतंत्रता के निश्चित आशय, आदि सब बातों को सहजनता से स्पष्ट किया है। शासन की अत्यधिक प्रभुता एवं राष्ट्र की दुर्बलता एवं आपतिजनक विकृति है, ऐसी स्पष्ट चेतावनी भी उन्होनें दी है निःसंदेह उनके इस चिंतन ने अनेक प्रचलित परिकल्पनाओं को धक्का दिया है ।आगे चलकर जयप्रकश जी ने भी कहा कि भारत, पाकिस्तान तथा बंगलादेश यद्यपि तीन पृथक राज्य हो गये है। फिर भी इस संपूर्ण भूभाग का राष्ट्र तो एक ही है। राज्य राष्ट्र नहीं है, इसी सिद्धांत के अनुसार पं. दीनदयाल जी अंखड भारत का विचार दो टूक शब्दों में प्रस्तुत किया करते थे। उनके विवेचन से यह भी ध्यान में आता है कि एक राज्य में अनेक राष्ट्रों को ठूँसने अथवा एक राष्ट्र को कृत्रिमता से अनेक राज्यों में विभाजित करने के कारण ही विश्व के अनेक जनसमाजों एवं भूखंडों में आंदोलन या उत्पात हो रहे है। अतः महत्वाकॉक्षी पराये राष्ट्रों के स्वार्थवश निर्मित देशविभाजनों को नष्ट करने की इच्छा जर्मनी, कोरिया, अथवा भारत की जनता में हो तो उसे स्वाभाविक ही मानना पड़ेगा। विश्व में

अन्यत्र व्यवच्छेदक राष्ट्रीय विशेषताएँ उन राष्ट्रों की अपनी प्रकृति, उनका जीवन लक्ष्य आदि की परिकल्पनाएँ पर्याप्त मात्रा में स्पष्ट हों या न हों भारत में वे बिल्कुल स्पष्ट है।

इसकी तुलना में हिंदु राष्ट्र की प्राचीनता एवं उसकी जीवनधारा की अद्भुत निरंततर के कारण यहाँ सांस्कृतिक राष्ट्रीयता हजारों वर्ष से परिपक्व हे। हिंदुत्व के सूत्र की उपेक्षा कर हिदुस्तान के एक राष्ट्रीत्व की कल्पना भी नहीं की जा सकती। आज कल की राजनीति भारत के जनसमाजों को जोड़ने के स्थान पर एक दूसरे से तोड़ने का ही काम अधिक कर रही है। इसलिए राष्ट्र के परिप्रेक्ष्य में राजनीति और शासनसत्ता की परिसीमाओं एवं कर्तव्य का क्या स्थान है, ठीक से समझने की आवश्यकता है। हिंदू ईसाई या इस्लामी संपद्रायों की पंक्ति में बिठाया जा सकने वाला एक संप्रदाय नहीं है। वह तो विशिष्ट जीवन–शैली और जीवन प्रवाह का बोध जगाने वाला और सबको अपने अंदर समा सकने वाला एक अत्यंत गौरवशली शब्द है। हिंदु अभियधान से पहचाने जाने वाले समाज ने भारत भूमि में इसी एकात्म सांस्कृकि जीवनप्रवाह का विकास किया है और इसीलिए स्वाभाविकतः यह हिंदू राष्ट्र है। क्योंकि हिंदू शब्द उपर है, व्यापक है, जीवणशैली है। कश्मीर से कन्याकुमारी तक और बंबई से कलकता तक देश को जोड़ने वाला यही शब्द है। या आस पास के अन्य एशियाई देशों को भी।

अततः कहा जा सकता है कि पं. दीनदयाल जी के विवेचन के इस के इस केन्द्रवर्ती सूत्र को ध्यान में रखने से आज के संभ्रम एवं राष्ट्रीय पतन के सम्पूर्ण इतिहास का कारण स्पष्ट हो जाता है। साथही इस पर भी प्रकाश प़ता है कि आज राष्ट्रीय पुनरूत्थान एवं स्वतंत्रता की सच्ची सुखानुभूति के लिए क्या करना चाहिए। आज आवश्यकता इस बात की है कि हम परावलोकन करने के बजाय आत्मावलोकन करने वाले बने। आत्मसाक्षात्कार की दिशा में मनन, चिंतन, अध्ययन एवं प्रतयक्षा आचरण करने के लिए अग्रसर हों। राष्ट्र जब तक अपने आत्मस्वरूप को नही पहचानता, उसमें चेतना को जायेगा नहीं जा सकेगा, उसके सारे सुप्तासुप्त गुणों का यथार्थ आहवान नहीं किया जा सकेगा न ही भावात्मक आशय से परिपूर्ण राष्ट्रनिर्माण संभव हो पायेगा।

अंत में इस कवीता का स्मरण किया जा सकता है। पंडित दिनदयाल उपाध्याय जी के विशाल कार्यो हेतु।

काबा हो या प्रयाग, प्रेम की बहती धार है।
अस्त्रों की जगह नही, सब जगह तिरस्कार है।
मंदिर हो या मस्जिद, जीवन के संस्कार हैं।
धर्म की लड़ाई ना करें, राष्ट्र ही परिवार है।।

संदर्भ ग्रंथ सूची

1. श्री सी. पी. भिसीकर –राष्ट्र की अवधारणां
2. एकात्म मानव दर्शन – सुरूचि प्रकाशन
3. घोष अरविन्दो – वन नेशन
4. हावर्उ माइकल – वार एण्ड नेशनस
5. कोटील्य –अर्थशास्त्र
6. गील्बर्ट पाओल – दी फिलोस्फी ऑफ नेशनलीज्म
7. ए. एल. बाथन– अदभूत भारत
8. ब्रूएली जान– नेशनलीज्म एण्ड स्टेट 1985
9. देसाई ए. आर– शोसल बैंकग्राउण्ड ऑफ इंडियन नेशनलीज्म 1946
10. गेलनर इरनेस्ट –नेशनल एण्ड नेशलीज्म 1989
11. सांस्कृतिक राष्ट्रवाद – प्रभात झा
12. राष्ट्रवाद –रवीन्द्र नाथ टैगोर – (अनुवाद) सौमीत्र मोहन

Chapter - 18

आत्मनिर्भर भारत की संकल्पना के संदर्भ में भारतीय परिवारों के उपभोग– संबंधित निर्णयों का अध्ययन

डॉ. हरिकिशनी

संक्षिप्त सार

वर्तमान शोध का मुख्य उद्देश्य आत्मनिर्भर भारत की संकल्पना के संदर्भ में भारतीय परिवारों के उपभोग–संबंधित निर्णयों का अध्ययन करना एवं उसके अनुरूप शोधकर्ताओं, नीति निर्धारकों, विज्ञापन कर्ताओं, व व्यवसायियों को महत्वपूर्ण दिशा निर्देश प्रदान करना है। इस शोध के परिणाम प्राथमिक और द्वितीयक स्रोतों से प्राप्त सूचनाओं पर आधारित हैं। प्राथमिक आंकड़े, भारत की राजधानी दिल्ली के विभिन्न क्षेत्रों में रहने वाले 13 से 18 वर्ष के 225 बच्चों से प्रश्नपत्रों (गूगल फॉर्म) के माध्यम से एकत्र किए गए हैं। प्राथमिक आंकड़ों का अध्ययन और विश्लेषण उचित सांख्यिकी उपकरणों जैसे माध्य, मानक विचलन, युग्मित टी–परीक्षण, तथा "विभिन्नता विश्लेषण" इत्यादि की सहायता से किया गया है। इस शोध के प्रमुख निष्कर्ष हैं (i) आत्मनिर्भर भारत की संकल्पना के केंद्र में परिवारों के उपभोग–संबंधित निर्णयों का अध्ययन निहित है, (ii) वर्तमान परिस्थितियों में, परिवार के उपभोग–संबंधित निर्णयों में बच्चे महत्वपूर्ण भूमिका अदा करते हैं, (iii) यह भूमिका, खरीद निर्णय प्रक्रिया के चरणों में भिन्न–भिन्न होती है, और (iv) परिवार के खरीद निर्णयों में बच्चों की भूमिका उनकी जनसांख्यिकी से प्रभावित होती है। इस शोध के निष्कर्षों

से शोधकर्ताओं, नीति निर्धारकों, विज्ञापन कर्ताओं, व व्यवसायियों को आत्मनिर्भरता की संकल्पना के संदर्भ में प्रभावशाली रणनीतियां बनाने व लागू करने में निश्चित तौर पर मार्गदर्शन मिलेगा।

भूमिका

कोविड–19 या कोरोनावाइरस महामारी की पहचान पहली बार दिसंबर 2019 में वुहान, चीन में हुई थी। इसके प्रकोप के मद्देनजर, मार्च 2020 में विश्व स्वास्थ्य संगठन ने इसे एक महामारी घोषित किया। 2 मार्च 2021 तक, 114 मिलियन से अधिक मामलों की पुष्टि की गई है, जिसमें कोविड–19 से 2.53 मिलियन से अधिक मौतें हुई हैं। निसंदेह यह इतिहास की सबसे घातक महामारियों में से एक है। इस महामारी के तीव्र प्रसार को रोकने के लिए जनवरी 2020 में चीन के हुबेई प्रांत में लॉकडाउन के बाद, 2020 और 2021 के दौरान विश्व के लगभग सभी देशों में लॉकडाउन जारी रहा तथा अप्रैल 2020 तक, दुनिया की लगभग आधी आबादी लॉकडाउन के अधीन थी, जिसमें 90 से अधिक देशों में 3.9 बिलियन से अधिक लोगों को उनकी सरकारों द्वारा घर पर रहने के लिए कहा गया था। इसी श्रृंखला में भारत ने पहले 21 दिवसीय लॉकडाउन की घोषणा 24 मार्च को "जान है तो जहान है" के नारे के साथ की गई तत्पश्चात दूसरा लॉकडाउन 15 अप्रैल से 3 मई, तीसरा 4 से 17 मई, तथा चौथा लॉकडाउन 18 से 31 मई तक चला (द इकोनॉमिक टाइम्स, 2020)।

भारत में कोरोनावायरस महामारी का आर्थिक प्रभाव काफी हद तक विघटनकारी रहा है। सांख्यिकी मंत्रालय के अनुसार वित्त वर्ष 2020 की चौथी तिमाही में भारत की वृद्धि दर घटकर 3.1ः रह गई । इस महामारी के आर्थिक प्रभाव का मुकाबला करने के लिए भारत सरकार द्वारा समय–समय पर विभिन्न उपायों की घोषणा की गई है जिनमें से प्रमुख हैं 17 अप्रैल को भारतीय रिजर्व बैंक द्वारा विभिन्न अन्य बैंकों को 50,000 करोड रुपए के वित्तीय सहायता की घोषणा, 18 अप्रैल को महामारी के दौरान भारतीय कंपनियों को बचाने के लिए प्रत्यक्ष विदेशी निवेश नीति में बदलाव, और 12 मई को प्रधानमंत्री द्वारा "आत्मनिर्भर भारत" की संकल्पना

का प्रस्तुतीकरण जिसके तहत 20 लाख करोड़ रुपए के आर्थिक प्रोत्साहन पैकेज की घोषणा की गई है (अनिल, 2020)।

"आत्मनिर्भर भारत" अभियान एक महत्वाकांक्षी परियोजना है जिसके मूल उद्देश्य कोविड–19 महामारी के दुष्प्रभावों को खत्म करना व भविष्य के भारत का पुनर्निर्माण करना हैं । यह महत्वाकांक्षी परियोजना पांच प्रमुख स्तंभों पर आधारित हैरू अर्थव्यवस्था, बुनियादी ढाँचा, प्रणाली, जीवंत लोकतंत्र, और माँग (द इकोनॉमिक टाइम्स, 2020)। आत्मनिर्भर भारत की इस परिकल्पना में स्वदेशी वस्तुओं का वृहत पैमाने पर अंगीकरण किया जाना भी सम्मिलित है (चित्र 1)। यह तभी संभव है जब उपभोक्ताओं में स्वदेशी वस्तुओं की गुणवत्ता संबंधी अपेक्षाएं संतुष्ट होती हैं जिससे स्वदेशी वस्तुओं की मांग बढ़ेगी जिसकी पूर्ति करने के लिए उत्पादन बढ़ाया जाएगा। फलस्वरुप लोगों को रोजगार मिलेगा उनकी आय में वृद्धि होगी और परिवारोंध्व्यक्तियों द्वारा उपयोग की जाने वाली वस्तुओं की मांग में वृद्धि होगी व लोगों का रहन–सहन स्तर बढ़ेगा और फलस्वरुप आर्थिक विकास की दर में वृद्धि होगी। यह एक निरंतर चलने वाली प्रक्रिया है इससे देश की आर्थिक संरचना को सुदृढ़ बनाया जा सकता है।

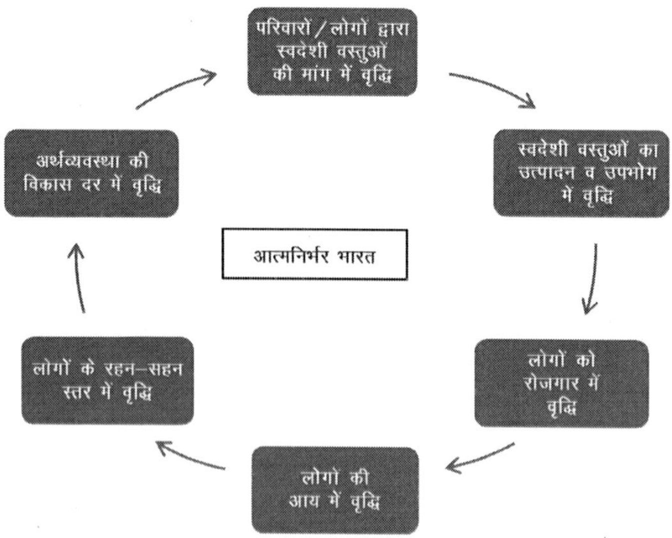

चित्र 1: आत्मनिर्भर भारत की परिकल्पना

प्रस्तुत शोध का मुख्य उद्देश्य आत्मनिर्भर भारत की संकल्पना के प्रमुख स्तंभ "मांग" का सूक्ष्म अध्ययन, भारतीय परिवारों के उपभोग– संबंधित निर्णयों के संदर्भ में अध्ययन करना एवं उसके अनुरूप शोधकर्ताओं, नीति निर्धारकों, विज्ञापन कर्ताओं, व व्यवसायियों को महत्वपूर्ण दिशा निर्देश प्रदान करना है।

साहित्य समीक्षा

पूर्व शोधों में परिवार को एक महत्वपूर्ण उपभोग व खपत इकाई माना गया है (चौधरी एट अल, 2018य वेबस्टर, 1994)। औद्योगिक क्रांति के पश्चात से ही परिवार विशेष में उपभोग संबंधी निर्णय कैसे लिए जाते हैं, व परिवार का कौन–कौन सा सदस्य इन निर्णयों में किस प्रकार की व कितनी भूमिका अदा करता है, यह विषय शोधकर्ताओं, व्यवसायियों, व नीति निर्माताओं के गहन अध्ययन–मनन का एक लोकप्रिय विषय रहा है (प्रताप, 2019य चौधरी एट अल, 2018)। परिवार उपभोग संबंधित प्रारंभिक अनुसंधान इन निर्णयों में पति–पत्नी की भूमिका के अध्ययन तक ही सीमित थे, परंतु 1980 के पश्चात परिवारों में बच्चों के बढ़ते हुए महत्व को व प्रभाव को देखते हुए, बच्चों को भी इन शोधों में शामिल किया जाने लगा (गुनेरी एट अल., 2009)।

बच्चों की भूमिका संबंधित विगत शोध इस तथ्य का खुलासा करते हैं कि परिवार में बहुत सारी वस्तुओं व सेवाओं के खरीद निर्णयों में बच्चे न सिर्फ महत्वपूर्ण भूमिका अदा कर रहे हैं, अपितु उनका यह प्रभाव दिनों–दिन इस सीमा तक बढ़ रहा है कि अधिकांश घरों में अब वस्तुएं बच्चों की पसंद अनुरूप ही खरीदी जाती हैं (मित्तल एट अल, 2020)। खरीद निर्णयों में बच्चों की यह भूमिका दो तरफा होती है जिसमें स्वयं उनके माता–पिता भी उन्हें सक्रिय भूमिका अदा करने के लिए प्रोत्साहित करते हैं।

बच्चे कई प्रकार से अपने परिवार के उपभोग संबंधी निर्णयों को प्रभावित करते हैं या कर सकते हैं जैसे अपने स्वयं के उपभोग की वस्तुओं के सभी निर्णय स्वयं लेकर या अपनी पॉकेट मनी के द्वारा वस्तुओं को स्वयं ही खरीदकर या अपने परिवार द्वारा इस्तेमाल की जाने वाली वस्तुओं

के संबंध में निर्णय लेकर या अपने माता–पिता के द्वारा इस्तेमाल की जाने वाली वस्तुओं के निर्णयों में सक्रिय भूमिका निभाकर (मैकनील, 1992)। बच्चे उपभोग निर्णयों में अपना योगदान कई तरह से देते हैं जैसे – व्यक्तिगत खरीदारी करके, घर पर सीधे अनुरोध करके, दुकान पर अनुरोध करके या "अप्रत्यक्ष रूप" से जबकि वे स्वयं अपने माता पिता को कुछ नहीं कहते परंतु "अवलोकन व अनुभव" के आधार पर माता पिता को पता होता है कि बच्चों को क्या वस्तु ज्यादा पसंद है और क्या उन्हें पसंद नहीं है और वे उसी के अनुरूप वस्तुओं की खरीदारी करते हैं।

विगत कुछ वर्षों में परिवारों में बच्चों के तीव्र गति से बढ़ते महत्व के मुख्य कारण हैं – कामकाजी महिलाओं की संख्या में वृद्धि, संयुक्त परिवारों की संख्या में कमी, प्रत्येक परिवार बच्चों की कम संख्या, पाश्चात्य संस्कृति का अनुमोदन, अंग्रेजी शिक्षा का प्रचार–प्रसार, परिवार के सदस्यों के बीच खुला वार्तालाप, परिवारों का साधन--संपन्न परंतु समय–निर्धन होना, मास मीडिया खासकर इंटरनेट का अधिक उपभोग इत्यादि। इन सभी कारणों की वजह से परिवार के खरीद निर्णयों में बच्चों की भूमिका का महत्व काफी बढ़ गया है। साथ ही, बच्चे परिवार में सूचना के एक "मूल्यवान स्त्रोत" के रूप में भी उभर रहे हैं इसलिए उन वस्तुओं के निर्णयों में जहां उन्हें ज्यादा ज्ञान है, बच्चे और भी ज्यादा महत्वपूर्ण भूमिका अदा करते हैं। बच्चों की भूमिका सभी वस्तुओं के उपभोग निर्णयों में एक समान नहीं होती अपितु वस्तु की प्रकृति, वस्तु की कीमत, निर्णय प्रक्रिया के चरण, बच्चे व उसके परिवार की जनसांख्यिकी जैसे तत्वों पर आधारित होती है (इशाक और तुफैल, 2014)।

भारत तेजी से बढ़ती बाजार अर्थव्यवस्थाओं में से एक है, जहां उपभोक्ता बाजार लगातार तेज गति से विकसित हो रहे हैं, जिसके परिणामस्वरूप भारतीय समाज में कुछ संरचनात्मक परिवर्तन दृष्टिगोचर हो रहे हैं जैसे कि पारिवारिक संरचना में परिवर्तन (संयुक्त परिवार से एकल परिवार), घर से बाहर काम करने वाली महिलाओं की बढ़ती भागीदारी, शिक्षा का बढ़ता स्तर, आय वितरण में परिवर्तन, उत्पादों की उपलब्धता में वृद्धि, प्रतिस्पर्धा में वृद्धि, मीडिया कवरेज में वृद्धि। इन सभी परिवर्तनों से परिवार के उपभोग निर्णयों का आंतरिक समीकरण भी

परिवर्तित हुआ है और परिवार के प्रत्येक सदस्य की भूमिका में भी कुछ परिवर्तन आया है।

वर्तमान शोध का मुख्य उद्देश्य आत्मनिर्भर भारत की संकल्पना व भारतीय परिवारों की मांग में आए संरचनात्मक परिवर्तनों के संदर्भ में, भारतीय परिवारों के उपभोग संबंधी निर्णयों में बच्चों की भूमिका के विभिन्न पहलुओं का अध्ययन करना, भावी शोध के नए अवसरों की खोज करना, तथा व्यवसायियों को नीति निर्माण में महत्वपूर्ण दिशा निर्देश प्रदान करना है। अध्ययन व विश्लेषण हेतु शोध उद्देश्यों को निम्न शोध प्रश्नों में परिवर्तित किया गया हैः

शोध प्रश्न 1 – क्या परिवारों के उपभोग–निर्णयों में बच्चों की कोई भूमिका होती है?

शोध प्रश्न 2 – क्या बच्चों की उपभोग–निर्णयों में भूमिका खरीद निर्णय प्रक्रिया के प्रत्येक चरण में एक जैसी होती है?

शोध प्रश्न 3 – बच्चों की जनसांख्यिकी का उनकी उपभोग–निर्णयों में भूमिका पर क्या प्रभाव पड़ता है?

शोध प्रणाली

इस शोध में प्राथमिक और द्वितीयक दोनों स्रोतों से प्राप्त सूचनाओं का इस्तेमाल किया गया है। इस शोध के लिए प्राथमिक आंकड़े भारत की राजधानी दिल्ली के विभिन्न क्षेत्रों में रहने वाले 13 से 18 वर्ष के 225 बच्चों से प्रश्नपत्रों (गूगल फॉर्म) के माध्यम से एकत्र किए गए हैं। प्रत्येक प्रश्नपत्र दो भागों में विभक्त था। पहले भाग में बच्चे व उसके परिवार की व्यक्तिगत सुचना संबंधित प्रश्न पूछे गए थे तथा दूसरे भाग में बच्चे की उपभोग निर्णयों में भूमिका से संबंधित प्रश्न। सभी प्रश्न सरल, स्पष्ट, व शोध उद्देश्य आधारित थे। प्रतिदर्श सैंपल का चुनाव सुविधा–प्रतिदर्श तकनीक के माध्यम से किया गया और इस बात का पूरा ध्यान रखा गया है कि चयन किया गया सैंपल एक प्रतिनिधित्व सैंपल हो। शोध में प्रयुक्त सैंपल की जनसांख्यिकी को तालिका एक में सूचीबद्ध किया गया है। प्रयुक्त सैंपल में बच्चों की औसत आयु 15.7 वर्ष, लड़के 60ः व लड़कियां 40ः, तथा पब्लिक विद्यालय में पढ़ने वाले बच्चों की संख्या (छ = 129)

सरकारी विद्यालय में पढ़ने वाले बच्चों की संख्या (छ = 96) से अधिक थी। प्राथमिक आंकड़ों को जनवरी 2021 में गूगल फॉर्म की मदद से एकत्र किया गया था।

तालिका 1: शोध में प्रयुक्त जनसांख्यिकी

विशेषताएँ	कुल संख्या (N = 225)	प्रतिशत (%)
बच्चों की आयु (वर्ष)		
13–14	72	32%
15–16	63	28%
17–18	90	40%
बच्चों का लिंग		
बालक	135	60%
बालिकाएं	90	40%
बच्चों का विद्यालय		
सरकारी विद्यालय	96	42.7%
पब्लिक विद्यालय	129	57.3%

शोध वस्तु

पिछले शोधों में यह पाया गया है कि बच्चों की भूमिका सभी वस्तुओं के खरीद–निर्णयों में एक समान नहीं होती है। बच्चे स्वयं के उपयोग के लिए खरीदी गई वस्तुओं के खरीद–निर्णयों में ज्यादा सक्रिय भूमिका निभाते हैं और परिवार संबंधित महंगी वस्तुओं के खरीद–निर्णयों में अपेक्षाकृत रूप से कम सक्रिय भूमिका निभाते हैं। अतः इस शोध के लिए बच्चे के स्वयं के उपभोग हेतु वस्तु (कंप्यूटर, मोबाइल टेलीफोन, गेम वीडियो, साइकिल) का चयन किया गया है। बच्चों ने इसी वस्तु को ध्यान में रखकर प्रश्न पत्रों को पूरा किया है। बच्चों को इन वस्तुओं में से किसी एक वस्तु जो उनके परिवार में पिछले 1 वर्ष में खरीदी गई हो, का चुनाव करना था तत्पश्चात प्रश्नों का उत्तर इसी वस्तु को ध्यान में रखकर देना था। इस शोध में केवल उन्हीं बच्चों को शामिल किया गया है जिनके परिवार में यह वस्तु पिछले 2 वर्ष के अंदर खरीदी गई हो ताकि बच्चों के जवाब वास्तविकता के ज्यादा नजदीक हो। इस संबंध में बच्चों से आवश्यक

प्रतिक्रियाओं के लिए "बहुत उच्च" से "शून्य" तक के पांच–बिंदु पैमाने का उपयोग किया गया है।

खरीद–निर्णयों में बच्चों की भूमिका का मूल्यांकन, निर्णय प्रक्रिया के चार चरणों के अनुसार तलपड़े तथा तलपड़े (1995) द्वारा विकसित पैमाने (11–आइटम) का उपयोग करके किया गया है। स्केल आइटमों की विश्वसनीयता का विश्लेषण करने के लिए विश्वसनीयता गुणांक, अल्फा की गणना की गई व संबंधित परिणामों को तालिका 2 में सूचीबद्ध किया गया है । स्केल पूरी तरह से विश्वसनीय पाया गया क्योंकि सभी क्रोनबैक अल्फा गुणांक (α) स्वीकृत सीमा 0.60 से अधिक हैं (नूननली, 1978)।

तालिका 2: स्केल आइटमों की विश्वसनीयता का विश्लेषण

स्केल आइटम	आइटमों की संख्या	क्रोनबैक अल्फा (α)
– खरीद आवश्यकता चरण	3	0.81
– सूचना खोज व मूल्यांकन चरण	2	0.74
– निर्णय लेने का चरण	5	0.63
– वास्तविक खरीद चरण 1	1	–

नोटः 1. विश्वसनीयता गुणांक, अल्फा, की गणना नहीं की जा सकती है क्योंकि स्केल में केवल एक आइटम है।

शोध परिणाम

शोध प्रश्न 1 का केंद्र भारतीय परिवारों के उपभोग संबंधी निर्णयों में बच्चों की भूमिका का अवलोकन करना था। इसके लिए सर्वप्रथम, खरीद निर्णय प्रक्रिया के चारों चरणों में बच्चों की भूमिका के माध्य व मानक विचलन ज्ञात किए गए तत्पश्चात उन्हें संक्षिप्त रूप से तालिका 3 में सूचीबद्ध किया गया है। अपेक्षानुसार, बच्चों की भूमिका के माध्य, सैद्धांतिक रूप से अपेक्षित मध्य–मान (2.5) से काफी ज्यादा हैं (1 से 5 के स्केल पर) जो इस बात की पुष्टि करते हैं कि बच्चे परिवार के खरीद निर्णय प्रक्रिया के प्रत्येक चरण में सक्रिय भूमिका अदा करते हैं।

उम्मीद के अनुसार, बच्चों की सबसे अहम भूमिका प्रथम चरण अर्थात खरीद आवश्यकता चरण ($M = 3.22$) में व न्यूनतम भूमिका निर्णय लेने

के चरण (M = 2.76) पर पाई गई जोकि पूर्व शोध परिणामों के अनुरूप है।

तालिका 3: खरीद निर्णय प्रक्रिया में बच्चों की भूमिका संबंधित माध्य और मानक विचलन

निर्णय प्रक्रिया के चरण	माध्य और मानक विचलन
चरण 1 – खरीद आवश्यकता चरण	3.22 (0.88)
चरण 2 – सूचना खोज व मूल्यांकन चरण	3.17 (1.10)
चरण 3 – निर्णय लेने का चरण	2.76 (0.85)
चरण 4 – वास्तविक खरीद चरण	3.11 (1.26)

शोध प्रश्न 2 के तहत बच्चों की भूमिका का खरीद निर्णय प्रक्रिया के प्रत्येक चरण में आकलन करना था । इसके लिए बच्चों की निर्णय प्रक्रिया के प्रत्येक चरण में भूमिका के माध्य परिणामों पर युग्मित टी–परीक्षण किए गए व संबंधित परिणाम तालिका 4 में प्रस्तुत किए गए हैं। तालिका 4 के आंकड़ों से स्पष्ट है कि सभी चरणों के मध्य अंतर $p < 0.05$ पर महत्वपूर्ण है जो इस जो इस तथ्य को सिद्ध करते हैं कि बच्चे निर्णय प्रक्रिया के प्रत्येक चरण पर एक जैसी भूमिका अदा नहीं करते हैं।

तालिका 4: खरीद निर्णय प्रक्रिया में बच्चों की भूमिका – युग्मित टी–परीक्षण

निर्णय प्रक्रिया के चरण	माध्य और मानक विचलन	युग्मित टी–परीक्षण		
		चरण 2	चरण 3	चरण 4
चरण 1 – खरीद आवश्यकता चरण	3.22(0.88)			
चरण 2 – सूचना खोज व मूल्यांकन चरण	3.17 (1.10)	2.774 (0.040)*		
चरण 3 – निर्णय लेने का चरण	2.76 (0.85)	9.429 (0.000)*	8.764 (0.000)*	
चरण 4 – वास्तविक खरीद चरण	3.11 (1.26)	1.733 (0.044)*	2.168 (0.031)*	6.496 (0.000)*

Note: 1- p < 0-05 पर महत्वपूर्ण

शोध प्रश्न 3 का अध्ययन क्षेत्र बच्चों की जनसांख्यिकी व उनकी उपभोग संबंधी निर्णयों में भूमिका का निरीक्षण करना था । इसके लिए बच्चों की जनसांख्यिकी (आयु, लिंग, व विद्यालय) तथा उनकी उपभोग संबंधी निर्णयों में भूमिका के मध्य "विभिन्नता विश्लेषण" किया गया और संबंधित परिणामों को तालिका 5 में सूचीबद्ध किया गया है । तालिका 5 के तथ्य इस बात को सिद्ध करते हैं कि बच्चों की जनसांख्यिकी जैसे वे किस आयु वर्ग (वर्ष 13–14य 15–16य 17–18) के हैं या उनका लिंग क्या है (बालक / बालिका) और वह किस विद्यालय (सरकारी / पब्लिक विद्यालय) में पढ़ते हैं, इन तथ्यों का उसकी उपभोग संबंधी निर्णयों में भूमिका पर प्रभाव पड़ता है।

तालिका 5: खरीद निर्णय प्रक्रिया में बच्चों की भूमिका व जनसांख्यिकी

जनसांख्यिकी	वर्गों का योग	df1	df2	माध्य वर्ग	F-ratio1	महत्व
बच्चों की आयु	2.274	2	1.137	.392	.676	.002′
बच्चों का लिंग	6.297	1	6.297	2.186	.140	.006′
बच्चों का विद्यालय	21.097	1	10.548	3.702	.026	.019′

Note: 1- p < 0-05 पर महत्वपूर्ण

परिणाम और निहितार्थ

इस शोध के प्रमुख निष्कर्ष हैं (i) भारतीय बच्चे पारिवारिक खरीद निर्णयों में प्रभाव डालते हैं, (ii) यह प्रभाव, खरीद निर्णय प्रक्रिया के चरणों में भिन्न–भिन्न होता है, (iii) और परिवार के खरीद निर्णयों में बच्चों की भूमिका उनकी जनसांख्यिकी (आयु, लिंग, और विद्यालय) से प्रभावित होती है। इस शोध के सभी निष्कर्ष इस विषय से संबंधित साहित्य के समानांतर हैं (चौधरी एट अल, 2018; विमलसिरी, 2004)। निश्चित तौर पर, इस शोध के निष्कर्षों से आत्मनिर्भर भारत की परिकल्पना को चरितार्थ करने की दिशा में नीति निर्माताओं, व्यवसायिक संगठनों, और शोधकर्ताओं को भविष्य के लिए अधिक कारगर ढंग से रणनीतियों के निर्माण व कार्यान्वयन में मदद मिलेगी। वर्तमान शोध के अनुसार, भारतीय परिवारों की स्वदेशी वस्तु के प्रति मांग के निर्धारण में बच्चे एक महत्वपूर्ण भूमिका

निभा सकते हैं क्योंकि बच्चे लगभग सभी प्रकार की वस्तुओं के उपभोग निर्णय में सक्रिय व अहम भूमिका अदा करते हैं। भारतीय परिवारों के उपभोग निर्णयों में बच्चों की यह भूमिका कैसे वह किस प्रकार की होगी इसकी जानकारी से निश्चित रूप से भारतीय व्यवसायियों को न सिर्फ नए उत्पादों को बनाने, विद्यमान उत्पादों की गुणवत्ता को बढ़ाने व सटीक ढंग से विज्ञापन रणनीतियां तय करने में मार्गदर्शन प्राप्त होगा अपितु विदेशी वस्तुओं की तुलना में उन्हें भारतीय लोगों का समर्थन भी प्राप्त होगा जिससे बाजार में इन वस्तुओं की मांग बढ़ेगी और देश आत्मनिर्भरता की दिशा में अग्रसर हो सकेगा ।

भावी शोध हेतु विकल्प

इस शोध ने आत्मनिर्भर भारत की संकल्पना के चरितार्थ में भारतीय परिवारों के उपभोग निर्णयों में बच्चों की भूमिका के संदर्भ में नई अंत–दृष्टि उत्पन्न की है। हालांकि अध्ययन दिलचस्प निष्कर्षों और प्रबंधकीय निहितार्थों को उपलब्ध करवाता है परंतु फिर भी भविष्य के अध्ययनों को इस अध्ययन में प्राप्त परिणामों की उपयोगिता वर्धन हेतु विस्तृत पैमाने पर जांच की जानी चाहिए। साथ ही, इस क्षेत्र में व्यापक सामान्यता के साथ निष्कर्ष निकालने के लिए, भविष्य के अनुसंधान को अन्य राज्यों के परिवारों को भी शामिल करके विस्तृत किया जाना चाहिए।

संदर्भ

अनिल, पी. (2020), ''राय। नई दिल्ली ने जीवन बनाम आजीविका बहस को फिर से दर्शाया'', लाइवमिंट, 12 अप्रैल, एक्सेस किया गया 15 फरवरी 2021.

इशाक, ए., और तुफैल, एम. (2014), "इनफ्लुएंस ऑफ चिल्ड्रन ऑन फैमिली परचेज डिसिशनरू इंपीरियल एविडेंस फ्रॉम पाकिस्तान", इंटरनेशनल रिव्यू ऑफ मैनेजमेंट एंड बिजनेस रिसर्च, 3 (1), 150–161.

गुनेरी, बी., यर्ट, ओ., कपलान, एम. डी., और डेलेन, एम. (2009), "द इनफ्लुएंस ऑफ चिल्ड्रन ऑन फैमिली परचेसिंग डिसीजंस इन टर्की", एशियन जर्नल आफ मार्केटिंग, 2 (1), 20–32.

चौधरी, एम, गोहाउस, एस.एम. और दुर्राह, ओ. (2018), "यंग अरब कंज्यूमर्सः ओमान में परिवार की खरीद प्रक्रिया का विश्लेषण, यंग कंज्यूमर्स, 19 (1), 1–18.

तलपड़े, एस., और तलपड़े, एम. (1995), "डेवलपमेंट ऑफ ए मल्टी आइटम स्केल टू मेजर टीनएजर इनफ्लुएंस ऑन फैमिली परचेज एन एक्सप्लोरेट्री स्टडी", जर्नल ऑफ मार्केटिंग थ्योरी एंड प्रैक्टिस, 3 (4), 41– 45.

द इकॉनॉमिक टाइम्स. (2020), भारत की आर्थिक गतिविधि लगभग पूर्व–लॉकडाउन स्तरों पर लेकिन कोविद करघेरू नोमुरा, एक्सेस किया गया 15 फरवरी 2021.

नुनली, जे. सी. (1978), "साइकोमेट्रिक थ्योरी (सेकंड एडिशन), न्यूयॉकरू मैकग्रा–हिल।

प्रताप, ए. (2019), ''उपभोक्ता व्यवहार में परिवार क्या भूमिका निभाता है?'' यहाँ उपलब्ध हैः https://notesmatic-com/2019/7/ (एक्सेस किया गया 16 फरवरी, 2021).

मित्तल, एम., चौधरी, एम. और गर्ग, एस. (2020), ''मोबाइल विकास के सबसे उपयुक्त सिद्धांत के लिए एक मूल्यांकन ढांचा'', जर्नल ऑफ मार्केटिंग एंड रिटेल मैनेजमेंट, वॉल्यूम, 1(1), 141–155.

मैकनील, जं. यू. (1992), "किड्स एंड कंज्यूमर्स हैंडबुक ऑफ मार्केटिंग टू चिल्ड्रन", न्यूयॉकरू लेक्सिंगटन पुस्तकें।

विमलसिरी, एस.जे. (2004), "क्रॉस नेशनल स्टडी ऑन चिल्ड्रंस परचेसिंग बिहेवियर एंड पैरंटरल रिस्पांस", जर्नल ऑफ कंजूमर मार्केटिंग, 21 (4), 274 दृ 284.

वेबस्टर, सी. (1994), "इफेक्ट्स ऑफ हिस्पैनिक एथेनिक आइडेंटिटी ऑन मैरिटल रोल्स इन द परचेज डिसीजन प्रोरोस", जर्नल ऑफ कंज्यूमर रिसर्च, 21 (2), 319–331.

Chapter - 19

Changing Scenario of MSME in Atmanirbhar Bharat

ARCHANA KUMARI & SANDEEP KUMAR PANDEY

Abstract: MSME is the "Backbone of Indian Economy" contributes 45% of industrial output, 48% of export, employing 60 million people, create 1.3 million job every year and produce more than 8000 quality products for the Indian and international market. MSME's contribution towards GDP in 2019 was 29%. Despite of these contributions MSMEs are suffering from problems like absence of adequate & timely finance, inadequate physical infrastructure, low technology level, lack of skilled manpower etc. The COVID-19 pandemic has worsened the situation even more. For revival and sustainability of MSMEs, the government has announced economic Package for MSME under Atmanirbhar Bharat.

The Hon'ble Finance Minister announced in her press briefing regarding various allotment of funds for MSMEs under various heads and she also elaborated the new definition of MSME.

Covid-19 pandemic and an appeal made by Honorable PM Modi JI on Go Local for Vocal has made us realized to substitute foreign brands with Indian Brands to make Indian Economy a self-reliant economy. This pandemic has affected the customers' perception towards Swadeshi products and has also provided different opportunities to MSMEs to fill the gap created by global disruption. This research Paper is an initiative in this regard and reveals that Indian MSMEs should focus on providing high quality customized products with right pricing and their easy availability as

Indians are ready to switch to Swadeshi products. Measures taken by Government for revival of MSMEs and changed perception of customers will definitely work for upliftment of MSMEs and will flow a wave of fulfilment of dream of "ATMANIRBHAR BHARAT".

Slogans initiated under Atmanirbhar Bharat include 'vocal for local', 'local for global' and 'make for world

Key word: Growth of MSME, Atmanirbhar Bharat, Growth of Economy, Infrastructure Development, System, Vibrant Demography, Demand Increase, Tranche.

Introduction

The covid-19 pandemic has changed the economic and social infrastructure of whole world. The world is now standing at the edge of a heavy economical breakdown. A swadeshi movement has been started by launching the "Aatmnirbhar Bharat campaign. In history, when India believed in the Gandhi's model of self-reliance, wonders happened. He articulated it as a social interdependence and mutual cooperation in a society. Now the same thing has been started in new model.

MSME the backbone of Indian economy will play avital role in attaining self-reliant goal. Enterprises in the micro small medium sector are complementary to large scale industries as subsidiary units and this sector are regarded as transformer and major contributor of the economy. This sector plays an important role in the areas of investment in infrastructure, generating more employment, developing innovative skills and competency, ensuring balanced regional development, developing backward areas, making economy self-sufficient through import substitution and making possible the development of the nation. The Union Ministry of Micro, Small & Medium Enterprises (MSME) India, envision a vibrant MSME sector by promoting growth and development of the MSME Sector, including Khadi, Village and Coir Industries, in cooperation with concerned Ministries/Departments, State Governments and other Stakeholders, through providing support to existing enterprises.

- India, the enterprises have been classified broadly into two categories: (i)Manufacturing
- (ii) Those engaged in providing/rendering of services.

Both the categories of enterprises have been further classified into micro, small and medium enterprises not based on their investment and turnover both. The present definition has taken away the existing difference between manufacturing and services sector units. The present ceiling on investment and turnover to be classified as micro, small or medium enterprises is as under encouraging creation of new enterprises.

The much-awaited relief package for MSME was announced on 13th may 2020 by the Finance Minister and there is enough information to understand how these might play out in the operationalization stage.

Review of Literature

According to the literature the Indian Government has not concentrated on providing relief measures to help business entrepreneurs of MSMEs to manage the threat of the COVID-19 pandemic. Additionally, the status of the national budget could not favour the Indian Government to announce relief measures for protecting business entrepreneurs of MSMEs, operating in rural and urban regions. The extending tenure of lockdown made the government to realize the need of economic package relief. The Indian Government announced a fiscal stimulus package worth a nominal amount and withdrew distribution of dividend taxes up to 0.3% of GDP. The relief package was not sufficient to compensate for the losses that were faced by business entrepreneurs of MSMEs in India. Therefore, the economic impact of

COVID-19 is expected on every sphere including growth, international trade, financial markets, unemployment, income, poverty and many more variables. The impact of the vir us spread is expected to lead to a huge loss as global trade is severely affected. The Indian growth model is based upon export-led-growth (Mishra, 2019), so it is quite possible that Indian economy will hit severely. On the international trade front, it is expected to plunge in a range of 13–32 per cent under optimistic and pessimistic scenarios, respectively (WTO, 2020). In another estimation, McKibben and Fernando (2020) utilized the computable general equilibrium (CGE) modelling and reported that global GDP would be reduced by around US$2.4 trillion in 2020 under a low-end pandemic considering the Hong Kong Flu as a reference point. However, the fall can extend to the tune of over US$9 trillion in 2020 in case of a serious outbreak similar to the Spanish flu.

Ozili and Arun (2020) noted the spill over effects of COVID-19 and hailed that the social distancing measure of virus controlling led to the shutdown of financial markets, corporate offices, businesses and events which in turn may have significant impact on economic growth. As per the International Labour Organization (ILO) estimation, the total value added of industrial enterprises in China declined by 13.5 per cent during the first 2 months of 2020 (National Bureau of Statistics of China, 2020). There are many projections and estimations by institutions and scholars on the economic fallout of COVID-19 pandemic. Though there are variations in degree and magnitude of the fall out, now there is a reasonable amount of coconscious that the economic impact would be severe on the world economy and also on Indian economic growth, much more than the global financial crisis (GFC) of 2008. IMF in its latest estimate in June 2020 projected that the global economy may shirk by 4.9 per cent, almost three times more than GFC, and the Indian economy is likely to witness 4.5 per cent negative growth for the 2020. With regard to the impact on employment and income, ILO (2020) estimated that global unemployment can range between 5.3 million and 24.7 million from a base level of 188 million in 2019 pushing these people towards below poverty line. Most of existing studies have focused on global growth, trade and unemployment, a few are country specific especially India. In this context, the present study aims to make an assessment of COVID-19 on Indian economy and highlights key policy measures to control the possible fallout on the economy. The study contributes the existing literature while analysing the impact on Indian economy with more focus on growth, trade, manufacturing and MSMEs. The detailed procedure of the assessment is reported in the next section.

Pooja Khatri (2019) conducts a descriptive study on the challenges of the Indian MSME sector. She studies the major five challenges faced by MSME. In which she covers finance, technology, human resources, marketing, operational, export related area of economy. She finds out that MSME contributes good amount of contribution to the GDP of the country. Major challenge is to manage the working capital in the MSME sector due to lack of the finance. Entrepreneurs and workers need to be trained properly to understand the market properly

Dinesh Kumar V & Dharaneedharan S (2017) analysed A Statistical study on Challenges and issues in MSME start-ups of Manufacturing Units. They studied Cosmo craft Technologies, Coimbatore Tamandu 's company for their research paper. They covered different areas of the company like financial, operational, marketing, technology for their survey. As per their survey the main factor is the knowledge and experience of the entrepreneurs affects whole MSME.

This research paper clearly says that every entrepreneur should concentrate on Employees development so that their business can growth easily

Ashok Kumar Panigrahi (2012) analysed that proper training and development for enhancing manager's knowledge and awareness about risk management can help in systematic handling of risks in MSMEs. As per his research MSMEs face issues like recruitment of skilful employees, technical issues, financial issues, marketing related issues and etc. Mainly entrepreneur had big challenge to manage small size unit with lack of professional touch of industry

Objective

1. To understand the role of MSME in economic growth.
2. To understand why aatmnirbhar package is suitable for Msme during COVID-19 pandemic.
3. To identify what government and support institution are doing to facilitate and encourage MSME under Aatmnirbhar Bharat.
4. To evaluate the role of each five pillar of Aatmnirbhar Bharat in the view of MSME
5. To understand the financial implication under each tranche Atmanirbhar Bharat.

Methodology

According to the above research framework, the main constructs are Financial Literacy, Access to Finance, and Growth of CHANGING SCENARIO OF MSME IN ATMANIRBHAR BHARAT for the purposes of changing the scenario OF MSME under the Aatmnirbhar Bharat. This study is a descriptive analysis was conducted to clarify the Financial Literacy ,Access to Finance, and Growth of MSMEs under the ATMANIRBHAR BHARAT package in 5 phases for MSMEs . Therefore, this study the annual balance sheet of MSMEs for the period 2019-20. The measurement of each indicator of the research data consists of 9-item that includes MSMEs' Financial Literacy measure; MSMEs' Access to Finance measure; and 4-items of MSMEs; pattern of MSMEs presence state wise; and finally, how much progress has been achieved so far under Aatmnirbhar Bharat.

- Secondary data.

Themes

Aatmnirbhar Bharat Yojana is a great step to save the economy of our nation. With the help of this economic financial package, crores of people will be able to financially stable again those who hardly hit by COVID19 situation in the past 2-3 months. Pm Modi Ji envisioned it by encompassing the whole member of the society, but young entrepreneurs are the first line warrior. Keeping this point in view new education policy was introduced to inculcate innovation, skill, research aptitude at early stage of life. Apart from these is EDP scheme, ATI scheme, NSIC, ni-msme, MGIRI, ETC. To reduce the gap between elite and non-elite member the government has setup the national SC&ST tribal platform for capacity building, skill development, and financial assistance under NSSH. Ana also special focus is given to northern region to reduce regional gap. Indian MSMEs match to world standard, digitalisation is given significant by introducing MY MSME, MSME SAMADHAN, MSME SAMBANDH, UDYOG AADHAR MEMORANDUM, and MSME DATABANK providing different solution to different problem digitally. Indian govt has signed MOU with Singapore, South Korea and other countries for boosting export of MSMEs and collaboration and meeting with foreign dignitaries. And all these activities will be financed through window of PMEGP, CLCSS, CGTMSE, SFURTI, etc.

India's self-reliance to be based on five pillars, says PM Modi

1. **Economy:** We need an economy that doesn't bring incremental change but makes quantum jumps.

2. **Infrastructure:** We need infrastructure that will become the identity of modern India.

3. **System:** We need a system that is no longer based on the rules and rituals of the past but one that actualises the dreams of the 21st century. This system needs to be technology-based.

Democracy: We are the world's biggest democracy. A vibrant demography is our strength. It is the source of energy for our efforts to make India self-reliant.

Demand: The cycle of demand and supply in our economy is an asset. We need to utilise this power fully. In a big push to revive the Coved-hit economy, Prime Minister Narendra Modi on also announced massive new financial incentives on top of the previously announced packages for a combined stimulus of Rs 20 lakh crore, saying the coronavirus crisis has provided India an opportunity to become self-reliant and emerge as the best in the world.

In a televised address to the nation, Modi also said there will be a fourth phase of the lockdown which will be very different from the earlier three phases. The third phase of the lockdown is scheduled to end on May 17.

Growth of MSME in economic: Central government of India allocated amount of Rs. 3 lakh crores to help MSMEs in this crisis. This initiative will help to act as seed money for small businesses to start again via purchasing raw materials, paying initial bills and wages to workers etc. In short, it will act as a working capital in businesses to start over again. Earlier, banks were unwilling to disburse such loans to firms because they already have pledged their assets and took loans against it, but, now, the central government has taken full guarantee of all Rs. 3 lakh crore and need no collateral for this loan, especially for MSMEs. In detail, finance minister Nirmala Sitharaman had announced economic relief package for MSMEs as it offers collateral free automatic loans worth Rs. 3 lakh crores with tenure up to 4 years and moratorium of 12 months. This scheme covers 100% guarantee to banks and on principal and interest aiming to benefit 45 lakhs of MSMEs and this will be available till 31st October 2020. The government also infusing Rs. 50,000 crores as equity to MSMEs as fund of funds, to be considered as mother fund and a few daughter funds in order to increase the capacity as well as size of MSMEs. Global tenders up to Rs. 200 will be offered to MSMEs only. Government has also redefined the MSMEs based on investment as well as their turnover. The new definition has replaced the earlier distinction between production and services units. Henceforth, investment up to Rs. 1 crore and turnover up to 5 crores will be called as micro units, investment up to Rs. 10 crore and turnover up to Rs. 50 crores will be known as small units, and investment up to Rs. 20 crore and turnover up to Rs. 100 crores will be called as medium business units . Moreover, the central government announces a partial credit guarantee scheme of Rs. 20,000 crores for the MSMEs' promoters in order to increase the business equity. It is expected about 2 lakh MSMEs along with non-performing units will be benefitted from this initiative. In addition, the existing partial credit guarantee scheme is extended in order to assist low rated finance companies aiming to raise debt by covering debt papers of primary market in which the government will bear the first 20% loss. A total of Rs. 45,000 crores have been allocated for the partial credit guarantee scheme 2.0 to offer liquidity in paper rated AA and below and even unrated paper. All MSMEs having turnover of up to Rs. 100 crore and with outstanding credit of up to

Rs. 25 crores will be permitted to borrow 20% of their total outstanding credits as on February 29, 2020. This scheme will have four-year tenure and is open till 31st October, NBFCs (Non-Banking Finance Company), micro finance institutions and housing finance companies are facing difficulties in order to increase the debt capital as the debt market is under confidence crisis. Therefore, the government stepped into with Rs. 30,000 crore as special liquidity scheme lift up investment grade debt paper from both primary and secondary markets. The government has guaranteed such papers and is expecting to increase the confidence level in the debt market. Finance minister had announced in March 26, 2020 as the workers earning Rs. 15,000 per month in business units where working people are less than 100 are at the biggest risk of losing jobs. Therefore, the government declared a proposal that EPF (employee provident fund) contribution of both employer and employee i.e., 12% will be reduced to 10% for March, April and May months aiming to increase the cash take away home. Now, the scheme has extended to further three months i.e., June, July and August and expecting a benefit of 4.3 crore people and 6.5 lakh business units which releases a total amount of Rs. 6,750 crore liquidity . However, for government PSUs, the employers' contribution will be 12% same as before whereas employees can pay 10% as per their interest.

Experts on MSMEs' Current Scenario and Economic Relief Package

Firms are in terrible situation where they are expecting ways to fix the demand problem and government is offering collateral-free loans to sail through the crisis. However, looking at the declining demand scenario, firms would not prefer to borrow more loans. Even finance minister had also acknowledged that the firms were asking to bank to not to disburse any loans.

Notably, where millions of people have lost their employment and declined purchasing power amid corona virus crisis, firms would not produce more product or services without effective demand. As they know that supply itself does not create any demand i.e., they would not show any eagerness in taking up more loans. This creates a vicious cycle, where lowering the production rate decreases the employment opportunities which leads to further compression of demand . An immediate relief to MSMEs could be given by the repayment of Rs. 5 lakh crores of dues owed by central government and private sector as the shortage in working capital has become the biggest issue for MSMEs. However, the government declared on 13th May 2020 to return the remaining dues to MSMEs within 45 days. Along with this, GST refunds are required to be expedited. These measures would make the firms 'Aatmnirbhar' (self-dependent) . A public provision for MSME workers as offering a partial wage guarantee for the lockdown period and another for three months in unlock period could directly assist employers along with guaranteeing incomes. Without effective demand, firms will produce lesser which lead to provide employment to fewer people, assisting business units with some wage guarantee scheme along with firms would provide a greater relief to MSME workers amid corona virus crisis. The Supreme Court has also said that firms, who are not able to pay full wages to workers during the lockdown period, will not be prosecuted in court . Amid corona virus crisis, standing at the verge of collapse due to nearly no demand in the market (especially for small businesses) and being prosecuted for not paying full wages to workers hardly seems fair. In addition, a huge majority of MSMEs provide employment to contractual, piece-rate paid labours. It becomes easier for the firms to decrease the workers' wages as if they would not provide adequate papers of their association with enterprise.

Hence, a wage guarantee program becomes significant in these conditions A bailout or relief from paying heavy electricity charges for a certain period of time amid corona virus crisis would greatly help in sustaining businesses of MSMEs. Only infusing liquidity would not help small businesses and could push their balance sheet to further deterioration if the demand does not revive However, MSMEs financing mostly comes from informal sources and this fact explains the MSMEs in COVID-19 Crisis and India's Economic Relief Package: A Critical Review Page 4 of 5 AIJR Preprints Available online at preprints.aijr.org effort made by Reserve Bank of India to increase liquidity in the market have had created very limited impact on MSMEs . In the interview with The Wire, former RBI governor Raghuram Rajan stated that Indian economy would become a shadow of its former self, if further measures would not be taken by the government soon. Considering the extent of catastrophe, the government should consult the opposition talent in order to tackle the situation as it can't be handled by the PMO (Prime Minister Office) itself. Situation demands to work on full strengths at all ends. He suggested to the government to not bow under the pressure of different rating agencies. In response to the "Atmanirbhar Bharat" economic package, he said that no measure is adequate in this crisis, especially in India's case. Loans provided to MSMEs in the proposed package takes time to work, but, on the other hand, hunger is an immediate problem which needs to be addressed first. Similarly, Prof. Abhijit Banerjee, Nobel Prize winner in Economics stated that purchasing power in India is not very high and due to lockdown, the poor people of country, now, do not have much money in their pocket and hardly have any purchasing power today. Currently, there is a huge decline in demand in the market. He also suggested the direct income support to the common people because they are the one who runs the economy, not the rich ones. Rajani admitted that the US style bailout is not possible in India, debt relief can be offered to industries such as airlines. Financial sector has already been in the deep distress way before the corona virus stroke. It needs re-capitalisation, restructuring and the hole in the leaking bucket must be plugged. He clearly added that the public sector banks need better management . Rajan said that MSME sector is already in most indebted conditions, and loans will only add to this. There is also an anticipation that bank will not permit loans to such MSMEs but using credit guarantee system will help to bail them out. He added that in order to help out MSMEs, a far better way is repayment of their dues. Union Minister of MSME Mr. Nitin Gadkari stated that the private sector and the government owed Rs. 5 trillion in dues to MSMEs. However, while announcing the economic package, finance minister Nirmala Sitharaman said that the government and public sector enterprises will return their dues to MSMEs within 45 days. Rajan questioned the state governments who were suspending labour laws for three years. Firstly, they must go for the wider consultation and micro-management by centre before imposing such laws on labour. Secondly, without adequate discussion, protest may happen against it which will further disrupt the economy. And finally, the government should take care of migrant workers in cities as they are enticed to return to their villages. However, offering food grains to poor and unemployed migrant workers is not enough, they need other essential commodities too such as vegetables, cooking oil, and most importantly, money and shelter

Relief measure as part of the Atmanirbhar Bharath Abhiyan

The much-awaited relief package for MSME was announced on 13thmay 2020 by the Finance Minister and there is enough information to understand how these might play out in the operationalisation stage. At the top level, these measures are substantive in terms of its magnitude, deal with multiple categories of MSMEs, and implicitly acknowledge the drawbacks noticed from past measures such as feeble credit transmission done through the mechanisms of the banking channel.

Six Major benefits for MSMEs

- A collateral-free automatic loan for MSMEs worth Rs. 3 Lakh Crores has been announced for a time period of 4 years. 45 Lakh MSMEs are to be benefited from this scheme.
- Emergency Credit line 20, 000 Crore subordinate debts will be facilitated by the government for the problem and stress of equity and around 2 Lakh MSMEs with below-average performance can benefit from the scheme.
- Tenders for Government procurement up to 200 crores will no longer be allowed globally.
- MSMEs will also be allowed to utilize E-commerce platforms via market links. They will be given their dues within 45 days whether from government agencies. An EPF support of Rs. 2500 Crore for business and workers for three more months was also announced.
- Definition of MSME is revised to their benefit like investment limit have been raised upwards, turnover of MSMEs have been taken into consideration and distinction between manufacturing and service sectors are removed.
- A Funds of funds will be set up to be operated through the Mother Fund, this will help to extend the MSMEs size and capacity.

Increase in credit guarantees, subordinated debts, clearing of outstanding dues and a wider definition would go a long way to revive the growth of MSMEs and boost the efforts to make the country self-reliant under the Atmanirbhar Bharat Abhiyan.

Financial implication As per the 'Atmanirbhar Bharat' scheme announced on 13th May, 2020

Sources of Msmes website

Existing and Revised Definition of MSMEs

Existing MSME Classification			
Criteria : Investment in Plant & Machinery or Equipment			
Classification	Micro	Small	Medium
Mfg. Enterprises	Investment<Rs. 25 lac	Investment<Rs. 5 cr.	Investment <Rs. 10 cr.
Services Enterprise	Investment<Rs. 10 lac	Investment< Rs. 2 cr.	Investment<Rs. 5 cr.
Revised MSME Classification			
Composite Criteria : Investment And Annual Turnover			
Classification	Micro	Small	Medium
Manufacturing & Services	Investment< Rs. 1 cr. and Turnover < Rs.5 cr.	Investment< Rs. 10 cr. and Turnover < Rs.50 cr.	Investment< Rs. 20 cr. and Turnover < Rs.100 cr.

1. Collateral Free loans from banks: The Credit Guarantee Fund Scheme (CGS) for Micro and Small Enterprises was launched by the GOI to make available collateral-free credit to the micro and small enterprise sector. Both the existing and the new enterprises are eligible to be covered under the scheme. The Ministry of Micro, Small and Medium Enterprises, Government of India and Small Industries Development Bank of India (SIDBI), established a Trust named Credit Guarantee Fund Trust for Micro and Small Enterprises (CGTMSE) to implement the Credit Guarantee Fund Scheme for Micro and Small Enterprises.

2. Protection against delayed payments: A payment due to a micro or small enterprise cannot exceed forty-five days from the day of acceptance or the day of deemed acceptance. In case of failure by the buyer to make payment on time, the buyer is required to pay compound interest with monthly interest rests to the supplier on that amount from the agreed date of payment or fifteen days of acceptance of goods or service. The penal interest chargeable for delayed payment to a MSME enterprise is three times of the bank rate notified by the Reserve Bank of India.

Mandatory reporting in Tax Audit report along with non-allowance of Interest paid under Income Tax.

3. Credit Linked Capital Subsidy Scheme: Under this scheme, new technology is provided to the business owners to replace their old and obsolete technology. A capital subsidy is given to the business to upgrade and have better means to do their business. The small, micro and medium enterprises can directly approach the banks for these subsidies.

4. Incubation: This scheme helps innovators with the implementation of their new design, ideas or products. Under this from 75% to 80% of the project cost can be financed by the government. This scheme promotes new ideas, designs, products etc.

5. Bank Interest: Rate of Interests are lower for the registered ones as compared to other enterprises. Public sector banks are permitted to categorize their MSME general banking branches as specialized MSME branches having 60% or more of their advances to MSME sector. This is to provide for a better service to this sector as a whole

Emergency Credit Line to Businesses/MSMEs from Banks and NBFCs up to 20% of entire outstanding credit as on 29.2.2020

- Borrowers with up to Rs. 25 crores outstanding and Rs. 100 crore turnover eligible
- Loans to have 4-year tenor with moratorium of 12 months on Principal repayment
- Interest to be capped
- 100% credit guarantee cover to Banks and NBFCs on principal and interest

- Scheme can be availed till 31st Oct 2020
- No guarantee fee, no fresh collateral

-Rs 20,000 crores Subordinate Debt for Functioning MSMEs which are NPA or are stressed

-Rs 50,000 cr. Equity infusion for MSMEs through Fund of Funds

-Global tenders will be disallowed in Government procurement tenders up to Rs 200 crore.

Overview of Performance of the MSME Sector

Table 1
Estimated contribution of MSMEs

Year	*MSME GVA*	*Growth (%)*	*Total GVA*	*Share of MSME in GVA (%)*	*Total GDP*	*Share of MSME in GDP (in %)*
2011-12	2622574	-	8106946	32.35	8736329	30.00
2012-13	3020528	15.17	9202692	32.82	9944013	30.40
2013-14	3389922	12.23	10363153	32.71	11233522	30.20
2014-15	3704956	9.29	11504279	32.21	12467959	29.70
2015-16	4025595	8.65	12566646	32.03	13764037	29.20
2016-17	4405753	9.44	13841591	31.83	15253714	28.90

Source: Annual Report of Ministry of MSME for the year 2019-20

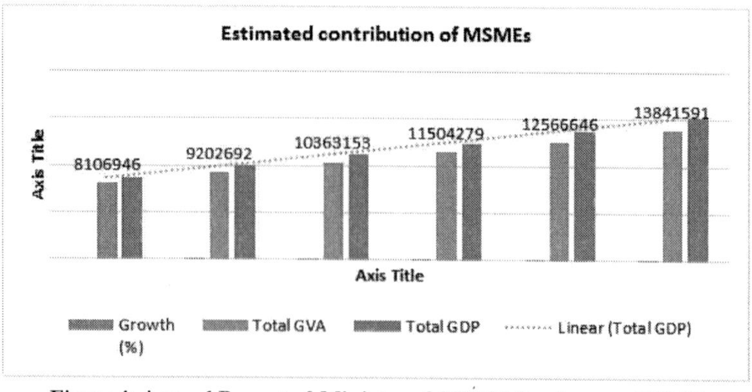

Figure 1: Annual Report of Ministry of MSME for the year 2019-20

- The approximate share of MSMEs in the GVA and GDP is 30% . there has been some decline in percentage but actual figure is increasing every year. MsMEs contribution in GVA and GDP from 2011-2017 has given.

Table 2
Estimated Number of MSMEs (Activity Wise)

Activity Category		Estimated Number of Enterprises (in lakh)	Share (%)	
Rural		Urban	Total	
(1)	(2)	(3)	(4)	(5)
Manufacturing	114.14	82.50	196.65	31
Electricity*	0.03	0.01	0.03	-
Trade	108.71	121.64	230.35	36
Other Services	102.00	104.85	206.85	33
All	324.88	309.00	633.88	100

Source: Annual Report of Ministry of MSME for the year 2019-20

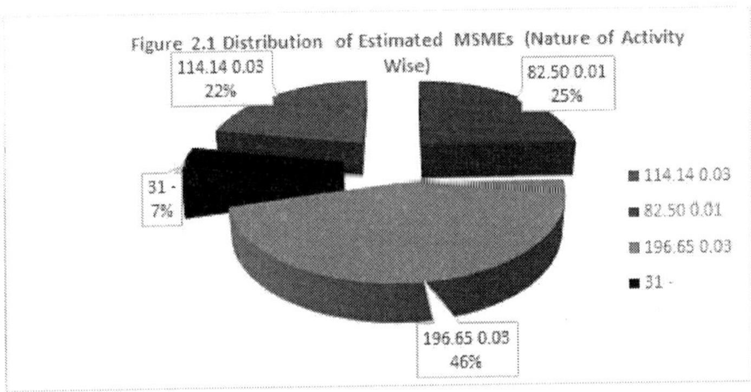

Figure 2: Non-captive electricity generation and transmission

As per the annual report of MSME RELEASED in 2020 total no. Of MSME in India are 633.88 lakh (196.65 lakh in manufacturing with 31% share, 0.03 lakh in electricity, and 230.35 lakh in trade with share of 36%, 206.85 lakh with 33% share in other services) across the country including both urban and rural area.

Table 3
Distribution of Estimated MSMEs (Nature of Activity Wise)

	Micro	*Small*	*Medium*	*Total*	*Share (%)*
(1)	(2)	(3)	(4)	(5)	(6)
Ruler	324.09	0.78	0.01	324.88	51
Urban	306.43	2.53	0.04	309.00	49
All	630.52	3.31	0.05	633.88	100

Source: Annual Report of Ministry of MSME for the year 2019-20

Micro sector with 630.52 estimated enterprise account for more than 90% enterprise under MSMEs. Small sector with 3.31 lakh and medium sector with 0.05 lakh estimated enterprise accounted for 0.52% and 0.01% of total MSMEs respectively. Out of total 633.88 lakh enterprise in MSMEs 324.88 lakh (51.25%) are situated in rural area and 309 lakh (48.75%) are situated in urban area.

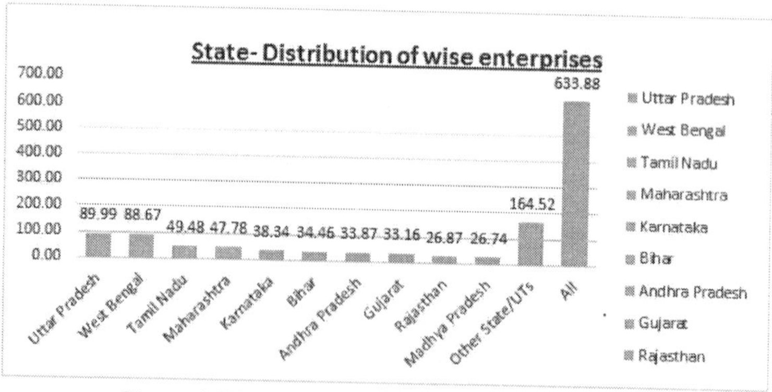

Figure 4: Distribution of MSMEs in Top Ten States

- Uttar Pradesh has retained the largest share (14.20%) in MSMEs enterprise. Top ten states account for 74.05% share in estimated MSMEs enterprise in the country.

Table 4 :State-wise distribution of MSMEs enterprises

Sl. No.		Estimate Number of MSMEs	
		Number (in lakh)	**Share (in %)**
1	Uttar Pradesh	89.99	14
2	West Bengal	88.67	14
3	Tamil Nadu	49.48	8
4	Maharashtra	47.78	8
5	Karnataka	38.34	6
6	Bihar	34.46	5
7	Andhra Pradesh	33.87	5
8	Gujarat	33.16	5
9	Rajasthan	26.87	4
10	Madhya Pradesh	26.74	4
11	Total of above ten States	469.36	74
1	Other State/UTs	164.52	26
13	All	633.88	100

Source: Annual Report of Ministry of MSME for the year 2019-20

Table 5

Distribution of employment by type of Enterprises in Rural and Urban Areas

	Micro	*Small*	*Medium*	*Total*	*Share (%)*
Rural	489.30	7.88	0.60	497.78	45
Urban	586.88	24.06	1.16	612.10	55
All	1076.19	31.95	1.75	1109.89	100

Source: Annual Report of Ministry of MSME for the year 2019-20

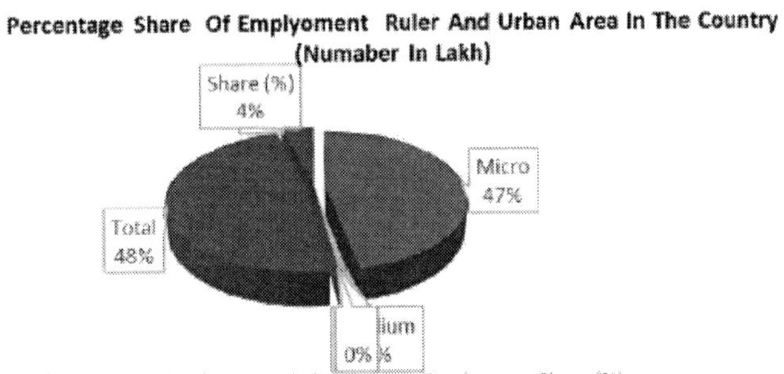

Figure 5: Percentage Share of Rural and Urban MSMEs in the Country

Micro sector with estimated 630.52 lakh enterprise provided employment to 1076.19 lakh person which account for 97% employment in MSMEs sector. Small sector with 3.31 lakh and medium sector with 0.05 lakh estimated enterprise provided employment to 31.95 lakh (2.88%) and 1.75 lakh (0.16%) person of total employment in MSMEs sector, respectively.

Micro, Small & Medium Enterprises with Udyog Aadhaar Registration Highlights

Table 6
Year wise and MSME wise Registration

Year/ Category	*2015-16**	*2016-17*	*2017-18*	*2018-19*	*2019-20#*	*Total*
Micro	4,21,516	21,47,908	13,44,612	18,70,932	16,32,644	74,17,612
Small	70,866	2,16,558	1,66,259	2,41,187	2,22,226	9,17,096
Medium	2,631	8,592	6,584	9,426	8,506	35,739
Total	4,95,013	23,73,058	15,17,455	21,21,545	18,63,376	**83,70,447**

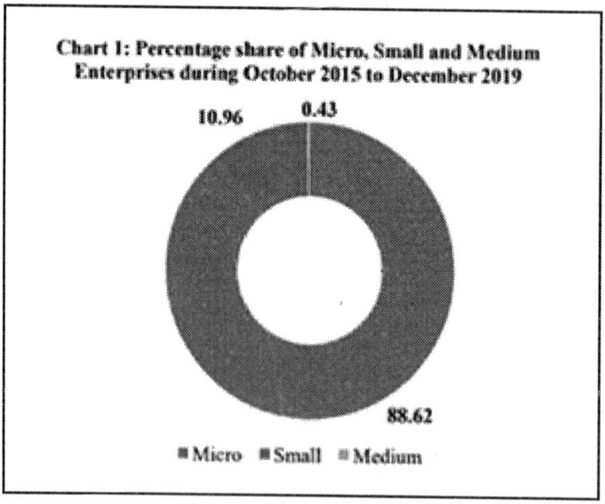

Figure 6: Micro, Small and Medium Enterprises (MSMEs) in India (Udyog Aadhaar -Memorandum)

I. Micro, Small & Medium Enterprises with Udyog Aadhaar Registration

II. Employment in MSMEs registered on Udyog Aadhaar Portal

Highlights: The percentage share of Micro Enterprises registered out of the total MSMEs registered during 2015-16(from Oct., 2015), 2016-17, 2017-18, 2018-19 and 2019-20 (till Dec., 2019) are 85.15%, 90.51%, 88.60%, 88.18% and 87.61% respectively. The percentage share of Micro Enterprises registered out of total MSMEs registered from 2015-16(from Oct., 2015) to 2019-20 (till Dec., 2019) is 88%. The percentage share of Small Enterprises registered out of total MSMEs registered during 2015-16(from Oct., 2015), 2016-17, 2017-18, 2018-19 and 2019-20 (till Dec., 2019) are 14.31%, 9.12%, 10.95%, 11.36% and 11.92% respectively. The percentage share of Medium Enterprises in the MSMEs during 2015-16 (from Oct., 2015), 2016-17, 2017-18, 2018-19 and 2019-20 (till Dec., 2019) are 0.53%, 0.36%, 0.43%, 0.44% and 0.46% respectively. Maharashtra tops the list of number of Micro, Small & Medium Enterprises registrations during 2015-16(from Oct., 2015) to 2019-20 (till Dec., 2019).

Growth in the Khadi Industry: Khadi is the unique programme of KVIC and a potent tool for creation of employment at the Artisans' doorstep being implemented by Khadi Institutions. The assistance provided through Market Development Assistance (MDA) and Interest Subsidy Eligibility Certificate (ISEC) Scheme are enabling Khadi Institutions to provide employment opportunities. Khadi sector Production and Sales have grown during previous years. Production and Sale of Khadi Sector during last 4 years and current year 2019-20 (up to December, 2019) is given below:

Table 7
Production and Sale of Khadi Sector

Year	*Production*	*Sales*
2015-16	1158.44 @	1663.98 @
2016-17	1520.83 @	2146.60 @
2017-18	1626.66 #	2510.21 #
2018-19	1963.30 #	3215.13 #
2019-20 (up to 31-12-2019)	1787.19 #	2883.71 #
2019-20 (Projected up to 31-03-2020)	2159.01 #	3753.45 #

Source: Annual Report of Ministry of MSME for the year 2019-20

Khadi sector Employment has grown from previous year, from 4.96 Lakh Khadi Artisans in 2018-19 to 4.98 Lakh Khadi Artisans in 2019-20 (Up to 31-12-20

Table 8
Budgetary Support to KVIC

Note: From FY 2017-18 onwards there is no separate allocation for Non-Plan.

Year	Allocation (R.E.)		Funds Released (in Crore)	
	Plan	Non- Plan	Plan	Non- Plan
2014 – 15	1452.00	229.09	1384.40	In crore
2015 – 16	1579.65	244.71	1520.49	244.18
2016 – 17	1647.40	258.74	1591.08	258.74
2017 – 18	2269.21	-	2125.51	-
2018-19	3082.22	-	3081.70	-
2019-20 R.E.(UP TO 31-12-2019)	3433.73	-	2897.30	-

Source: Annual Report of Ministry of MSME for the year 2019-20

The budgetary allocation of fund both (plan & non-plan) has been provided. It can be analysed that the budgetary allocation of fund is increasing year by year and also released fund in percentage part of allocation has been increased.

Coir Board: Coir Board is a statutory body established under the Coir Industry Act, 1953 for promoting the overall development of the coir industry and improvement of the living conditions of the workers engaged in this traditional industry.

Table 9
Exports of Coir during Last 5 Years (Volume and Value)

Year	*Quantity (MT)*	*Value (Rs. In Lakhs)*
2014-15	626666	163033.77
2015-16	752020	190142.52
2016-17	957045	228164.82
2017-18	1016564	253227.84
2018-19	964046	272804.59
2019-20 (Up-to Dec 2019)	764000	210000.00
2019-20 (Estimated Upto March 2020)	1000000	300000.00

Table 9 shows that the export quantity of coir product has increased over the period of time, but a fall has been seen during the year 2018-19 and 2019-20. But value of export has not declined much.

Table 10
The Top 5 coir importing countries from India are indicated in Coir Importers from India

Sl.No.	*Country*	*Quantity (Tonnes)*	*Percentage (%)*	*Value(Rs.in Lakhs)*	*Percentage (%)*
1	China	354268	36.75	71505.98	26.21
2	USA	122221	12.68	60134.19	22.04
3	Netherlands	96982	10.06	24841.02	9.11
4	South Korea	75186	7.80	11743.33	5.22
5	UK	22192	2.30	11306.73	4.30

Source: Annual Report of Ministry of MSME for the year 2019-20

This table indicates that Chinese market is the main importer of Indian coir products (36.75% in quantity and

26.21% in value). After that major importer is USA, Netherland, South Korea, and UK with 12.68%, 10.06%, 7 .80%, 2.30% share respectively in quantity imported.

Progress report of ATMANIRBHAR BHARAT

Table 11

Source: Press information bureau posted on 1st October 2020
Bank category - wise ECLGS/GECL daily reporting format (data -29.09.2020)
Non - individual sanction and Distribution daily reporting data

Bank	*No of account (actual figure)*		*No of account (actual figure)*	
	Cumulative sanctioned	*Cumulative disbursed*	*Cumulative sanctioned*	*Cumulative disbursement*
Public sector bank	33,75,007	21,87,793	80,060.50	66,848.34
Private sector bank	7,25,789	3,39,517	86,167.44	57,984.84
Sub- total- (PSBs+PVSBs)	41,00,796	25,27,310	1,66,227.94	1,24,833.18
NBFCs	50,440	30,777	293230	2,083.17
Total(non-individual)	41,51,236	25,58,087	1,69,160	1,26,916
Individual sanction and disbursement reporting				
Public sector bank	36,960	22,472	1,119.84	545.06
Private sector bank	2,51,454	38,162	8,893.35	2,755.88
Subtotal-PSBs+PVSBs	2,88,414	60,634	10,013.20	3,300.95
NBFCs	6,18,362	90,306	7,295.77	2,028.82
Total(individual)	9,06,776	1,50,940	17,309	5,330

a) Out of total amount (Rs 1,86,469 Crore) sanctioned under the 100% Emergency Credit Line Guarantee Scheme, Rs 1,32,246 crore has been already disbursed to 2,709,027 borrowers, by 12 Public sector banks, top 24 private banks, & individual by 29.09.2020.

b) Additional 3 months have been extended till 19.11.2020 for building portfolio and to increase ceiling for AA/ AA-rated bonds from 25% to 50% of total portfolio under revised guidelines issued on 17.08.2020

c) Purchase of Rs 25,505 crore portfolio and Rs 3,171 are currently in process of approval by the banks as on 25th September 2020. As per the report of PSBs portfolio of Rs 16,401 has been purchased so fair.

- **Under special liquidity scheme for NBFCs/HFCs/ MFIs as on 30th September 2020, detail are as follows:**
  - Approved amount (involving 39 proposal)- 11,120 crore
  - Amount disbursed out of sanctioned amount- 7,227 crore
  - Amount not availed- 182 core
  - Remaining amount of sanction that lapsed- 3,707 crore
  - Scheme closed on- 30th September 2020.
- **MUDRA-shishu loans** is currently consists of Rs 1.62 lakh crore (Maximum loan amount of Rs. 50,000). However , 86% of eligible accounts were on moratorium till 31.08.2020. Rs. 1,232 crores are allocated under FY 2020-21 budget and RS. 120 Crore released to SIDBI on 7th September 2020
- **Other Direct Tax Measures**

During the Current Financial Year, a number of 33, 53,898 refunds amounting to Rs.1,18,324 crore have been issued. Remaining refunds are under process.

Table 10
other direct tax measures

Summary Current Year		*Income Tax*	*Corporate Tax*		*Total*	
Total Refunds Issued Till 29/09/2020	*Count*	*Amount in Rs Crore*	*Count Rs*	*Amount in Rs Crore*	*Count*	*Amount in Crore*
	31,75,358	32,75,358	1,78,540	86,094.00	33,53,898	11,83,24.00

Source: Press information bureau posted on 1st October 2020

Under the ANBP, the following was announced:

i. Due date of all income-tax return for FY 2019-20 will be extended from 31st July, 2020 & 31st October, 2020 to 30th November, 2020 and Tax audit from 30th September, 2020 to 31st October, 2020

ii. Date of assessments getting barred on 30th September, 2020 will be extended to 31st December, 2020 and those getting barred on 31st March, 2021 will be extended to 30th September, 2021.

iii. Period of Vivadse Vishwas Scheme for making payment without additional amount will be extended to 31st December, 2020.

iv. Further enhancement of Ease of Doing business through IBC related measure :

v. A special resolution under section 240A of the Code, to provide relief to the MSMEs is being finalized and the same would be notified soon. suspension of the Insolvency and Bankruptcy Code up to one year and has also raised the threshold limit of default from 10. Decriminalization of Companies Act defaults

vi. The Companies (Amendment) Bill, 2020, has been passed by Lok Sabha on 19th September, 2020 and by Rajya Sabha on 22nd September,

2020. After, the assent of Hon'ble President, The Companies (Amendment) Act,2020 has been notified on 28th September, 2020.

vii. Ease of Doing Business for Corporates:

viii. The Companies (Amendment) Bill, 2020, has been passed by Lok Sabha on 19th September, 2020 and by Rajya Sabha on 22nd September, 2020. After, the assent of Hon'ble President, the Companies (Amendment) Act, 2020 has been notified on 28th September, 2020.

Conclusion

MSMEs, the engine of Indian economy is second largest employer after agriculture. Its major contributions are providing employment, reducing regional imbalance, major contributor in GDP, and export . Despite of these contributions MSMEs are suffering from problems like absence of adequate & timely finance, inadequate physical infrastructure, low technology level, lack of skilled manpower etc. The COVID-19 pandemic has worsened the situation even more To revive the Indian economy, the government has announced economic Package for MSME under Atmanirbhar Bharat. Like other sectors MSMEs have been hit severely due to lockdown as to counter attack covid-19 pandemic. But the problem faced by MSMEs are not the new, even before crisis the situation was somewhat the same.

The ECLGS scheme will infuse liquidity in MSMEs sectors and set the base for boosting MSMEs as their credit was going through tough time. NBFCs share the burden of financing the MSMEs with banks are also given major space in relief package. Special fund for Stressed MSMEs and infusion of equity fund for MSMEs, global tender is disallowed up to

Rs 200 crore to increase their operation in India. Government has been continuously monitoring the settlement of dues to MSMEs .promotion of e-marketing is compensatory scheme for trade, fair and exhibition definition will help in seamless expansion of Msme enterprises in India.

The Atmanirbhar economic package was criticized on the ground of that it mainly focuses on liquidity issue and it will not involve much fiscal spending by the government. The government under Atmanirbhar Bharat has mostly tried to ensure credit for MSMEs through different scheme.

But in a situation like this mere a stimulus economic package is not effective. Major reforms are needed to solve its pressing problem and make them fully potential. However, a better starting base has been provided through economic Atmanirbhar Bharat package that will lead to attainment of self-reliant goal.

References

Mali, D.D. (1998). Development of Micro, Small and Medium Enterprises of India: Current Scenario and Challenges, *SEDME (Small Enterprises Development, Management and Extension) Journal*, Vol.25, No.4

Bal Subrahmanyam, M. H. (2004). 'Small Industry and Globalization: Implications, Performance and Prospects', *Economic and Political Weekly*, Volume XXXIX, No.18, pp 1826-1834.

Bargal, H., Dash Mishra, M., and Sharma, A. (2009). *Performance Analysis of Small Scale.*

Financial Literacy and Growth of Micro, Small and Medium Enterprises in West Java, Indonesia : Marcella Susan

Issues of Micro, Small and Medium Enterprises (MSME) in India Dr. B. Chandra Mohan Patnaik Associate Professor, School of Management, KIIT University, Bhubaneswar, Odisha, India Dr. Ipseeta Satpathy, KIIT University, Bhubaneswar, Odisha, India Priti RachayeetaResearch Scholar, School of Management, KIIT

University, Bhubaneswar, Odisha, *India Business and Management*, Vol 1, No 2.

Online available at http://www.zenithresearch.org.in

Annual balance sheet of MSMEs 2019-20

Sources Press information bureau Released on September 2020

Registration of Micro, Small and Medium Enterprises (MSMEs) in India (Udyog Aadhaar Memorandum) 2019-20 (Up to December, 2019)

Google scholar

Shodhganga

Wikipedia

Yahoo finance

Sources Press Information Bureau posted on 1 October, 2020.

Annexure

Annexure

शहीद भगत सिंह सांध्य महाविद्यालय

N A A C मान्यता प्राप्त 'ए' ग्रेड

(दिल्ली विश्वविद्यालय)

शोध आलेख के लिए आमंत्रण

एक संपादित पुस्तक के लिए

" आत्मनिर्भर भारत:
युवा उद्यमशीलता एवम् कौशल और उसके
वित्तीय निहितार्थ के दृष्टिकोण से "

एक प्रयास

वाणिज्य विभाग-SBSEC

शहीद भगत सिंह सांध्य महाविद्यालय
NAAC मान्यता 'क' वर्ग
(दिल्ली विश्वविद्यालय)

"वाणिज्य-विभाग"

शोध आलेख के लिए आमंत्रण

(पुस्तक प्रकाशित हेतु)

"आत्मनिर्भर भारतः युवाओ की व्यवसायिक कुशलता तथा इसके वित्तीय पहलुओं के दृष्टिकोण से"

अंत:विषय शोध आलेख देश -विदेश के (हिंदी अथवा अंग्रेज़ी) शिक्षविदों, अनुसंधान विद्वानों, कंपनियों के कार्यकर्ताओं द्वारा आमंत्रित हैं।

आलेख सारांश जमा करवाने की अंतिम तिथि **10 फरवरी 2021**

सम्पूर्ण शोध आलेख जमा करवाने की अंतिम तिथि **25 फरवरी 2021**

academics.commerce@sbse.du.ac.in +91 98715 95627

महाविद्यालय का विवरण

शहीद भगत सिंह सांध्य महाविद्यालय (स्थापित,1973) दिल्ली विश्वविद्यालय के संघटक महाविद्यालयों में से एक है। सामान्यतः इसे SBSEC कहा जाता है , यह दिल्ली के दक्षिण में, शेख सराय क्षेत्र में स्थित है । इस महाविद्यालय के हरे-भरे परिसर इसमें पढ़ने के वातावरण को जीवंतता प्रदान करते हैं। यह वाणिज्य और मानविकी के विषयों में विभिन्न स्नातक पाठ्यक्रम प्रदान करता है। वर्तमान में इसमें लगभग 3000 छात्र विभिन्न पाठ्यक्रमों का अध्ययन कर रहे हैं। यह महाविद्यालय छात्रों की आकांक्षाओं में सामाजिक जिम्मेदारी एवं सांस्कृतिक जागरूकता की भावना को दर्शाता है।

हम 21 वीं सदी का एक चुनौती के रूप में सामना करने के लिए तत्पर हैं, हमारे कॉलेज के निर्माण हेतु परिवर्तन और विकास के वाहन के रूप में छात्रों को तैयार करने के लिए इस तेजी से बदलते वैश्विक वातावरण में भी कर्म निष्ठ बनाने के लिए प्रतिबद्ध हैं।

आत्मनिर्भर भारत

पृष्ठ 1

विभाग का विवरण

वाणिज्य विभाग दो पाठ्यक्रम प्रदान करता है: बी.कॉम (ऑनर्स) और बी.कॉम। 2011 में वाणिज्य संगठन- 'VARICO' का गठन किया गया और यह संगठन संपूर्ण वर्ष में विभिन्न प्रकार के कार्यक्रम आयोजित करता है जिसमें अतिथि व्याख्यान, गोष्ठियाँ, संगोष्ठीयाँ जैसे शैक्षणिक कार्यक्रम सम्मिलित हैं।

महामारी के कठिन समय के दौरान भी वाणिज्य विभाग गतिविधियों को व्यवस्थित करने और छात्रों और शैक्षणिक समाज के लिए अवसरों को बाहर लाने में सक्रिय रहा है। विभाग ने जून, 2020 के दौरान " आत्मनिर्भर भारत :युवा उद्यमशीलता, कौशल और उसके वित्तीय निहितार्थ के नजरिए से" पर द्वीदिवसीय अंतर्राष्ट्रीय वैबगोष्ठी का आयोजन किया। वैबगोष्ठी की गतिविधि को ई-बुकलेट में संकलित किया गया था और ऑनलाइन मंच के माध्यम से जारी किया गया था। । संपूर्ण गतिविधियों को ई-बुकलेट के माध्यम से शिक्षा मंत्रालय (तत्कालीन मानव संसाधन विकास) को प्रस्तुत किया गया था। शहीद भगत सिंह जी की 113 वीं जयंती के अवसर पर, वाणिज्य विभाग द्वारा पत्रिका " प्रबुद्ध" शीर्षक से पहली ई-पत्रिका, ऑनलाइन मंच के माध्यम से जारी की गई थी। इस कार्यक्रम का संपूर्ण विवरण समाचार पत्र-**राष्ट्रीय सहारा** द्वारा किया गया।

प्रतिष्ठित संपादकीय बोर्ड

प्रो. आर.के. सिंह, प्रमुख और डीन, वाणिज्य कर विभाग ,DSE, DU

प्रो. आरके सिंह वर्तमान में दिल्ली विश्वविद्यालय के दिल्ली स्कूल ऑफ इकोनॉमिक्स में वाणिज्य विभाग के प्रमुख और डीन हैं।आपने दिल्ली यूनिवर्सिटी से पोस्ट ग्रेजुएशन और एमफिल पीएचडी पूरी की। आपको अखिल भारतीय वाणिज्य, हाइड्रैड 2007 द्वारा सर्वश्रेष्ठ व्यवसाय अकादमिक पुरस्कार और ऑक्सफोर्ड यूके द्वारा सामाजिक उत्तरदायित्व और संगठनात्मक प्रतिबद्धता के लिए सर्वश्रेष्ठ पेपर पुरस्कार से सम्मानित किया गया।.

पृष्ठ 8

प्रो.अमिताभ कुंडू, JNU, दिल्ली

प्रो. अमिताभ कुंडू वर्तमान में विकासशील देशों के लिए अनुसंधान और सूचना विज्ञान में प्रतिष्ठित फेलो हैं । आप "स्वच्छ भारत अभियान" में सर्वेक्षण की अध्यक्षता कर रहे हैं। आप 2017 के दौरान यूएनईएससीडब्ल्यूए, बेरूत में गरीबी पर क्षेत्रीय सलाहकार और 2017 के दौरान श्रीलंका सरकार के सलाहकार रहे । जनवरी 2014 तक आप जवाहरलाल नेहरू विश्वविद्यालय ,नई दिल्ली में प्रोफेसर रहे ।

प्रतिष्ठित संपादकीय बोर्ड

प्रो. जयदीप शर्मा, IGNOU

प्रो. जयदीप शर्मा की शैक्षणिक योग्यता, लाइब्रेरी में पीएचडी और संबलपुर विश्वविद्यालय, उड़ीसा से सूचना विज्ञान। इससे पूर्व आपने दिल्ली विश्वविद्यालय से MLIS पूर्ण किया और आपको MLIS में अध्ययन के लिए छात्रवृत्ति से संमानित किया गया। आप पेशेवर गतिविधियों के साथ जुड़े रहे हैं, समीक्षक के रूप में समीक्षा पत्रिकाओं के साथ संबद्ध। आपने अन्य विश्वविद्यालयों में पीएचडी छात्रों के लिए सह-मार्गदर्शक के रूप में भी काम किया।

पृष्ठ 9

प्रो. नसीब अहमद, वाणिज्य एवं व्यवसाय अध्ययन विभाग, JMI

प्रो.नसीब अहमद ने गोरखपुर विश्वविद्यालय से स्नातक और स्नातकोत्तर की पढ़ाई पूरी की और उसी से वित्त में एमबीए की पढ़ाई पूरी की। आपको डीडीयू, गोरखपुर विश्वविद्यालय के एम.बी.ए प्रवेश परीक्षा में सेकंड रैंक के लिए यूजीसी, नई दिल्ली और मेरिट छात्रवृत्ति से जूनियर रिसर्च फ़ेल्लोशिप से सम्मानित किया गया हैं।आपने जम्मू विश्वविद्यालय के MCOM पाठ्यक्रम के लिए "ई-कॉमर्स" पर अध्ययन सामग्री भी तैयार की।

संपर्क

शहीद भगत सिंह(सांध्य)महाविद्यालय
NAAC 'ए' ग्रेड मान्यता प्राप्त
दिल्ली विश्वविद्यालय
शेख सराय फ़ेज़ -2, नितेणी, नई दिल्ली, 110017

दूरभाष : 29253430
फ़ैक्स: 011-29257 826
वेबसाइट : www.sbsec.org
: academics.commerce@sbse.du.ac.in
: +919871595627

पृष्ठ 11

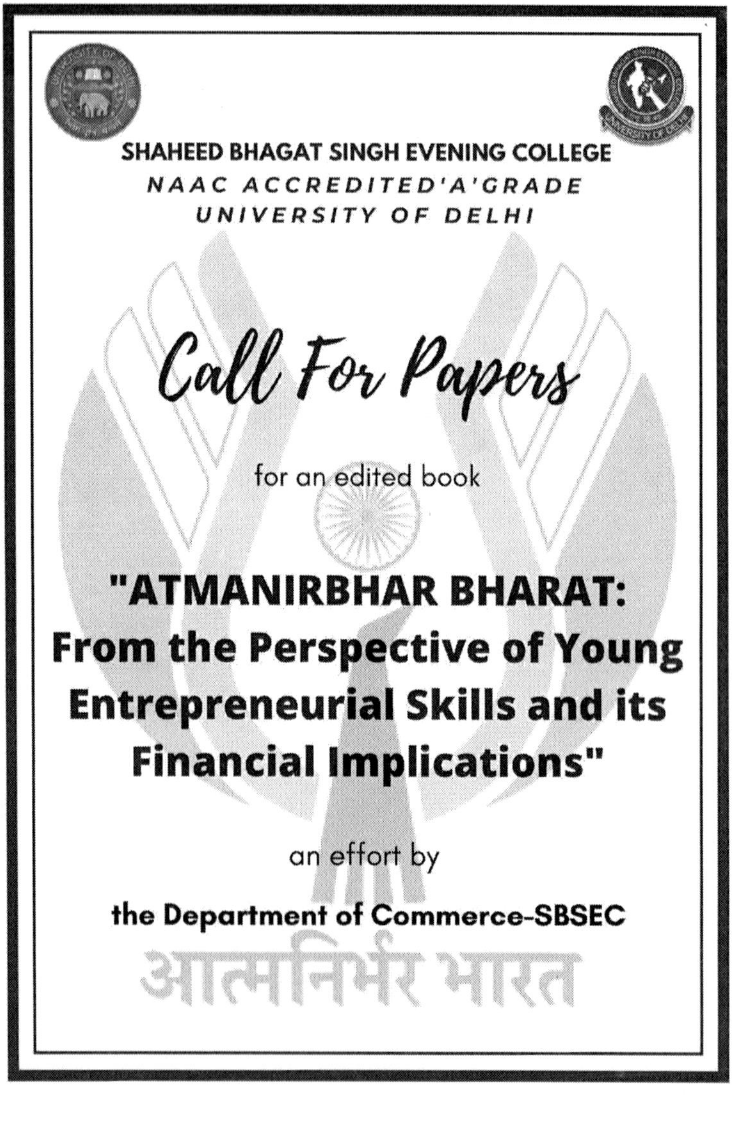
SHAHEED BHAGAT SINGH EVENING COLLEGE
NAAC ACCREDITED'A'GRADE
UNIVERSITY OF DELHI
Call For Papers
for an edited book
"ATMANIRBHAR BHARAT:
From the Perspective of Young
Entrepreneurial Skills and its
Financial Implications"
an effort by
the Department of Commerce-SBSEC
आत्मनिर्भर भारत

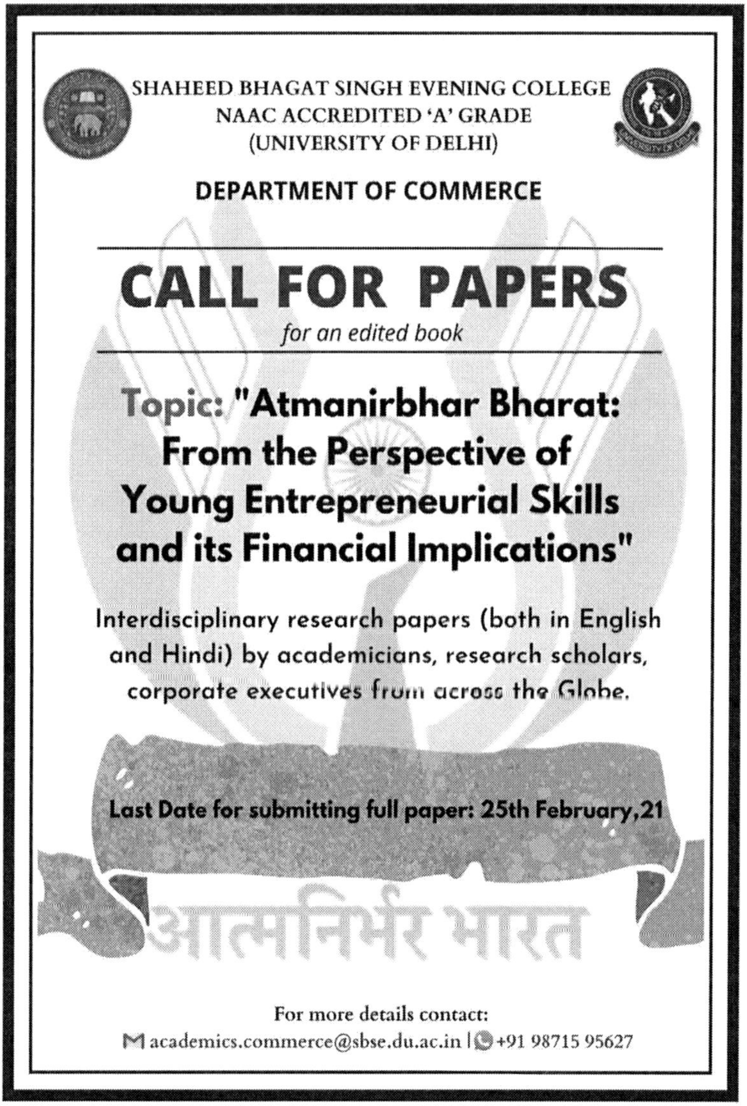
SHAHEED BHAGAT SINGH EVENING COLLEGE
NAAC ACCREDITED 'A' GRADE
(UNIVERSITY OF DELHI)
DEPARTMENT OF COMMERCE
CALL FOR PAPERS
for an edited book
Topic: "Atmanirbhar Bharat: From the Perspective of Young Entrepreneurial Skills and its Financial Implications"
Interdisciplinary research papers (both in English and Hindi) by academicians, research scholars, corporate executives from across the Globe.
Last Date for submitting full paper: 25th February,21
आत्मनिर्भर भारत
For more details contact:
academics.commerce@sbse.du.ac.in | +91 98715 95627

About the College

Shaheed Bhagat Singh Evening College (estd. 1973) is one of the constituent colleges of the University of Delhi. SBSEC, as we call it, is located in the south of Delhi, near Sheikh Sarai. It has a lush green campus along with a vibrant learning atmosphere. It offers various undergraduate courses in the disciplines of Commerce and Humanities. At present it has approximately 3000 students studying various courses.

The college embodies the spirit of social responsibility and cultural awareness reflecting the aspirations of the students.

We look forward to the 21st century as a challenge and an opportunity to build our college as a vehicle of change and growth to prepare students think critically and act responsibly in a rapidly changing global environment.

About the Department

The Department of Commerce offers two courses: B.Com (Hons.) and B.Com. The Commeree Association-VARICO, formed in 2011, organises and hosts a plethora of co-curricular activities and academic events throughout the year like Seminars, Workshops, Guest lectures and many more.

Even during the difficult times of pandemic the department of commerce has been active in organising activities and bringing out opportunities for the students and the academic fraternity. The department organised a Two-day International Webinar on "ATMANIRBHAR BHARAT: From the Perspective of Young Entrepreneurial Skills and It's Financial Implications" during June, 2020. The proceedings of the webinar were compiled in an e- booklet and was released through the online platform. The recommendations and the e-booklet were submitted to the Ministry of Education (erstwhile Human Resource Development). On the occasion of 113th Birth Anniversary of Shaheed Bhagat Singh, first e-magazine, by Department of Commerce titled 'PRABUDDHA' was released through the online platform. The event was reported by the National Newspaper-RASHTRIYA SAHARA.

आत्मनिर्भर भारत

Concept Note

The year 2020 has witnessed a once in a century global crisis engendered by the COVID-19 pandemic. Transforming the crisis into an 'opportunity', India has charted its own unique trajectory showing remarkable resilience in 'Saving Lives & Livelihoods'.

Faced with enormous uncertainty, India imposed the most stringent lockdown at the very onset of the pandemic even before 100 cases were recorded. India, then continually calibrated its response while gradually unlocking and easing economic activity. India's GDP is projected to record a growth of 11% in 2021 -22, while nominal GDP (excluding inflation) may expand 15.4% after the 7.7% pandemic-driven contraction in 2020 - 21, the Economic survey said on 29th January, 2021. These projections are in line with IMF, which also says that India is expected to emerge as the fastest growing economy in the next two years. **Atmanirbhar Bharat**, flagship Program of Government of India, subsequently announced a financial package of Rupees Twenty Lakh Crore in May 2020. It also includes coordinated efforts to boost the local and regional art & craft, indigenous & home-grown produces which are essential for the positive momentum in the recovery and growth. The year 2021 will require sustained and calibrated measures to facilitate the process of economic recovery and to enable the economy to get back to its long-term growth trajectory. The revival of the industrial and infrastructure sector will be key to the overall economic growth and macroeconomic stability. Enormous opportunities for the youngsters in entrepreneurship are visibly unearthed. Newer paradigms of excellence might be created and explored by requisite skills and competence.

Objectives

•To gauge the role and contribution of Global Economies in self-reliant India.
•To appraise the International-Relations and Global-Collaborations in Atmanirbhar Bharat.
•To examine the financial packages and fund's appropriation by the Government of India for Digitalised Atmanirbhar Bharat.
•To assess the upcoming prospects of Entrepreneurship for the youngsters in terms of skills, digitalisation, health and employability in post COVID-19 phase.

Themes

Atmanirbhar Bharat is panacea for the country's device to recover the bruised economy. The pre-emptive & timely decision (lockdown) taken by the Government of India, in curbing the ill-affect of pandemic on the life of its citizens brought the accolades for it, from across the globe. The humane side has been resiliently shown by India to the world in its action. The title of this proposed edited book is in consonance with the **Atmanirbhar Bharat**- Government of India's flagship program to be introduced in calibrated and coordinated manner in recovering the economy from this ongoing unprecedented corona-crisis. Newly introduced **NEP-20 (National Education Policy-20)**, focuses on innovation, research for resurgence, and enhancing youngsters' skills & competency at an early age of their life. Hence, following indicative themes are proposed in sync with the **aesthetic standards** of Government of India's vision for post pandemic phase.

Page 4

***HUMANITARIAN, PHILANTHROPIC AND MAITRIYI INITIATIVES**

CSR, Health-care Initiatives, Service to Mankind, Lesson on Dharma-Deeds. Prabuddha Bharat, Time-Management

***WOMEN, YOUTH AND MINORITY INCLUSIVITY & EMPOWERMENT**

In the light of Government's action-oriented programs and vigour, Indigenous Business Opportunities

***SUSTAINABLE ECONOMIC DEVELOPMENTS**

Efforts-Policies and programs to uplift the Economy, Agriculture & Food Processing, Automobile, Manufacturing, Infrastructure Industries, Vocal for Local, Clamour for Climatic Action

***IT, DIGITALISATION & COMMUNICATION**

HR, Leadership Policies, Satellites-Surveillance Communication and Transportation, Digital- Advancements, Literacy, Etiquettes, Ethics

***FINANCE, BANKING & SERVICE SECTOR**

NBFC, Investments, Reforms and newly- emerged financial designs, Stock Market- Performances & Behaviour, Services - Hotel, Hospitable, Entertainment, Education

***GLOBAL TIES & INTERNATIONAL RELATIONS**

International collaborations, Global Competiveness, Politics & Governance

***ENTREPRENEURSHIP & VOCATIONAL SKILLS**

Education, Management, Marketing, Health & Nutrition, Tourism, Fashion & Fabric

Distinguished Editorial Board

Prof. Jaideep Sharma,
IGNOU

Prof. Jaideep Sharma completed his Phd in Library and Information Science from Sambalpur University, Orissa. Prior to that he completed MLIS and BUS from University of Delhi and was awarded Scholarship for studies in MLIS respectively. He has been associated with professional peer review journals acting as reviewer. He also acted as co-guide for Phd students in various universities.

Prof. Naseeb Ahmad,
Department of Commerce and Business Studies, JMI

Dr. Naseeb Ahmed completed his graduation and post graduation from Gorakhpur University and also did his MBA in Finance from the same. He was awarded with Junior Research Fellowship from UGC, New Delhi and Merit Scholarship for securing second rank in MBA entrance exam of DDU, Gorakhpur University. He also prepared study material on "E-Commerce" for M.Com course of University of Jammu.

Visit Us

SHAHEED BHAGAT SINGH EVENING COLLEGE
NAAC ACCREDITED 'A' GRADE
UNIVERSITY OF DELHI
SHEIKH SARAI PHASE-2, (TRIVENI) NEW DELHI-110017
Phone: 29253430
Fax: 011-29257826
: www.sbsec.org
: academics.commerce@sbse.du.ac.in
: +91 98715 95627

आत्मनिर्भर भारत

UNDERTAKING CUM DECLARATION FROM THE AUTHOR

PERSONAL DETAILS

NAME

GENDER

DOB

ADDRESS

MOBILE

EMAIL

AADHAR

EDUCATIONAL DETAILS

M.PHIL./PH.D. - TOPIC

YEAR OF SUBMISSION

SUPERVISOR

UNIVERSITY

PROFESSIONAL DETAILS

DEPARTMENT

COLLEGE

UNIVERSITY

TITLE OF THE PAPER

LANGUAGE

DISCIPLINE

PLAGIARISM - SOFTWARE

PLAGIARISM PERCENTAGE

I hereby declare that the paper represents my original work, and have not been produced or considered for publication anywhere else. I have used no other sources except those that I've indicated in the References. All data, tables, figures and text citations, which have been reproduced from other sources, including the internet have been explicitly acknowledged as such I am aware of the consequences of non-compliance of my above declaration.

I've not been charged any cost for this paper by the Department of Commerce - SBSEC, University of Delhi, for its publication.

The content in the paper may only be used for academic discourse. I shall be held responsible for any error, omission, misrepresentation in the content and arise any consequences therefrom such an act, now or later in future. All the details submitted above are true and correct to the best of my knowledge.

NAME / (DIGITAL SIGNATURE)
DATE
PLACE

Bio Notes

Dr. Omkar Singh Deol
Associate Professor

Specialisation: International Business and Finance

Dr. Omkar Singh Deol is an Associate Professor in the Department of Commerce at Shaheed Bhagat Singh Evening College. He has done M.Phil. and Ph.D. in international business from the Department of Commerce, Delhi School of Economics. He is a member of many esteemed expert committees constituted by the UGC. He is also a member of the Editorial Board of the International Journal of Business and General Management (IJBGM); published by International Academy of Science, Engineering and Technology (IASET). He has written five books in the areas of international business and finance. He has presented several research papers in many national and international conferences and has many publications in many esteemed journals. He has also served as the Head of the Commerce Department, Shaheed Bhagat Singh Evening College for the academic year 2007 – 2008 apart from serving as a convenor for various academic and departmental committees.

E-mail: deolomkar@gmail.com

Dr. Kavita Yadav
Associate Professor

Dr Kavita Yadav, Associate Professor, symbol of grace, poise & elegance, has been rendering her services in teaching Under-Graduate Courses (Program & Honours) since her appointment as permanent faculty in Department of Commerce in 2008.

She has obtained Masters in Commerce, Education, Legislative Laws and Business Administration (Self-Management & Crisis Management) alongwith PG Diploma in Personnel Management & Labour Welfare, truly shows her distinct fondness for the academics.

She has been actively contributing in Research by attending national and international Conferences & seminars, presenting papers and co-Charing sessions nation-wide and around a dozen publications of repute justified her commitment and hard work in academics. Her interest in Strategic Management, Adolescent Healthcare, Management and Accounting is vehemently depicted in her work. Strategic Management and Healthcare Sector – A Study of Non-Government Hospitals of Delhi and Organisational Behaviour are two books to her credit.

Her incredible contribution in the college as convenor, Department of Commerce; Examination; Sandhyalok College annual magazine; and Women Development Centre-WDC is highly admired. She is appreciated for her meticulous planning skills of academic programs in college, her keen interest in the paper- Entrepreneurship, majestically brought Hon'ble Sh Manish Sisodia, Deputy CM, NCT, Delhi for an interactive session with students..

She is Liaison Officer OBC Cell, of the college. She had invited Sh Kaushlendra Singh Patel, Member, NCBC, Padamshri Dr Naresh Trehan, Prof Sushma Yadav, Vice-Chancellor, Bhagat Phool Singh Mahila University, Haryana at different programs to address student's inquisitiveness.

In order to imbibe disciplinary habits, she accompanied students during several academic trips and sight-seeing for their academic growth, visit to Pragati Maidan, New Delhi, JawaharLal Nehru Stadium, Mini Bharat Darshan Railway trip, Simla to name a few.

In the backdrop of the exodus of unprecedented corona crisis, she engaged students in bringing the first e-magazine entitled 'PRABUDDHA', a Department of Commerce venture which was being inaugurated on the pious occasion of 113th Birth Anniversary of martyr Shaheed Bhagat Singh by Prof Geeta Singh, Director, CPDHE, DU.

She convened a two day International online conference on 'ATMANIRBHAR BHARAT FROM THE PERSPECTIVE OF YOUNG ENTREPRENEURIAL SKILLS & IT'S FINANCIAL IMPLICATIONS', and also the 56-page proceedings in form of a booklet was ceremoniously released and same had been submitted into the respected offices of Government of India, afterwards. On the lines of NEP-20, she now profoundly motivates her students in organising more academic events in Mother Language, Hindi.

E-mail: drkavitayadav.sbsec@gmail.co m,
kavita yadav@sbse.du.ac.in

Dr. Amrita Kaur
Assistant Professor

Specialistion : International Trade, Taxation,, Sustainable Development

Dr. Kaur holds a Doctorate in Commerce from Jamia Millia Islamia University, New Delhi. She is a post graduate in commerce from University of Delhi. She has teaching experience of over 11 years at the University of Delhi, with a wide array of research work, publications in Scopus indexed/ABDC journals and paper presentations at national and international levels.

E-mail: amrita.kaur@sbse.du.ac.in

Dr Anshu Jain
Assistant Professor

Specialisation: Finance

Dr. Anshu Jain currently works at Shaheed Bhagat Singh Evening College, University of Delhi as an Assistant Professor in the Department of Commerce. She holds a B. Com (Hons.), M Com, M Phil degree from Delhi University and PhD from Mewar University, Chittorgarh, Rajasthan. Her specialization lies in the area of Finance. She has more than 20 years of teaching experience in the field of Commerce.

E-mail: anshu.jain@sbse.du.ac.in

Dr. Aditi Goel
Assistant Professor

Specialisation: International Business

Dr. Aditi Goel is currently an Assistant Professor at Shaheed Bhagat Singh Evening College, University of Delhi. She did her B. Com (Hons) and M. Com from University of Delhi and PhD from Singhania University. She has more than 9 years of experience in teaching undergraduate courses. She has actively participated in many administrative and extra-curricular activities of the college like organising seminars, webinars, student's fest etc. She is the co-convener of the Finance and Investment Cell of the college.

E-mail: aditi.goel@sbse.du.ac.in

Old order should change, always and ever, yielding place to new, so that one "good" order may not corrupt the world.

- Shaheed Bhagat Singh